SUPER SIMPLE
PHYSICS

Penguin Random House

DK LONDON
Senior editor Ben Morgan
Senior art editor Michelle Staples
Editors Edward Aves, Steven Carton, Alexandra Di Falco
Illustrators Adam Brackenbury, Gus Scott
Managing editor Lisa Gillespie
Managing art editor Owen Peyton Jones
Production editor Gillian Reid
Senior production controller Meskerem Berhane
Jacket designer Akiko Kato
Jackets design development manager Sophia MTT
Publisher Andrew Macintyre
Art director Karen Self
Associate publishing director Liz Wheeler
Publishing director Jonathan Metcalf

Authors Leo Ball, Ben Davies, Hilary Lamb, Penny Johnson, Ben Morgan, Robert Snedden, Giles Sparrow, Steve Woolley
Consultants Rutuparna Das, Penny Johnson

DK DELHI
Senior editor Virien Chopra
Senior art editor Vikas Chauhan
Project editor Bipasha Roy
Project art editor Sanjay Chauhan
Art editor Sifat Fatima
Assistant editors Sukriti Kapoor, Manjari Thakur
Assistant art editor Bhavnoor Kaur
Illustrator Aparajita Sen
Assistant picture researcher Geetika Bhandari
Picture research manager Taiyaba Khatoon
Managing editor Kingshuk Ghoshal
Managing art editor Govind Mittal
Senior DTP designer Vishal Bhatia
DTP designer Syed Mohammad Farhan
Pre-production manager Balwant Singh
Production manager Pankaj Sharma

First published in Great Britain in 2021 by
Dorling Kindersley Limited
DK, One Embassy Gardens, 8 Viaduct Gardens, London, SW11 7BW

The authorised representative in the EEA is
Dorling Kindersley Verlag GmbH. Arnulfstr. 124, 80636 Munich, Germany

Copyright © 2021 Dorling Kindersley Limited
A Penguin Random House Company
10 9 8 7 6 5 4 3 2
002–314297–Feb/2021

A CIP catalogue record for this book is available from the British Library.
ISBN: 978-0-2413-8143-4

Printed and bound in China

For the curious
www.dk.com

MIX
Paper from
responsible sources
FSC™ C018179

This book was made with Forest Stewardship Council™ certified paper – one small step in DK's commitment to a sustainable future. For more information go to www.dk.com/our-green-pledge

SUPER SIMPLE
PHYSICS

THE ULTIMATE BITESIZE STUDY GUIDE

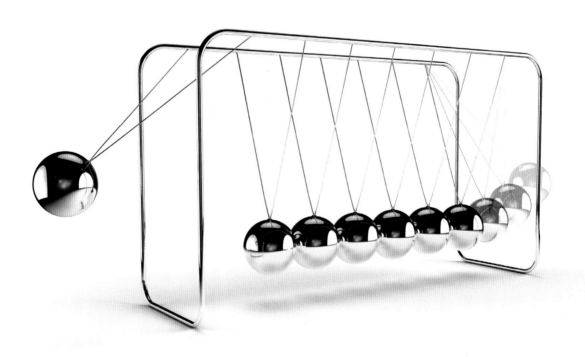

Contents

Energy

Working scientifically

Safety and teacher supervision

- The experiments outlined in this book describe the experiments required for the practicals set in the UK Physics GCSE curriculum. In undertaking these experiments you must follow the instructions on each page as well as the general instructions on "Working safely" on page 17.

- Some of the experiments require the additional supervision of a physics teacher, and they should therefore only be undertaken at school under such supervision. The experiments requiring teacher supervision are marked with this symbol:

Teacher supervision required

- DISCLAIMER: The publisher cannot accept any liability for any injury or losses arising from experiments where such instructions were not followed and/or that were undertaken without appropriate supervision.

Describing motion

Forces

Force and motion

Waves

Light

Electrical circuits

Using electricity

Static electricity

Magnetism and electromagnetism

Matter

Pressure

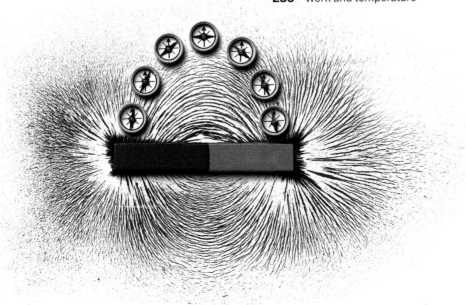

Atoms and radioactivity

Space

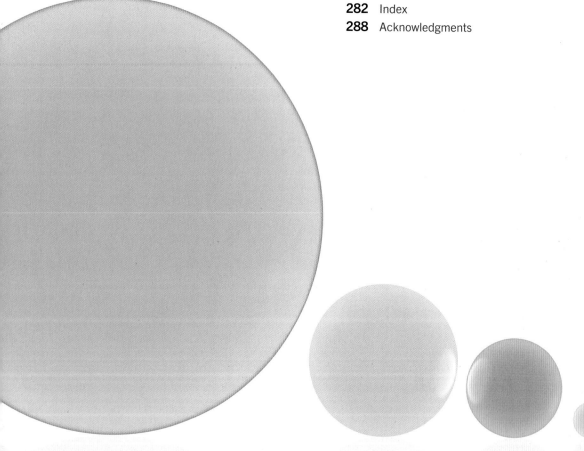

Working
scientifically

The scientific method

As scientists, we want to explain how and why things happen — such as what happens when a current flows through a wire, or when stars or planets form. We do this by thinking logically in a step-by-step process. The steps on this page are used in all fields of science.

1. Ask a scientific question
Scientists are curious and often ask questions about how things work. For instance, why does a kettle sometimes take longer to boil? A scientific question is one that can be answered by collecting data (information). A question such as "which kind of hot drink is nicest?" is not a scientific question.

2. Make a hypothesis
The next step is to come up with a possible explanation that can be tested. This is called a hypothesis. We can often write a hypothesis using the words "depends on". For instance, our hypothesis might be: the length of time the kettle takes to boil depends on how much water is in it.

Collect data
Some scientific questions can't be tested by experiments. Astronomers can't experiment with planets and stars, for instance. However, they can still make hypotheses and predictions and then test the predictions by making observations to collect data.

3. Make a prediction
To test a hypothesis, we use it to make a prediction. A prediction can often be written as "If… then…". For example: I predict that if I double the amount of water, it will take twice as long to boil.

4. Collect data
Hypotheses are usually tested by experiments. In this case, we might heat measured volumes of water and time how long each volume takes to boil. An experiment must be a fair test, which means the only variable we change is the one we're investigating (the volume of water, in this case). The information we collect in an experiment is called data.

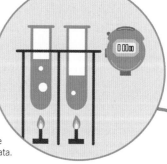

7. Theory
If the hypothesis is tested many times and never fails, it might eventually become accepted as a scientific theory.

Refine hypothesis or experiment
If the prediction was wrong, the hypothesis might be wrong too or the experiment might not have worked properly. Failed experiments are not a waste of time – they sometimes lead to new discoveries.

Many scientists repeat the experiment.

The conclusion does not support the hypothesis.

The conclusion supports the hypothesis.

6. Peer review
After a successful experiment, a scientist may write a report (called a paper) so that other scientists can find out about the experiment and check the details. The paper may be published in a scientific journal for all scientists to read.

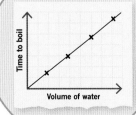

Time to boil / Volume of water

5. Analysis and conclusion
After collecting data, we analyse it carefully to check for errors and look for patterns. We use the analysis to decide whether the experiment supports the hypothesis. This forms our conclusion.

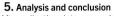

Key facts

✓ A hypothesis is a scientific idea that can be tested.
✓ A hypothesis is used to predict what may happen in an experiment.
✓ If a hypothesis is supported by an experiment, it may become part of a theory.
✓ Scientists present their discoveries to be checked by other scientists.

🔍 Scientific theories

People sometimes say "it's just a theory" when they don't believe something. However, in science, a scientific theory is an explanation that has been tested many times and become widely accepted as true. For example, the idea that Earth and other planets of the solar system orbit the Sun is a scientific theory based on many careful observations and predictions. If it weren't for science, we'd probably believe that the movement of the Sun across the sky meant that it was orbiting Earth, rather than vice versa.

Solar system

Scientific progress

Scientific methods and theories change over time. For example, the invention of the telescope changed the way people thought about the solar system. As telescopes became more powerful, new ideas about the stars and the Universe became accepted too.

Quadrant

Sun

Elliptical orbits
About 80 years after Copernicus died, a German astronomer called Johannes Kepler proposed a heliocentric model with elliptical (oval) orbits instead of circular ones. This matched the movements of the planets much better than older models.

Heliocentric model
Using observations made with the naked eye, the Polish astronomer Nicolaus Copernicus devised a new model. This had the Sun at the centre (heliocentric) and planets travelling around it in circular orbits. At first, it wasn't accepted because it didn't match observations perfectly.

Observing the skies
The first people known to study the night sky were the people of Mesopotamia (now Iraq), around 5000 years ago. Ancient astronomers used simple instruments like a quadrant to measure the angle stars or planets made with the horizon, and to predict when the Sun or Moon would rise and set.

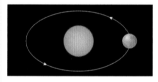

140 CE	1543	1609	1610

Earth in the middle
The people of the ancient world thought that the Sun moved around Earth and that Earth was the centre of the Universe. The Greek astronomer Ptolemy based his "geocentric model" of the solar system on this idea. Geocentric means Earth is in the middle. To make this model fit with the observation that planets sometimes appeared to move backwards through the sky, Ptolemy gave each planet a complex system of orbits within orbits (epicycles).

Ptolemy's model is called geocentric because it puts Earth in the centre.

Telescopes
After the telescope was invented in the early 1600s, the Italian scientist Galileo Galilei discovered mountains and craters on the Moon and four moons orbiting Jupiter. His observations supported the heliocentric model.

In a different light

Visible light is just one part of the electromagnetic spectrum. Astronomers can learn more about stars and galaxies by observing the other kinds of electromagnetic wave that they emit. Some of these waves are absorbed by Earth's atmosphere, so X-ray, ultraviolet, and infrared telescopes have to be launched into space. Radio telescopes can be built on the ground. The images here show what the Andromeda galaxy looks like at different wavelengths.

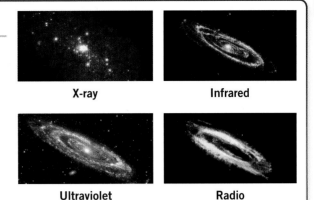

X-ray   **Infrared**

Ultraviolet   **Radio**

Theory of gravity
Inspired in part by Kepler's elliptical orbits, the English scientist Isaac Newton published a book that included his laws of gravity and motion. These mathematical models help to explain how the planets orbit the Sun and how moons orbit planets.

Newton also invented the reflecting telescope, which uses a curved mirror instead of lenses.

Andromeda galaxy

Discovering galaxies
In 1912 the American astronomer Henrietta Swan Leavitt worked out a way of calculating the distance from Earth to variable stars — stars whose brightness varies. In 1923 another American, Edwin Hubble, used her idea to demonstrate the existence of other galaxies beyond our own, revealing that the Universe was far bigger than anyone had realized.

1687   **1781**   **1908**   **Present day**

Better telescopes
As telescopes got bigger and better, astronomers discovered more distant objects. The German-born astronomer William Herschel discovered Uranus using a telescope 12 metres long. He also identified lots of nebulas — clouds of glowing material among the stars.

William Herschel constructed his giant telescope with his sister Caroline Herschel.

Modern observation methods
Today, astronomers can launch telescopes into space or build telescopes that detect radio waves or other forms of electromagnetic radiation instead of visible light. The information gathered has helped us explain how stars form and die, how gravity holds them together in galaxies, and how the Universe might have begun.

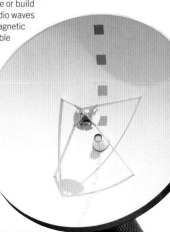

Radio telescope

Science and society

Scientific developments sometimes raise ethical questions that can't be answered by experiments, though gathering data can help people make informed decisions. The answers to questions such as the examples below depend on people's opinions, not on science.

Key facts

✓ Some scientific developments raise ethical questions.

✓ Questions about what is right or wrong cannot be answered by experiments and depend on people's opinions.

Cheap meat
Selective breeding can be used to produce farm animals that give better meat, cows that produce more milk, or hens that lay more eggs. However, changes that cut costs for farmers may be harmful to the animals. Chickens bred to grow very fast, for example, may be too heavy to walk. Are cheap meat and higher profits more important than animal welfare?

Clean energy
Climate change is happening because humans are adding too much carbon dioxide to the atmosphere. Tidal power generates electricity without producing carbon dioxide, but this sometimes involves building a barrage across a river estuary, preventing fish from migrating and changing natural habitats. Is clean energy more important than preserving wildlife habitats?

This golden rice is genetically engineered to produce extra vitamins.

Normal white rice

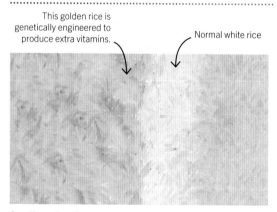

Genetic engineering
Genetic engineering can provide cures for diseases or alter crops to provide additional nutrients. These bring benefits to many people's lives, but genetically modified organisms are not natural. Is it wrong to modify life in this way?

Biofuel power station

Biofuels
Biofuels are fuels made from crops. Burning these fuels reduces carbon dioxide emissions compared with burning fossil fuels, as the crops absorb carbon dioxide as they grow. However, growing them uses land that could be used for food. Is clean energy more important than food supplies?

Risks and benefits

Science and technology can produce inventions that improve people's lives, but some technologies bring risks too. Benefits and risks need to be weighed up, taking all the evidence into account. Often the option that we think is more dangerous turns out not to be.

Key facts

✓ Modern technology can have great benefits, but some technologies can also cause harm.

✓ The risks and benefits of different technologies need to be assessed before deciding whether or not to use them.

Nuclear power or fossil fuels
Many people think nuclear power is dangerous because of the risk of accidents or radiation leaks. However, scientific studies suggest that fossil fuel power stations cause more illness and death through pollution, as well as contributing more to climate change. There are also more accidents caused by drilling for oil and mining coal than there are by obtaining nuclear fuel.

Walk or drive?
Which is safer – walking or driving? Accident statistics show that pedestrians suffer more fatal accidents per mile travelled than drivers. But this isn't the only factor. Walking is a form of exercise, and exercise can greatly reduce your chance of contracting illnesses such as heart disease and diabetes.

Flight safety
Air crashes are always big news and make some people afraid to fly. However, travelling by car is much more dangerous. For example, between the years 2000 and 2009, car occupants in the USA were more than 100 times more likely to have a fatal accident per mile travelled than passengers on commercial airliners.

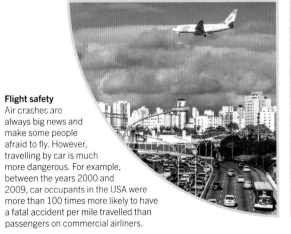

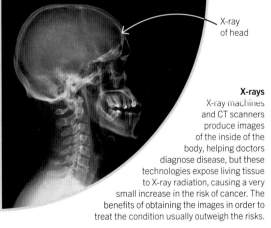

X-ray of head

X-rays
X-ray machines and CT scanners produce images of the inside of the body, helping doctors diagnose disease, but these technologies expose living tissue to X-ray radiation, causing a very small increase in the risk of cancer. The benefits of obtaining the images in order to treat the condition usually outweigh the risks.

Scientific models

We often use models to help us understand scientific ideas. Like hypotheses, models can be tested by experiments. There are five main types of scientific model: descriptive, computational, mathematical, spatial, and representational.

Key facts

✓ Models help us understand or describe a scientific idea.

✓ Models can be used to make predictions, which can then be tested by experiments.

✓ Types of model used in physics include descriptive, computational, mathematical, spatial, and representational.

Descriptive models
These models use words and sometimes diagrams to describe something. This diagram showing how electricity travels from power stations to our homes is a descriptive model.

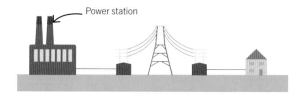
Power station

Computational models
Computational models use computers to simulate complex processes. Weather forecasts are made using computational models of the atmosphere. The image shown here is a forecast for the waves in the Atlantic Ocean.

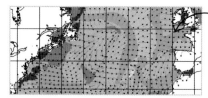
Yellow and green colours represent large waves.

Mathematical models
These are models that use equations to represent what happens in the real world. For example, a mathematical equation can model the fall in temperature as a hot object transfers heat to its surroundings. The results of mathematical models can be shown on graphs.

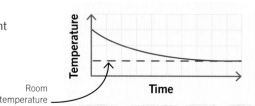
Temperature / Time / Room temperature

Spatial models
A spatial model shows how things are arranged in three-dimensional space, such as the way the parts of our ears fit together. This scale model is not the same size as a real human ear, but all the parts are the correct sizes relative to each other.

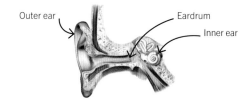
Outer ear / Eardrum / Inner ear

Representational models
These models use simplified shapes and symbols to represent more complex objects in the real world. For example, this circuit diagram helps us understand how the electrical circuit in a torch works.

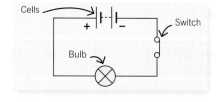
Cells / Switch / Bulb

Working safely

Physics experiments can involve electricity, moving objects, and heat, so there's a risk of being injured. It's important to conduct investigations safely, so be sure to follow these guidelines.

Protecting your eyes

Safety glasses or goggles protect your eyes against splashes of liquids or small particles such as iron filings. They should also be used if you are stretching wires or springs, in case the wire breaks and flies at your face.

Heating water

When heating water, take care to avoid splashing it on your skin. If scalded, run cold water over your skin as soon as possible.

Protecting your feet

Some physics experiments use weights that could fall on your feet and injure them. A cardboard box full of crumpled newspaper will catch a falling weight and stop you from putting your feet in the wrong place.

Slips and spills

If you spill water on the floor, clean it up straight away in case someone slips on it.

Working with electricity

When working with electricity, always switch off or disconnect the power supply or battery before making changes to a circuit. Ask your teacher to check the circuit before you switch it on.

Dangerous substances

Some science experiments involve radioactive materials or dangerous chemicals. These substances should only be handled by specially trained people wearing appropriate safety equipment. Experiments involving dangerous substances should not be carried out at home.

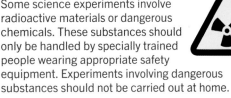

Bunsen burners

When using a Bunsen burner, keep the area around it clear. Tie back loose hair and clothing to keep them from getting near the flame. Allow hot equipment to cool before handling or use heat-resistant gloves.

Beware of the Sun

When doing experiments with light, never look directly at the Sun – it can permanently damage your eyes. The danger is even greater if using binoculars or a telescope.

Planning an experiment

To be a fair test, a scientific experiment should vary only one thing at a time to see what effect it has on something else. We call the thing you deliberately vary the independent variable. The thing it affects is the dependent variable, and things you need to keep constant are control variables.

Investigating insulation

In the scientific method, you test a hypothesis (an idea) by carrying out an experiment. Air is a poor conductor of heat, so you might form a hypothesis that materials containing lots of trapped air will be good insulators. To test this hypothesis, you could carry out an experiment like the one shown here. Three beakers of hot water are given different types of insulation, and the water temperature is measured regularly as the beakers cool down.

 Key facts

✓ Experiments must be carefully planned to ensure a fair test.

✓ Things that change in experiments are called variables.

✓ The independent variable is the thing you change.

✓ The dependent variable is the thing you measure.

✓ Control variables are the things you keep the same to ensure a fair test.

🔍 **Experimental controls**

The uninsulated beaker is an experimental control. It allows you to compare the temperature change with insulation to how it would change if no insulation had been used. Any differences must be due to the independent variable and not due to control variables such as the water volume or type of glass beaker.

The dependent variable is the water temperature. Measuring the temperature allows you to see if some kinds of insulation work better than others. Scientists collect data by measuring the dependent variable.

Thermometer

The independent variable is the type of insulation. This is the thing you vary to look for an effect. Each beaker of hot water has a different kind of insulation (or none).

Control variables include the water volume, its starting temperature, and the location of the beakers. These must be the same for every beaker to ensure a fair test.

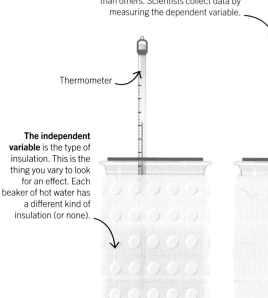

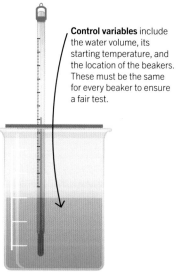

Bubble wrap　　　　**Fleece**　　　　**No insulation**

The planning process
Experiments should always be carefully planned in advance. The most important part of the planning process is to decide what the independent and dependent variables are. It's also important to work out what equipment you need and ensure the experiment can be conducted safely.

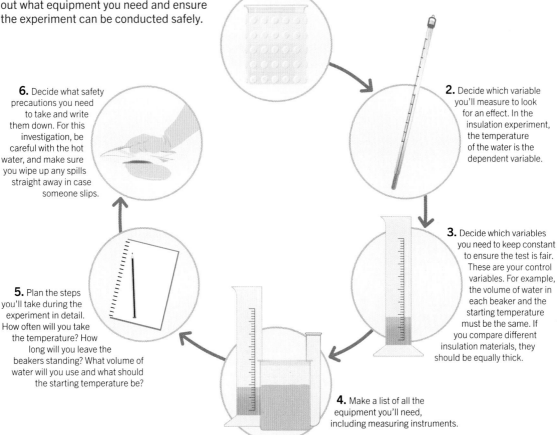

1. First decide which variable you will deliberately change. This is the independent variable. In the insulation experiment, the type of insulation is the independent variable.

2. Decide which variable you'll measure to look for an effect. In the insulation experiment, the temperature of the water is the dependent variable.

3. Decide which variables you need to keep constant to ensure the test is fair. These are your control variables. For example, the volume of water in each beaker and the starting temperature must be the same. If you compare different insulation materials, they should be equally thick.

4. Make a list of all the equipment you'll need, including measuring instruments.

5. Plan the steps you'll take during the experiment in detail. How often will you take the temperature? How long will you leave the beakers standing? What volume of water will you use and what should the starting temperature be?

6. Decide what safety precautions you need to take and write them down. For this investigation, be careful with the hot water, and make sure you wipe up any spills straight away in case someone slips.

Collecting data

All experiments involve collecting data, which we use to see if a hypothesis is supported or not. Planning how and when to collect data is important. For this experiment, taking the temperature regularly allows you to create a graph of your results. The graph helps you spot possible errors in the measurements, and it helps you reach a conclusion.

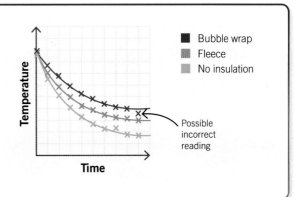

- Bubble wrap
- Fleece
- No insulation

Possible incorrect reading

Measuring

Most experiments involve taking measurements of physical quantities, such as temperature, volume, mass, or time. To obtain accurate data, you need to use an instrument suited to the size of the quantity you are measuring.

Key facts

✓ Most experiments involve measurements of physical quantities, such as temperature, volume, mass, or time.

✓ Instruments that can measure large quantities are usually not accurate when measuring small quantities.

Length and distance

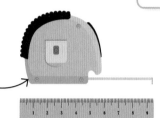

Use a tape to measure longer distances, such as when finding your walking speed over 10 metres.

Use a ruler to measure the length of a small object.

Volume

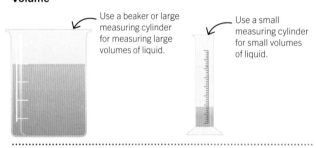

Use a beaker or large measuring cylinder for measuring large volumes of liquid.

Use a small measuring cylinder for small volumes of liquid.

Time

Use a stopwatch to measure periods of time greater than 10 seconds.

Use an electronic timer, like this light gate, to measure very small time intervals.

Force

This force meter has a stiff spring and can measure forces up to 50 N, but it is not very accurate for measuring very small forces.

This force meter has a stretchier spring and can accurately measure small forces. You will damage it if you try to measure a large force with it.

🔍 Electronic instruments

Electronic instruments are often more accurate than manual versions. However, this doesn't always make them the best choice. They are more expensive and easier to damage, so they should only be used in experiments where greater accuracy is necessary.

A digital multimeter can measure voltage, current, and resistance.

Test leads are connected to circuits.

Significant figures

The significant figures in a number are the digits that have meaningful information. More accurate measuring devices produce values with more significant figures. When collecting data or doing calculations, we often need to round numbers up or down to just a few significant figures.

Recording data

The number of significant figures depends on the measuring instruments you use. For instance, a ruler with a scale divided into centimetres gives fewer significant figures than a ruler with a scale divided into millimetres. Digital instruments often give more significant figures than traditional ones (but this doesn't necessarily mean they are more accurate).

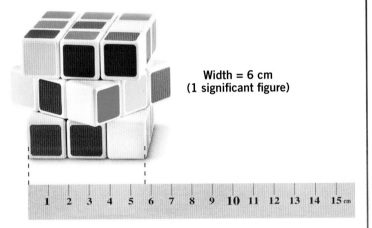

**Width = 6 cm
(1 significant figure)**

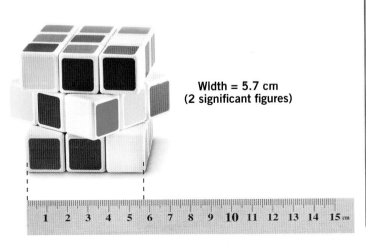

**Width = 5.7 cm
(2 significant figures)**

 Key facts

✓ **More accurate measuring instruments produce values with more significant figures.**

✓ **When multiplying or dividing, round answers to the same number of significant figures as the least accurate starting value.**

✓ **When adding or subtracting, round answers to the same number of decimal places as the least accurate starting value.**

Using calculators

Sums done on calculators may give you more significant figures than you need. Suppose you calculate the resistance of a light bulb using the formula below. You use readings from a voltmeter and an ammeter that each show values to three significant figures.

$$R = \frac{8.12 \text{ V}}{1.04 \text{ A}}$$

The answer on a calculator is 7.8076923.

Writing your answer like this implies you know the resistance to 8 significant figures, but the measuring instruments were only accurate to 3 significant figures, so your answer should be too:

$R = 7.81 \ \Omega$ (3 s.f.)

When multiplying or dividing, round your answer to the same number of significant figures as the least accurate starting value. When adding or subtracting, round your answer to the same number of decimal places as the least accurate starting value.

Presenting data

Data is the information you collect from experiments. It often consists of numbers such as measurements. Organizing data into tables, charts, or graphs helps you to make sense of it and spot patterns. The kind of chart or graph you use depends on the kind of data you collect.

Tables

Tables are useful for organizing data and for doing simple calculations, such as working out mean (average) values. This table shows results from an experiment investigating how mass added to a trolley affects its acceleration.

Independent variable

Dependent variable

Mass added to trolley (kg)	Acceleration (m/s²)			
	1st run	2nd run	3rd run	Mean
0.5	9.9	10.2	10.1	10.1
1.0	6.8	8.8	6.6	6.7
1.5	5.2	4.8	5.1	5.0

Tables help us spot "outliers". These are very different from the other values and may be mistakes. This value was ignored when calculating the mean.

Pie charts

Use a pie chart to show percentages or relative amounts. For example, this pie chart shows estimates of different sources of background radiation that people are exposed to worldwide.

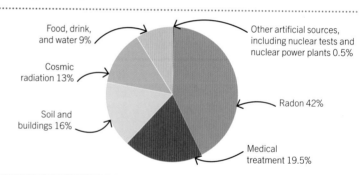

Food, drink, and water 9%

Other artificial sources, including nuclear tests and nuclear power plants 0.5%

Cosmic radiation 13%

Soil and buildings 16%

Radon 42%

Medical treatment 19.5%

Bar charts

Use a bar chart when the independent variable is made up of discrete (separate) categories. For example, this bar chart shows how much energy different groups of people need each day. You should also use a bar chart when the independent variable consists of discrete values, such as numbers of people or numbers of objects (which are always counted in whole numbers).

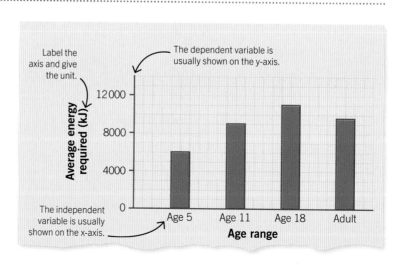

Label the axis and give the unit.

The dependent variable is usually shown on the y-axis.

The independent variable is usually shown on the x-axis.

Continuous and discrete variables

Discrete variables are variables that can only have certain values. For example, the number of passengers on a plane can only be a whole number, and the insulation around a container of hot water can only consist of certain materials. A continuous variable, however, can take any value and may not be a whole number. Length and weight, for example, are continuous variables.

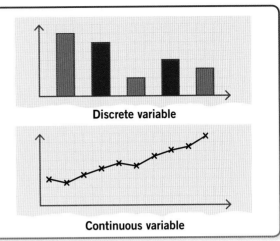

Discrete variable

Continuous variable

Line graphs

Use a line graph when both axes show numerical values that vary continuously rather than dividing into discrete (separate) categories. Line graphs are often used when one of your variables is time. This graph shows how the temperature of ice changes as it is heated.

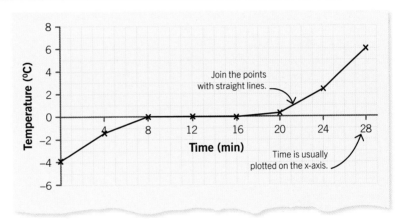

Join the points with straight lines.

Time is usually plotted on the x-axis.

Scatter graphs

Use a scatter graph to investigate a relationship between two variables. This graph shows how the current through a resistor and through a bulb varies when the voltage is changed. If the data points form a clear pattern when plotted on the graph, such as a line, we say the variables are correlated. When this is the case, draw a straight "line of best fit" or "curve of best fit" through the points.

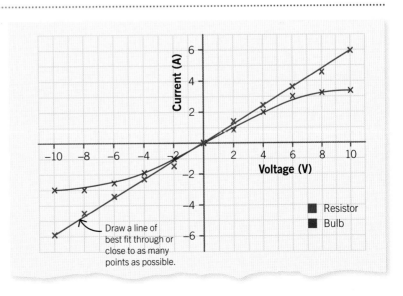

Draw a line of best fit through or close to as many points as possible.

Resistor
Bulb

Patterns in data

In some experiments you might look to see if there is a relationship between two variables. In other words, if you change one variable, how does it affect the other?

Correlation

When two variables appear to be linked, we say they are correlated. Plotting a scatter graph of your data is a good way to spot correlations. A correlation between two variables doesn't show that one causes the other. For example, ice cream sales and swimming accidents are positively correlated, but this is because ice cream and swimming are both more popular in hot weather and not because ice cream causes swimming accidents.

Key facts

✓ A correlation is when one variable changes as the other variable does.

✓ A correlation does not show that one change causes the other.

✓ A relationship between two variables is linear if the points form a straight line when plotted on a graph.

✓ A relationship is proportional if a straight line goes through the origin.

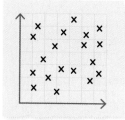

No correlation
The data points are scattered about randomly and show no pattern. There is no correlation between the variables.

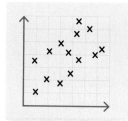

Weak correlation
The points look as if they might be grouped around a diagonal line. The large scatter means this is only a weak relationship.

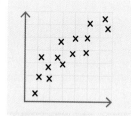

Strong positive correlation
The points form a diagonal line, showing that one variable increases as the other one does.

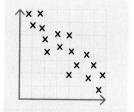

Strong negative correlation
The line formed by these points shows that one variable decreases as the other increases. This is a negative correlation.

Linear and proportional relationships

Graphs showing correlation can reveal other interesting patterns in a relationship, depending on their shape.

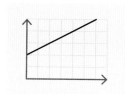

Linear
A correlation where the points form a straight line is described as linear.

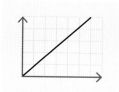

Proportional
If the points form a straight line through the origin (where x and y both equal zero), the relationship is described as proportional. This means that if one variable doubles, so does the other.

Inversely proportional
In an inversely proportional relationship, one variable halves when the other doubles. This forms a curved line.

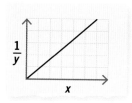

Checking
To check whether a relationship is inversely proportional, plot one variable against the inverse of the other (1 divided by the value). The graph should be a straight line through the origin.

Conclusions

The conclusion of an experiment describes what you found out, interprets the results, and says whether the experiment agrees with the prediction you made.

An electricity experiment
Three students carried out an experiment to test the prediction that the current flowing through a bulb is proportional to the voltage across it. By using an ammeter to measure current in the circuit and a voltmeter to measure voltage across the bulb, they obtained the results shown in the graph. Their conclusions are shown below.

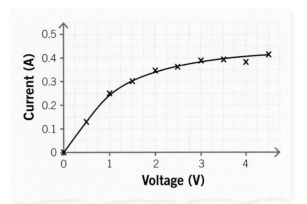

Conclusion 1
"The current does go up when the voltage goes up, so the prediction was correct."

An incorrect conclusion
The description is not detailed, and the graph does not show a proportional relationship, which would produce a straight line.

Conclusion 2
"The current increases as voltage increases, but the graph is a curve. A proportional relationship would produce a straight line, so the prediction was not correct."

A better conclusion
The description has more detail and the final conclusion is correct.

Conclusion 3
"The graph shows that the current increases as the voltage increases. At lower voltages, the relationship could be proportional, as the first few points fall on a straight line. However, at higher voltages there is a smaller increase in current for every increase in voltage. This shows that the resistance is increasing. The prediction was partially correct, as the current does increase with voltage, but the relationship is not proportional."

An excellent conclusion
The description is much more detailed. The student has used their knowledge of the link between current, resistance, and voltage to suggest what may be causing the change in shape of the graph.

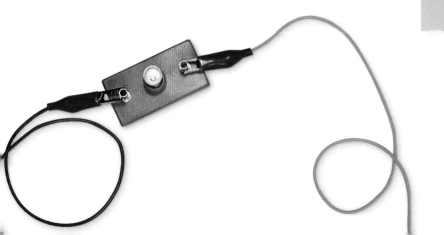

Accuracy and precision

When planning and evaluating an experiment, you need to think about the accuracy and precision of your measurements. The words accurate and precise have specific meanings in science.

Accurate or precise?

A measurement is considered more accurate if it is closer than other measurements to the true value being measured. It is precise if repeating the measurement several times produces values that are the same or very close to each other. To understand the difference, it helps to think of measurements as trying to hit a target.

Key facts

✓ Accurate measurements are ones that are close to the true value being measured.

✓ Precise measurements are those that give the same (or similar) values when the measurement is repeated.

✓ Errors in measurements can be random or systematic.

The centre of the target represents the true value being measured.

Inaccurate and imprecise
The measurements are inaccurate as they are not near the centre of the target, and imprecise as they are not close to each other.

Precise but inaccurate
These measurements are precise because they are all nearly the same value, but they are inaccurate because they aren't close to the centre.

Accurate but not precise
These are close to the centre but not to each other, so they are accurate but not precise.

Accurate and precise
These measurements are both accurate and precise.

🔍 Types of error

Systematic errors
The accuracy of some instruments depends on how they're used. Balances should be set to zero with a container on them so you only measure the mass of the contents. If a balance is not zeroed properly, all the measurements will be incorrect by the same amount. This is a systematic error and reduces the accuracy of the measurements.

This ought to be zero when the beaker is empty.

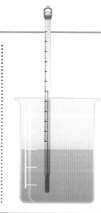

Random errors
Random errors are different for every reading. For example, if you take the temperature of water in a beaker, the thermometer might return a slightly different reading each time it dips into a different part of the water. This reduces the precision of your measurements.

Evaluations

We often evaluate our experiments to decide how much we can trust the results. An experiment has to be valid and fair, and the conclusions must be based on high-quality data. An evaluation may also suggest how the method could be improved.

Is the experiment valid?
An experiment is valid if you can answer "yes" to all of these questions.

Was it a fair test?
Did you control all the variables apart from the independent variable you were testing?

Is it reproducible?
If a different person carries out the experiment using different equipment, do they get the same results?

Is it repeatable?
If you repeat the experiment using the same equipment, do you get the same results?

Did it test the hypothesis?
Did you make a prediction from your hypothesis? Was the experiment a good test of the hypothesis?

Data quality
Good data is accurate and precise. You can assess the quality of your data by repeating an experiment, but sometimes you can also tell by looking carefully at the results. The graphs below are from an experiment measuring the extension of a spring holding different weights.

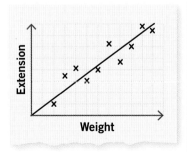

The data points are scattered about the line of best fit. The data is not precise.

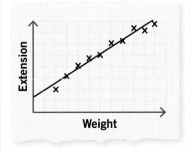

The points are closer to the line, so the data is precise. However, extension should be zero for zero weight, so it's odd that the line does not pass through the origin. There may be a systematic error (see page 26) causing inaccurate data.

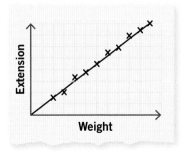

This data is very close to the line of best fit, and the line goes through the origin, as we expect. This data is both accurate and precise.

Using mathematical models

Mathematical models use equations to represent what happens in the real world. Sometimes we can work out a mathematical model from a graph of results. At other times, we might use an equation to predict a result.

Key facts

✓ Mathematical models use equations to represent what happens in the real world.

✓ Mathematical models can be used to describe graphs of results.

✓ We can rearrange equations to calculate particular quantities.

Linear equations

If a relationship between two variables produces a straight line on a graph, we call the relationship linear. Linear relationships can be described by equations written like this: $y = mx + c$. For instance, this graph shows how the length of a spring changes when different weights are hung on it. If you know the original length of the spring and the slope of the line, you can use the graph or the equation to work out the spring's length for any weight.

Length (m) vs **Weight (N)**

The line can be described by the following equation:
length = (spring constant × weight) + original length.

Original length of spring

Rearranging equations

Sometimes you need to rearrange an equation before doing a calculation. For example, the equation $F = m \times a$ tells you how to calculate force if you know mass and acceleration, but what if you're told the force and asked to calculate acceleration? You need to rearrange the formula so that a is the subject. You can do it by dividing each side by m. Remember that equations have to stay balanced, so the same operation must be carried out on both sides.

$$F = m \times a$$

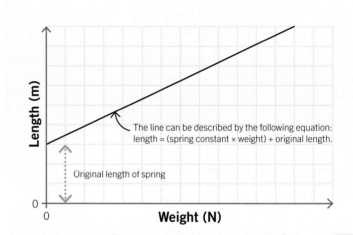

1. $F = m \times a$

2. $\dfrac{F}{m} = \dfrac{m \times a}{m}$ — Divide both sides by m.

3. $\dfrac{F}{m} = \dfrac{m \times a}{m}$ — These two m's cancel each other out.

4. $\dfrac{F}{m} = a$

5. $a = \dfrac{F}{m}$

Standard form

Saturn is about 1 400 000 000 000 metres from the Sun. A bacterium is about 0.000 001 metres wide. It's easy to make mistakes in calculations when numbers have lots of zeros, so we simplify them by writing them in "standard form". This shows a long number as a much shorter number (from 1 to under 10) multiplied by a power of 10. To work out the power of 10, count how many times the decimal point has to move.

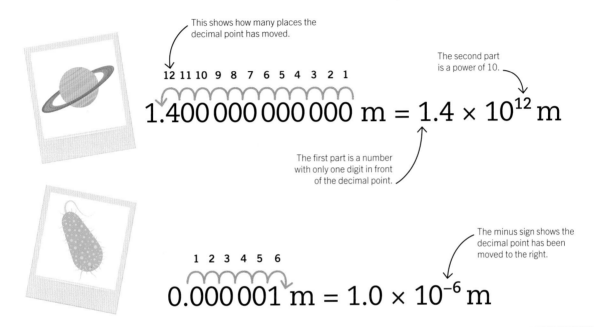

This shows how many places the decimal point has moved.

The second part is a power of 10.

12 11 10 9 8 7 6 5 4 3 2 1

$$1.400\,000\,000\,000 \text{ m} = 1.4 \times 10^{12}\,\text{m}$$

The first part is a number with only one digit in front of the decimal point.

The minus sign shows the decimal point has been moved to the right.

1 2 3 4 5 6

$$0.000\,001\,\text{m} = 1.0 \times 10^{-6}\,\text{m}$$

Calculating percentages

A percentage is a number shown as a fraction of 100. To turn any fraction into a percentage, work out the fraction on a calculator, multiply the answer by 100, and add a percentage symbol. For example, a 30 watt light bulb transfers 18 watts of power to light and wastes the other 12 watts as heat. What's its efficiency as a percentage?

$$\text{efficiency (\%)} = \frac{\text{useful power output (W)}}{\text{total power input (W)}} \times 100$$

$$= \frac{18\text{ W}}{30\text{ W}} \times 100$$

$$= 0.6 \times 100$$

$$= 60\%$$

SI units

Science is an international activity. Scientists from different countries work together on the same problems, so it helps if everyone uses the same units for measurements. Scientists around the world use the *Système International* (SI) system of units.

Base units
All SI units are based on a small number of base units. The five base units in the table below are used in this book.

Quantity	SI base unit	Symbol
time	second	s
length	metre	m
mass	kilogram	kg
current	ampere (amp)	A
temperature	kelvin	K

One unit on the Kelvin temperature scale is the same size as one degree on the Celsius scale, but the scales start at different points.

Derived units
Most SI units are derived from base units. For example, the unit for area (m^2) is based on the metre.

Quantity	SI unit
area	square metre (m^2)
volume	cubic metre (m^3)
speed and velocity	metres per second (m/s)
acceleration	metres per second squared (m/s^2)
frequency	hertz (Hz)
force	newton (N)
momentum	kilogram metres per second (kg m/s)
pressure	pascal (Pa)
energy	joule (J)
power	watt (W)
charge	coulomb (C)
potential difference (voltage)	volt (V)
resistance	ohm (Ω)

1 Hz = 1 per second

1 Pa = 1 N/m^2

1 W = 1 J/s

SI prefixes
A metre isn't a very useful unit for measuring the size of an atom or the distance to Mars, so we add prefixes to standard units to make bigger or smaller versions.

Prefix	Multiplies by	Example
nano (n)	10^{-9}	1 nanometre (nm) = 0.000 000 001 m
micro (μ)	10^{-6}	1 microsecond (μs) = 0.000 001 s
milli (m)	10^{-3}	1 milligram (mg) = 0.001 g
centi (c)	10^{-2}	1 centimetre (cm) = 0.01 m
kilo (k)	10^{3}	1 kilogram (kg) = 1000 g
mega (M)	10^{6}	1 megahertz (MHz) = 1 000 000 Hz
giga (G)	10^{9}	1 gigawatt (GW) = 1 000 000 000 W
tera (T)	10^{12}	1 terawatt (TW) = 1 000 000 000 000 W

Energy

Energy

Energy is the ability to make something happen. It moves your arms and legs, charges your phone, powers your TV, and makes the Sun shine. Energy can be stored in different ways or transferred from one store to another, but it can never be destroyed.

Key facts

✓ **Energy can be stored in many different ways.**

✓ **Energy can be transferred from one energy store to another.**

✓ **Energy cannot be destroyed.**

✓ **Movement energy is also called kinetic energy.**

Light transfers energy from a bulb to its surroundings.

The faster the clockwork robot walks, the greater its store of kinetic energy.

Energy stores
Energy can be stored in different ways. The energy stored by a moving object is called kinetic energy. The faster an object is moving, the greater its kinetic energy.

Energy transfers
Energy can be transferred from one energy store to another. When you switch on a lamp, the bulb transfers energy to the surroundings by light and heating.

Energy and food

The food we eat supplies our bodies with energy. We measure the amount of energy in food using units called kilojoules.

Energy in different foods

Different foods store different amounts of energy. We sometimes measure food energy in Calories, but the scientific unit for energy is the joule. Food contains thousands of joules, so we use units called kilojoules (1 kJ = 1000 J). The chart here shows how long you would have to run for to use up the energy in different foods.

Key facts

✓ The scientific unit for energy is the joule (J).

✓ The energy in food is often shown in kilojoules (1 kJ = 1000 J).

✓ A person's daily energy requirement depends on their age, size, and level of physical activity.

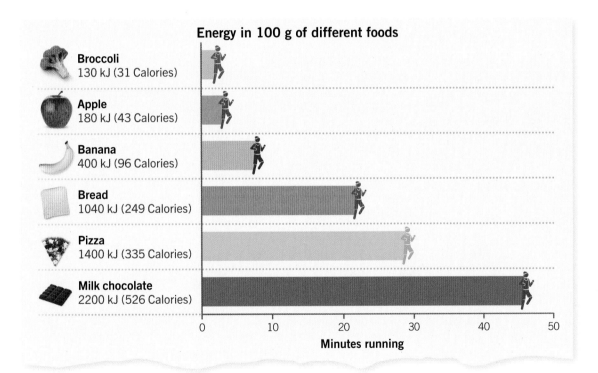

Energy in 100 g of different foods

Broccoli
130 kJ (31 Calories)

Apple
180 kJ (43 Calories)

Banana
400 kJ (96 Calories)

Bread
1040 kJ (249 Calories)

Pizza
1400 kJ (335 Calories)

Milk chocolate
2200 kJ (526 Calories)

Minutes running

🔍 Energy and exercise

The average adult needs around 10000 kJ of energy a day, but the figure varies from person to person and from day to day. In general, the greater a person's mass, the more energy they need – so adults use more energy than children. How physically active you are also affects how much energy your body uses.

Walking
800–1700 kJ
per hour

Swimming
1200–3000 kJ
per hour

Jogging
1900–4000 kJ
per hour

Energy stores

Energy isn't just stored in batteries — it can be stored in many different ways, from the kinetic energy stored in a moving car to the potential energy of a diver on a high diving board. When energy moves from one store to another, we say the energy is transferred.

Key facts

✓ Energy can be stored in many different ways, including thermal energy, chemical energy, gravitational potential energy, kinetic energy, elastic energy, and nuclear energy.

✓ An energy transfer is the movement of energy from one store to another.

Thermal energy
When energy is stored in hot objects, we call it heat energy or thermal energy. When you heat water to make tea or coffee, its store of thermal energy increases.

Kinetic energy
A moving object has kinetic energy. The faster it moves or the greater its mass, the greater its store of kinetic energy.

Chemical energy
Energy stored in chemical bonds is called chemical energy. The energy stored in batteries and food is stored as chemical energy. Explosives and fuels store large amounts of chemical energy that transfers to thermal energy when they burn.

Elastic potential energy
Stretch a rubber band or squeeze a spring and it will store elastic potential energy until you release it. Elastic potential energy can also be stored in objects when they're squashed or twisted.

Nuclear energy
The energy stored inside atoms is called nuclear energy or atomic energy. This store of energy powers nuclear reactors, nuclear bombs, and the Sun.

Gravitational potential energy
An object or a person raised to a high position stores gravitational potential energy (GPE). When a diver falls, their GPE is transferred to kinetic energy.

🔍 Hydroelectric power

Hydroelectric power stations use gravitational potential energy to make electricity. A dam is built to hold back a river in a valley, forming a deep artificial lake. Water from the lake flows downhill through pipes inside the dam, turning machines called turbines, which drive electricity generators. Gravitational potential energy transfers to kinetic energy in the turbines and ultimately to electrical energy, which is used to power homes.

Energy transfers

When you switch on a light, ride a bike, cook a meal, or do anything at all, you transfer energy from one energy store to another. Energy transfers make everything happen.

Energy transfer by heating
Heating an object transfers energy to its thermal energy store. This either makes the object warmer or causes a change of state to happen. Here, chemical energy stored in fuel is transferred by heating to water in a kettle. The hot water will eventually cool down as energy escapes, but the total amount of energy shared by the fuel, stove, kettle, water, and their surroundings remains constant. This is called the law of conservation of energy.

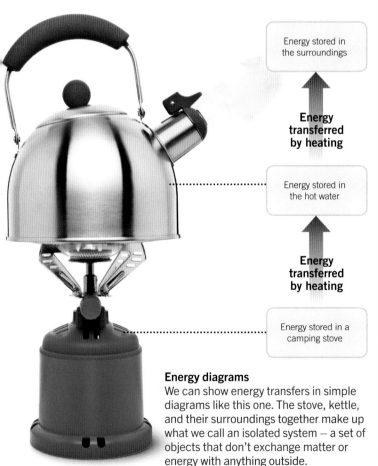

Energy stored in the surroundings

Energy transferred by heating

Energy stored in the hot water

Energy transferred by heating

Energy stored in a camping stove

Energy diagrams
We can show energy transfers in simple diagrams like this one. The stove, kettle, and their surroundings together make up what we call an isolated system – a set of objects that don't exchange matter or energy with anything outside.

Other energy transfers

Heating isn't the only way to transfer energy. Energy can also be transferred by forces, electricity, radiation, and sound.

By forces
If a force acts on an object, for example by moving it, it transfers energy to the object. We call the energy transferred in this way work.

By electricity
Whenever you switch on an electric device, energy is transferred along the wires by electricity.

By radiation
Different forms of radiation – such as visible light, X-rays, and microwaves – transfer energy at incredible speeds. Our planet gets most of its energy in this way from the Sun.

By sound
Like all types of wave, sound waves transfer energy as they travel. When sound waves reach your ears, the energy is transferred to your eardrums, which vibrate.

Renewable energy resources

Sources of energy that will never run out are called renewable energy resources. These energy resources are becoming more widely used because they contribute far less to climate change than fossil fuels. All sources of renewable energy have advantages and disadvantages.

Key facts

- ✓ Sources of energy that will never run out are called renewable.
- ✓ Renewable energy resources contribute far less to climate change than fossil fuels.
- ✓ Sources of renewable energy include solar, biofuels, wind, hydroelectric, tidal, wave, and geothermal.

Solar energy

A solar power station uses the Sun's energy to generate electricity. At a concentrated solar power plant, mirrors arranged in circles focus sunlight onto a central receiver, where the heat is used to boil water and make steam, which drives a generator. Electricity can also be produced directly using solar cells (photovoltaic cells). Solar power plants and solar cells work best in sunny climates and can't generate electricity at night.

Biofuels

In some parts of the world, biofuels are used to power cars rather than petrol or diesel. Biofuels can be made from fast-growing crops like sugar cane. The sugar is fermented to make ethanol, which can be burned in car engines. Although biofuels contribute less to global warming than fossil fuels, their production takes up land that could be used to grow food and has led to deforestation in tropical areas.

Wind energy

Warmed by the Sun, the air in Earth's atmosphere is continually moving, and this kinetic energy can be captured by wind turbines and used to generate electricity. Wind turbines require suitable weather and must be high above the ground or sea to work well. Many wind farms are built offshore (in the sea), where they don't spoil the appearance of natural landscapes.

Hydroelectricity
Hydroelectric dams hold back rivers to form artificial lakes. Water from the lake flows through pipes to turbines at the bottom of the dam. The turbines drive generators, which produce electricity. One disadvantage of hydroelectricity is that the natural habitat of the valley is lost when it's flooded to make the lake.

Wave and tidal energy
Wave and tidal power stations use the motion of sea water to drive turbines placed in water. Wave power is still experimental. Tidal power stations are difficult and expensive to build but can produce large amounts of electricity at predictable times, though not constantly. One disadvantage is that they can change tidal patterns upstream, affecting the wildlife there.

Geothermal energy
At a geothermal power station, cold water is pumped deep underground, where it is heated to make steam by energy from Earth's interior. The steam is then used to drive electricity generators. Geothermal power stations produce very little pollution but work best in volcanically active places.

🔍 Power stations

Most power stations use the same system to generate electricity. Energy from fuels or from the Sun is used to turn water into steam, which flows through pipes and turns spinning fans called turbines. The turbines drive generators, which create electricity. In wind farms, hydroelectric power stations, and wave or tidal power stations, moving water or air turns the turbines directly.

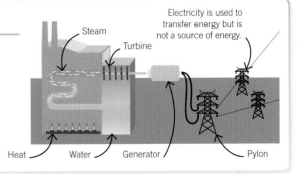

Electricity is used to transfer energy but is not a source of energy.

Steam · Turbine · Heat · Water · Generator · Pylon

Non-renewable energy

The modern world uses a lot of energy to power everything from cars and planes to the gadgets in our homes. Most of our energy comes from non-renewable resources (resources that will run out one day), such as fossil fuels.

Fossil fuels

Fossil fuels formed from the remains of plants and algae that lived in the distant past. For millions of years, these organisms transferred energy from sunlight to stored chemical energy. These fuels are very useful because a small mass of fossil fuel stores a large quantity of energy. However, burning fossil fuels pollutes the atmosphere with carbon dioxide and is the main cause of climate change.

Key facts

✓ Non-renewable energy comes from energy resources that will run out.

✓ Most of our energy comes from non-renewable sources.

✓ Burning fossil fuels pollutes the atmosphere and causes climate change.

Oil
Oil (petroleum) comes from tiny fossilized sea organisms. Crude oil obtained from underground is used to make petrol, diesel, and kerosene (a liquid fuel used to power jet engines in aircraft). These fuels are very convenient to store, transport, refill tanks, and burn in engines.

Coal
This solid fuel formed from the fossilized remains of trees and other plants. Coal is burned in power stations and generates much of the world's electricity. As well as producing carbon dioxide when it burns, it produces a pollutant called sulphur dioxide, which causes acid rain.

Natural gas
Natural gas is burned in power stations to make electricity and in homes to power central heating systems or cook food. It transfers about twice as much energy per kilogram as coal, which means it releases only half as much carbon dioxide when burned, causing less pollution.

🔍 Nuclear power

Nuclear power stations use the energy stored in the atomic nuclei of radioactive elements such as uranium. Nuclear fuels are non-renewable but they store huge amounts of energy and do not emit greenhouse gases such as carbon dioxide. Disadvantages of nuclear power include the production of radioactive waste that remains harmful for thousands of years and requires burial deep underground, and the risk of widespread contamination of the environment if there is an accident.

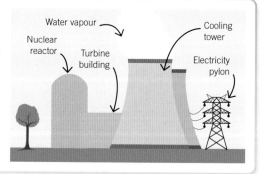

Water vapour · Nuclear reactor · Turbine building · Cooling tower · Electricity pylon

Climate change

Much of the energy we use comes from fossil fuels, which release carbon dioxide gas (CO_2) when we burn them. CO_2 is a greenhouse gas — it traps heat in Earth's atmosphere. As atmospheric levels of CO_2 have risen, the planet's climate has changed.

The greenhouse effect

The main cause of climate change is pollution of the atmosphere with greenhouse gases, such as CO_2 from fossil fuels and methane from agriculture. These gases absorb heat radiated from Earth's surface and reradiate it into the air, making the atmosphere warmer (much as glass traps warmth in a greenhouse). Without any greenhouse effect, Earth would be too cold for most life. However, human activity is making the effect too strong.

Key facts

✓ The use of fossil fuels as an energy resource releases carbon dioxide (CO_2) into the atmosphere.

✓ Rising levels of atmospheric CO_2 and other greenhouse gases cause climate change through the greenhouse effect.

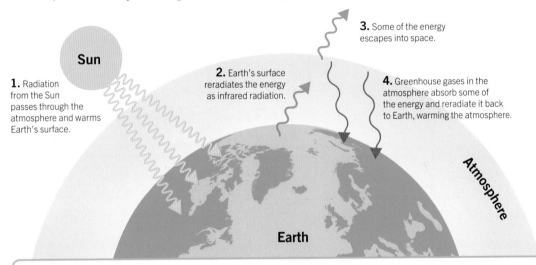

1. Radiation from the Sun passes through the atmosphere and warms Earth's surface.

2. Earth's surface reradiates the energy as infrared radiation.

3. Some of the energy escapes into space.

4. Greenhouse gases in the atmosphere absorb some of the energy and reradiate it back to Earth, warming the atmosphere.

Sun

Earth

Atmosphere

⚙ Atmospheric CO_2

Measurements of CO_2 levels in the atmosphere show they are currently rising steeply. Levels of CO_2 in the distant past can also be measured by sampling bubbles of air trapped in ancient ice sheets. These studies show that CO_2 levels were stable until about 200 years ago, when the use of fossil fuels began rising rapidly.

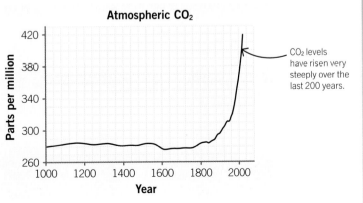

Atmospheric CO_2

Parts per million

420

380

340

300

260

1000 1200 1400 1600 1800 2000

Year

CO_2 levels have risen very steeply over the last 200 years.

Trends in energy use

Our consumption of energy resources — especially fossil fuels — has increased dramatically in the last 200 years. Because fossil fuels are non-renewable and harm the environment, many countries are now trying to increase their use of renewable energy instead.

Energy consumption
The graph shows how consumption of different energy resources has grown since the year 1800, when the world was starting to industrialize. The rise in the use of fossil fuels has caused a rise in the level of carbon dioxide in the atmosphere — the main cause of climate change.

Key facts

✓ The use of fossil fuels has increased dramatically in the last 200 years.

✓ The use of fossil fuels is one of the causes of climate change.

✓ Many countries are now trying to reduce their use of fossil fuels and increase their use of renewable energy.

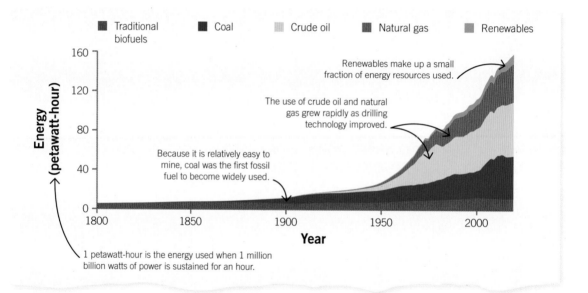

Renewables make up a small fraction of energy resources used.

The use of crude oil and natural gas grew rapidly as drilling technology improved.

Because it is relatively easy to mine, coal was the first fossil fuel to become widely used.

1 petawatt-hour is the energy used when 1 million billion watts of power is sustained for an hour.

🔍 Carbon capture and storage

Carbon dioxide released when fossil fuels are burned is the main cause of climate change. One idea proposed to reduce emissions is carbon capture. The carbon dioxide in waste gases from power stations is made to react with chemicals called amines to form a liquid that can be stored underground. Power stations could cut emissions by 90 per cent this way, but the electricity they produce would be more expensive.

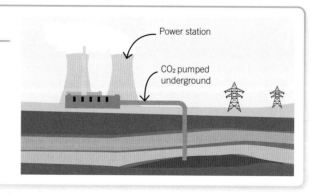

Efficiency

When you switch on a light, not all the energy is transferred to the surroundings by light – some of it is transferred to the air by heating. This is wasted energy. An efficient device is one that wastes only a small percentage of the energy it transfers.

Sankey diagrams

We can show how efficient a device is with a Sankey diagram. The diagrams here show that old-fashioned filament light bulbs have very low efficiency because most of the energy is transferred to the surroundings as heat. In contrast, an LED light bulb transfers most of its electrical energy to light and wastes only a small amount as heat.

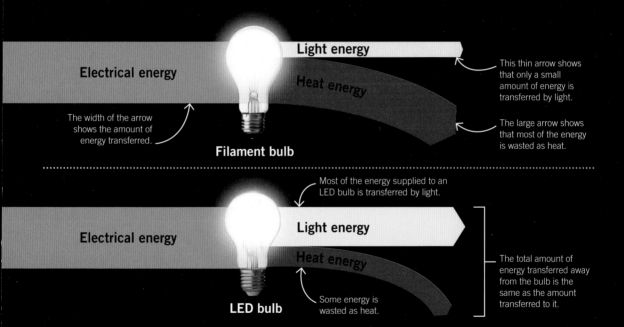

Light energy

Electrical energy

Heat energy

This thin arrow shows that only a small amount of energy is transferred by light.

The width of the arrow shows the amount of energy transferred.

Filament bulb

The large arrow shows that most of the energy is wasted as heat.

Most of the energy supplied to an LED bulb is transferred by light.

Electrical energy

Light energy

Heat energy

LED bulb

Some energy is wasted as heat.

The total amount of energy transferred away from the bulb is the same as the amount transferred to it.

🔍 Improving efficiency

All machines and devices waste energy, and that wasted energy ultimately escapes to the surroundings as heat. For example, bicycles waste energy through friction between moving parts. This can be reduced by keeping the chain and other moving parts lubricated. By using energy-efficient electrical devices in our homes, we can reduce how much energy we waste and so reduce our consumption of fossil fuels, which is good for the environment.

Efficiency

Many household appliances have energy-efficiency labels that help people choose the most efficient product to buy.

Heat transfers

Why do hot drinks cool down? Stores of thermal energy (heat) never stay in one place — the energy always transfers from hot things to colder things. These transfers can happen in different ways.

Heating water
When water is heated on a gas hob, energy is transferred is three ways: by conduction, convection, and radiation.

Cold water sinks

Hot water rises

Convection is the transfer of heat by currents moving within a fluid. As water in the bottom of the jug heats up, it expands and becomes less dense. This makes it rise, creating convection currents.

Conduction is the transfer of thermal energy through solids or between materials that are in physical contact. Heat from the burning fuel transfers through the glass to the water by conduction.

Radiation is the transfer of energy by electromagnetic waves, which travel at the speed of light. As well as emitting light that we can see, the flames emit infrared radiation.

🔍 Thermal equilibrium

If you leave a hot drink standing, it will cool down until it's the same temperature as its surroundings. Similarly, a cold drink will warm up. This is because energy continually transfers from hotter objects to colder objects until they are at the same temperature as each other. When that happens, we say that they are in thermal equilibrium.

Hot drink

Cold drink

Radiation

When you put your hand near a hot teapot, you can feel its heat warm your skin. That's because your skin can sense something your eyes can't see: infrared radiation. All objects emit infrared radiation, but the hotter an object is, the more radiation it gives out.

Thermal images

Although infrared radiation is invisible to our eyes, thermal cameras can detect it. This thermal image shows the radiation emitted by hot tea in a cup and a teapot. Like visible light, infrared radiation is a form of electromagnetic radiation and can travel through space. When it strikes an object, some of the infrared radiation is absorbed and transfers energy to the object's thermal energy store, making it warmer. You can feel this warmth on your skin when you put your hand close to a hot cup without touching it.

Key facts

- ✓ Hotter objects emit more infrared radiation than cooler objects.
- ✓ When infrared radiation strikes an object, it transfers energy to its thermal energy store.
- ✓ Matt black surfaces are better at absorbing and emitting infrared radiation than shiny or white surfaces.

Cooler areas appear blue.

Hotter areas are represented by white or pink in this thermal image.

Some of the infrared radiation emitted by the teapot is reflected by the table top.

Thermal energy has spread into the teapot's handle by conduction.

🔍 Absorbers and reflectors

The amount of energy an object absorbs from infrared radiation depends on the colour and texture of its surface. Matt (non-shiny) and black surfaces are good at absorbing and emitting infrared radiation. White or shiny objects, however, reflect radiation, so they absorb relatively little thermal energy.

Black absorbs and emits infrared radiation well

White reflects infrared radiation well

Investigating radiation

This experiment allows you to compare the rates at which black, white, and shiny surfaces absorb infrared radiation. You can also use the same equipment to investigate how different surfaces emit radiation.

Absorbing radiation

Infrared radiation from the Sun transfers energy to the cans, heating the water inside them. Matt black surfaces absorb more infrared radiation than white or shiny surfaces, so the water in the black can should heat up the fastest.

Method

1. Empty and rinse three drink cans or food tins. Paint one tin matt black, another white, and the third shiny silver. The colour of the can is the independent variable in this experiment.

2. Pour an equal amount of cold water into each can. Insert a thermometer and put some cotton wool around it to reduce loss of heat.

3. Place the cans outside on a sunny day. The quantity of water in the cans and the amount of heat they receive from the Sun are both control variables.

4. Note the temperature of the water in each can. Temperature is the dependent variable in the experiment.

5. Leave the cans in the Sun for 90 minutes, and record the temperature of the water every 10 minutes.

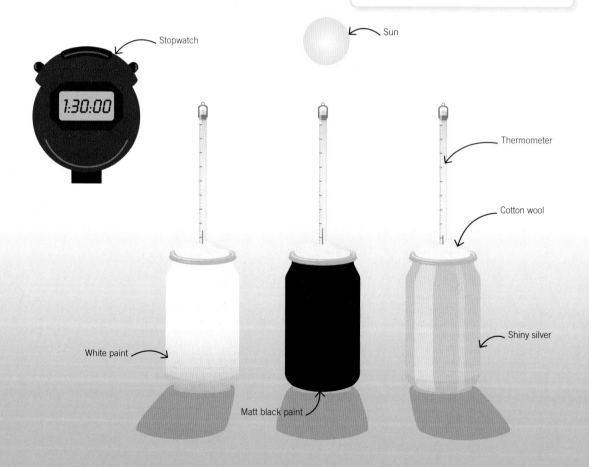

Stopwatch

Sun

Thermometer

Cotton wool

Shiny silver

White paint

Matt black paint

Results

Record your data in a table and then plot the results on a graph. The graph shows that the temperature rises quickly in all three cans but climbs fastest and highest in the black can. The silver and white cans show similar results.

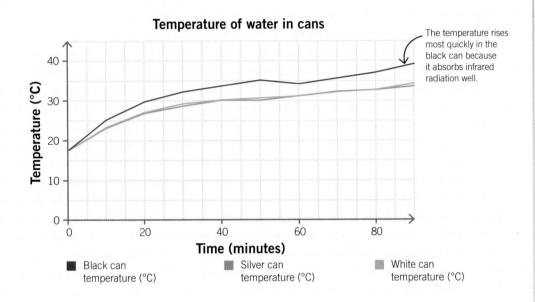

Temperature of water in cans

The temperature rises most quickly in the black can because it absorbs infrared radiation well.

Time (minutes)

Temperature (°C)

■ Black can temperature (°C) ■ Silver can temperature (°C) ■ White can temperature (°C)

Conclusion

The black can absorbed more radiation than the silver and white ones. The only difference between the cans was colour, so this means black absorbs radiation more easily than white or silver. The temperature of the water in the cans did not rise steadily. This might be because there was a breeze or a cloud passing in front of the Sun. The temperature and radiation reaching the cans could be controlled more easily indoors by using a heat lamp instead of the Sun.

Emitting radiation

You can use the same equipment to investigate how hot objects lose energy by radiation to their surroundings. This experiment is much quicker, so use one can at a time. Fill the first can with exactly 300 ml of water heated to 50°C, insert a thermometer, and put some cotton wool around it. Wait for the temperature to reach 45°C and then record the temperature every 30 seconds for 10 minutes. Repeat with the other two cans, making sure the room temperature stays the same, and show your results on a graph.

Conduction

Metal objects often feel cold to the touch because metals are good at transferring energy away from your body. The spread of thermal energy through physical contact is called conduction.

Conduction in metals

When a metal bar is heated, the extra energy makes the particles vibrate more. Because the particles in metals are arranged in a tight lattice, vibrations spread from particles to their neighbours, transferring kinetic energy and so causing heat to spread through the object. Metals also conduct heat well because some of their electrons can move freely, which also transfers kinetic energy.

Key facts

- ✓ Conduction is the transfer of energy by touch.
- ✓ Metals are good thermal conductors because the particles are arranged in a lattice and because electrons can move freely.
- ✓ Materials that are poor thermal conductors are called insulators.

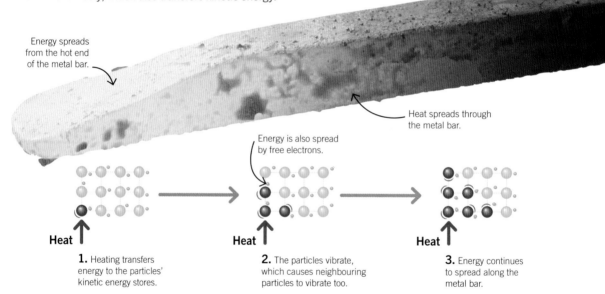

Energy spreads from the hot end of the metal bar.

Heat spreads through the metal bar.

Energy is also spread by free electrons.

Heat

1. Heating transfers energy to the particles' kinetic energy stores.

Heat

2. The particles vibrate, which causes neighbouring particles to vibrate too.

Heat

3. Energy continues to spread along the metal bar.

🔍 Conductors and insulators

Solids that are dense and crystalline, such as metals, are good thermal conductors because the particles are packed tightly and locked in a lattice, which helps them transfer energy to their neighbours. In contrast, air is a very poor thermal conductor because the particles are far apart. Materials that contain trapped air, such as woolly jumpers and foam coffee cups, are also poor conductors. We call these materials insulators and use them to slow the transfer of thermal energy. One of the best insulators is aerogel, a silicon-based insulator that is more than 99 per cent air.

Aerogel blocks heat from a flame

Investigating insulators

Some materials, like metals, conduct thermal energy well. Other materials are poor conductors (good insulators). These materials can be used to reduce the energy transferred from a hot object to its surroundings, or to keep something cool by reducing the transfer of energy into it.

Method

1. Set up the apparatus as shown below. All the beakers must be the same size, and you should try to keep the thickness of the insulation the same.

2. When you're ready to start, pour the same volume of hot water from a kettle into each beaker. Put the thermometers in and start the stopwatch.

3. Write down the starting temperatures, then record the temperature of the water in each beaker every minute for 10 minutes.

Investigating insulation
You can test the insulating properties of different materials by using them to insulate beakers of hot water. The best insulator is the one that keeps the water warm the longest. You also need to measure how quickly the temperature falls with no insulation.

Teacher supervision required

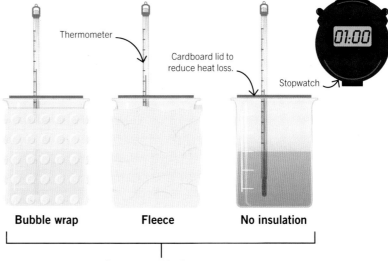

Thermometer

Cardboard lid to reduce heat loss.

Stopwatch

Bubble wrap   **Fleece**   **No insulation**

Beakers containing hot water

Results

Plot the data for all three beakers on the same graph. Draw a smooth curve through the points for each beaker. The graph should show that both the bubble wrap and the fleece kept the water warmer than having no insulation, and that bubble wrap was best at keeping the water hot. You could have carried out this investigation more simply by recording just the start and end temperatures. However, if you'd also made an incorrect final reading like the one in this graph, you might then have wrongly concluded that bubble wrap has the same insulating properties as fleece.

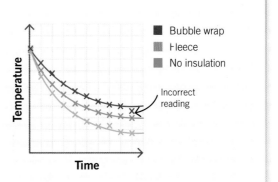

- Bubble wrap
- Fleece
- No insulation

Incorrect reading

Temperature

Time

Convection

Convection is the transfer of thermal energy by currents moving in a fluid (a liquid or a gas). When a region of air or water is heated, it becomes less dense than the surrounding fluid and rises, creating a convection current.

Key facts

✓ Convection is the transfer of heat by currents moving in a fluid.

✓ Convection occurs because heating makes parts of a fluid less dense than the surrounding fluid.

✓ Thermals are rising columns of warm air produced by convection.

Convection in water

We can watch convection happen by adding a coloured dye to water before heating it. In the experiment shown here, the dye is placed at the bottom of the beaker and gradually dissolves. When the water over the flame is heated, it becomes less dense than the surrounding water and rises.

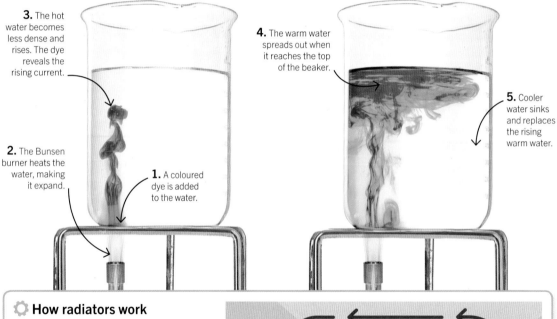

3. The hot water becomes less dense and rises. The dye reveals the rising current.

4. The warm water spreads out when it reaches the top of the beaker.

5. Cooler water sinks and replaces the rising warm water.

2. The Bunsen burner heats the water, making it expand.

1. A coloured dye is added to the water.

How radiators work

Modern central heating systems use convection to heat the air inside houses. Hot water in radiators transfers energy to the air, which warms and becomes less dense. The warm air rises and cooler air replaces it. Eventually the warm air cools and sinks back down, completing the cycle. This circulation of air is a convection current.

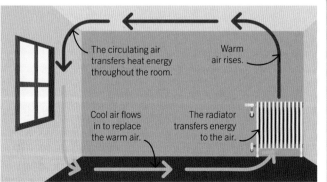

The circulating air transfers heat energy throughout the room.

Warm air rises.

Cool air flows in to replace the warm air.

The radiator transfers energy to the air.

⚙ How thermals work

Roads, buildings, and areas of darker ground (such as ploughed fields) heat up more quickly in the Sun than areas of vegetation. They transfer energy to the air above them, creating rising columns of warm air called thermals, which are often topped by fluffy white cumulus clouds. Gliders can stay airborne for long periods by circling in a thermal to climb and then following the clouds to find another thermal.

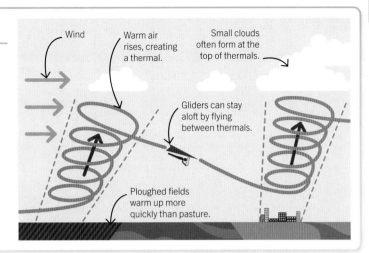

Wind

Warm air rises, creating a thermal.

Small clouds often form at the top of thermals.

Gliders can stay aloft by flying between thermals.

Ploughed fields warm up more quickly than pasture.

Thermals
This hang-glider needs no engine to stay airborne. It gets all the lift it needs from thermals — convection currents rising from the sun-warmed ground.

Reducing energy transfers

Heating a house can be expensive, so modern buildings are designed to minimize the transfer of energy to their surroundings. Well-insulated buildings also reduce our need for fossil fuels to supply energy for heating.

Insulating houses

Houses can transfer heat to the environment by conduction, convection, and radiation, so designers of modern buildings aim to reduce all three. Good insulation not only helps keep houses warm in winter but keeps them cooler in summer, making them more comfortable.

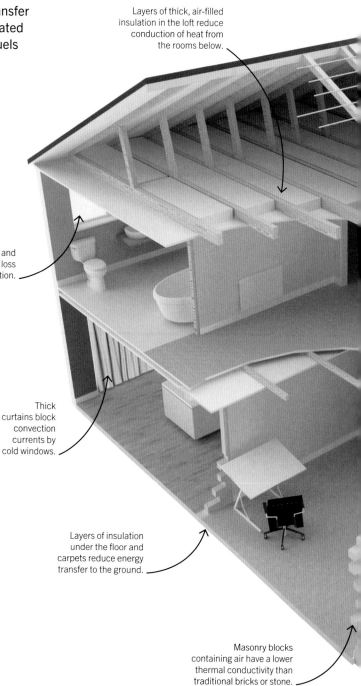

Layers of thick, air-filled insulation in the loft reduce conduction of heat from the rooms below.

Small windows and coated glass reduce loss of heat by radiation.

Thick curtains block convection currents by cold windows.

Layers of insulation under the floor and carpets reduce energy transfer to the ground.

Masonry blocks containing air have a lower thermal conductivity than traditional bricks or stone.

🔍 Heat loss

A house usually loses most of its energy through the roof and walls, but heat is also lost through windows, doors, and the ground. The greater the difference in temperature between the inside and outside of the house, the faster the rate of energy loss.

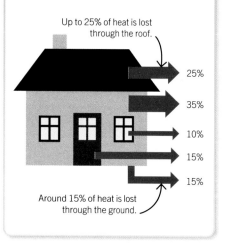

Up to 25% of heat is lost through the roof.

25%

35%

10%

15%

15%

Around 15% of heat is lost through the ground.

Key facts

✓ Energy can be transferred from the inside of a house to its surroundings by conduction, convection, and radiation.

✓ Good insulation reduces heating bills and reduces the use of fossil fuels.

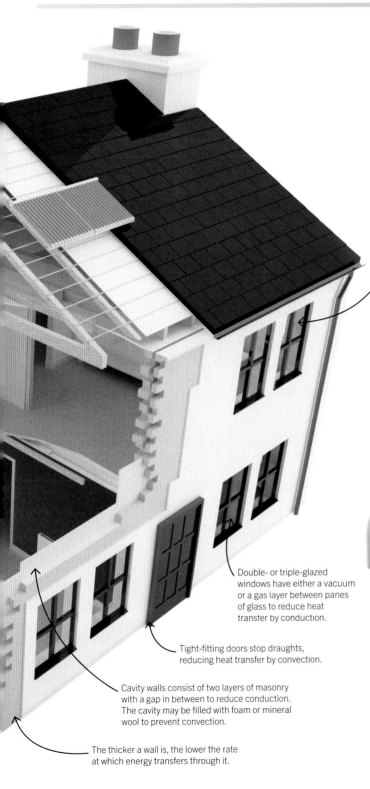

Windows on the sunny side of the building may be larger to let more sunlight enter, reducing the need for heating in winter.

Double- or triple-glazed windows have either a vacuum or a gas layer between panes of glass to reduce heat transfer by conduction.

Tight-fitting doors stop draughts, reducing heat transfer by convection.

Cavity walls consist of two layers of masonry with a gap in between to reduce conduction. The cavity may be filled with foam or mineral wool to prevent convection.

The thicker a wall is, the lower the rate at which energy transfers through it.

⚙ Vacuum flask

Vacuum flasks were invented by Scottish chemist James Dewar in 1892 to keep chemicals cold, but today we use them more often to keep hot drinks hot. The inner flask has a double wall made of glass or aluminium with a vacuum between the two walls, which reduces transfer of energy by conduction or convection. The silvery inner surface also reflects radiation.

Outer lid used as cup

Insulated stopper

Plastic outer layer

Silvery inner surface

A vacuum between the two inner walls cuts heat loss by conduction and convection.

Kinetic and potential energy

As a roller-coaster races up and down, energy is transferred back and forth between its stores of kinetic energy (KE) and gravitational potential energy (GPE). The equations on these pages show you how to calculate both quantities.

Kinetic energy
A moving object stores kinetic energy. When it speeds up, energy is transferred to this store, and when it slows down, energy is transferred away. The faster the object moves, or the greater its mass, the greater its store of kinetic energy. The equation here shows how to calculate kinetic energy.

$$\text{kinetic energy (J)} = \frac{1}{2} \times \text{mass (kg)} \times \text{speed}^2 \text{ (m/s)}^2$$

$$E_k = \frac{1}{2} \times m \times v^2$$

The carriage has maximum GPE at the peak of a hill.

As the carriage goes downhill, GPE is transferred to KE and it speeds up.

Key facts

✓ The faster an object moves, or the greater its mass, the greater its store of kinetic energy (KE).

✓ The higher an object is, or the greater its mass, the greater its store of gravitational potential energy (GPE).

✓ When a roller-coaster accelerates downhill, energy is transferred from its store of GPE to its store of KE.

Calculating kinetic energy

Question
A paper plane has a mass of 5 g (0.005 kg) and travels at 12 m/s. How much kinetic energy does it store?

Answer

$E = \frac{1}{2} \times m \times v^2$

$= \frac{1}{2} \times 0.005 \text{ kg} \times (12 \text{ m/s})^2$

$= 0.36 \text{ J}$

Gravitational potential energy

When you raise an object, the lifting force does work and transfers energy to the object's store of gravitational potential energy (GPE). The higher an object is, or the greater its mass, the greater its store of GPE. This equation shows how to calculate the change in an object's GPE from a change in its height.

On Earth, this figure is approximately 10 N/kg. On the Moon, it would be about a sixth of this figure.

$$\text{change in GPE (J)} = \text{mass (kg)} \times \frac{\text{gravitational field}}{\text{strength (N/kg)}} \times \frac{\text{change in}}{\text{height (m)}}$$

$$\Delta\text{GPE} = m \times g \times \Delta h$$

The Greek letter delta means "change in".

📑 Calculating GPE

Question
A woman with a mass of 70 kg climbs 30 m up a cliff. How much gravitational potential energy does she gain?

Answer
$\Delta\text{GPE} = m \times g \times \Delta h$
$\quad\quad\quad = 70 \text{ kg} \times 10 \text{ N/kg} \times 30 \text{ m}$
$\quad\quad\quad = 21\,000 \text{ J}$

The carriage needs a lot of KE to travel around the loop.

Climbing causes the carriage to slow down. Energy is transferred from its KE store to its store of GPE.

Air resistance and friction between the carriage and track continually transfer energy away, slowing the ride.

The carriage reaches top speed and maximum KE at the bottom of the hill.

Conservation of energy

Energy can be transferred or stored, but it cannot be created or destroyed. The total amount of energy in an isolated system remains the same before and after energy transfers. This is known as the law of conservation of energy.

Friction with the hook and with air causes energy to be transferred away, reducing the height the pendulum reaches.

Energy transfers in a pendulum
A pendulum is a mass suspended freely from a fixed point. Energy is transferred between the pendulum's store of kinetic energy (KE) and its store of gravitational potential energy (GPE). The pendulum, hook, and air make up what we call a system. The total amount of energy within an isolated system (one that energy does not enter or leave) remains constant.

Key facts

✓ Energy can be transferred or stored, but it cannot be created or destroyed.

✓ The total amount of energy within an isolated system remains the same before and after energy transfers.

✓ As a pendulum swings, energy is transferred between its stores of kinetic energy and gravitational potential energy.

Maximum GPE (pendulum is stationary)

Maximum GPE (stationary again)

GPE transfers to KE

KE transfers to GPE

Maximum KE (pendulum at maximum speed)

⚙ Harmonic motion

The pendulum's repetitive, back-and-forth movement is known as simple harmonic motion. Each swing takes exactly the same length of time, which is why pendulums are used as timekeepers in mechanical clocks. When the pendulum's angle of swing is plotted on the y-axis of a graph against time, it shows a pattern called a sine wave. Plotting GPE and KE on a graph also produces sine waves. When added, these form a straight line, showing that energy is transferred between them but conserved.

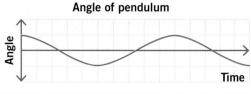

Angle of pendulum

Angle

Time

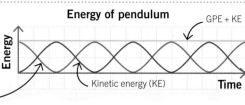

Energy of pendulum

GPE + KE

Energy

Gravitational potential energy (GPE)

Kinetic energy (KE)

Time

Transferring energy by forces

It takes energy to power a car, make a plane fly, or ride a bike. The energy transferred when a force moves an object is called work.

Work done

The scientific meaning of "work" is different from its everyday meaning. When you push an object, the force does work to move it and transfers energy from your body to the object's kinetic energy store. As work done is a measure of energy, the units are joules (J). You can work out the total energy transferred by multiplying the force by the distance moved in the direction of the force.

$$\text{work (J)} = \text{force (N)} \times \text{distance (m)}$$
$$W = F \times d$$

For instance, if you push a loaded shopping trolley for 4 m with a continuous force of 14 N, you've done 56 J of work.

$$W = F \times d$$
$$= 14\,N \times 4\,m$$
$$= 56\,J$$

A force of 14 newtons acts continuously for 4 metres.

14 N

4 m

Key facts

✓ The energy transferred when a force moves an object is called work.

✓ As work done is a measure of energy, the units are joules (J).

✓ Work done equals force multiplied by distance moved in the direction of the force.

🔍 Examples of work

Work is done whenever energy is transferred.

When you pull the brakes on a bike, the force of friction between the brakes and wheel does negative work. Friction transfers energy from the bike's kinetic energy store to thermal energy, making the bike slow down.

When you drop a ball, the force of gravity does work and energy is transferred to the ball's kinetic energy store, making it accelerate.

When you stretch a spring, the force transfers energy to the spring's store of elastic potential energy. The force needed increases as the spring gets harder to stretch (see page 82).

Energy and power

Power is a measure of how quickly energy is transferred (how quickly work is done). The more energy transferred per second, the greater the power.

Lifting power

Two cranes use motorized pulleys to lift heavy loads from a ship. Both loads have the same mass, so the same energy is needed to lift them a certain distance. However, the orange crane lifts the cargo to twice the height of the yellow crane in the same time. Its motor has twice the power.

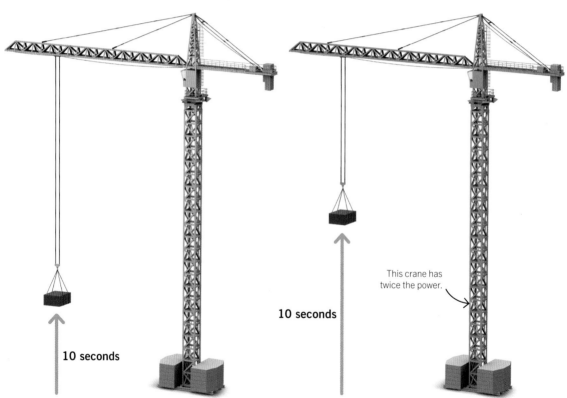

This crane has twice the power.

10 seconds

10 seconds

Power equation

The equation here shows how to calculate power. We measure power in units called watts (W). A power of 1 watt means 1 joule of energy is transferred in 1 second.

$$\text{power (W)} = \frac{\text{energy transferred (J)}}{\text{time (s)}}$$

$$P = \frac{E}{t}$$

Calculating power

Question
A boy weighing 400 newtons climbs 2.6 m up a ladder in 4 seconds. Use the formula work = force × distance to calculate how much energy was transferred. What was the boy's power?

Answer
First calculate energy transferred (work done).

$E = f \times d$
$= 400\ N \times 2.6\ m$
$= 1040\ J$

Then use the power formula to calculate his power.

$P = \dfrac{E}{t}$
$= \dfrac{1040\ J}{4\ s}$
$= 260\ W$

Calculating energy

Question
A microwave oven with a power rating of 800 W heats a bowl of soup for 3 minutes. How much energy does it use?

Answer
First rearrange the power equation to make energy the subject, then put in the numbers. Don't forget to convert minutes to seconds (3 minutes = 180 s).

$P = \dfrac{E}{t}$
$E = P \times t$
$= 800\ W \times 180\ s$
$= 144\,000\ J$

Rocket power
To escape the pull of gravity and reach orbit, massive rockets require engines with up to 60 gigawatts (60 billion watts) of power.

Calculating energy efficiency

Efficient devices are good at transferring energy to useful energy stores. An efficient light bulb, for instance, transfers energy mostly as light rather than wasting it as heat. The efficiency of a device is the percentage of energy transferred usefully.

Key facts

✓ The efficiency of a device is the percentage of energy transferred usefully.

✓ Efficiency can be calculated from either energy or power.

Energy efficiency equation

This noisy old lawnmower is inefficient. It transfers most of the energy it receives to sound and heat. Only 30 per cent of the energy is output usefully to cut grass, so its efficiency is 30 per cent. You can calculate the efficiency of a device using the equation shown here.

$$\text{efficiency (\%)} = \frac{\text{useful energy output (J)}}{\text{total energy input (J)}} \times 100$$

Multiplying by 100 converts the answer to a percentage.

Useful energy transfer

4500 J kinetic energy

15000 J energy

10500 J heat and sound

Wasted energy

Efficiency and power

You can also calculate efficiency if you know the total power input and useful power output of a device. Use this equation instead.

$$\text{efficiency (\%)} = \frac{\text{useful power output (W)}}{\text{total power input (W)}} \times 100$$

 ## Efficiency calculations

Question 1

A 75 watt fan runs for 1 minute, transferring 4500 joules of energy. 200 joules is transferred to thermal energy stores, 700 joules is transferred through sound waves, and the rest is transferred to useful kinetic energy stores. What is the efficiency of the fan?

Answer 1

Useful energy transfer = 4500 J − (200 J + 700 J)
= 3600 J

Wasted energy

$$\text{Efficiency} = \frac{3600 \text{ J}}{4500 \text{ J}} \times 100$$

= 80%

Total energy transferred

Check your answer makes sense. Nothing can be more than 100% efficient, so your answer must be less than 100.

Question 2

A 5 watt light bulb has an efficiency rating of 60%. What is its useful power output?

Answer 2

Rearrange the second efficiency equation to make useful power output the subject.

Useful power output = efficiency × total power input

$$= \frac{60}{100} \times 5 \text{ W}$$

= 3 W

Improving efficiency

Machines with moving parts generate frictional forces that transfer energy to useless energy stores, such as sound and heat. Adding lubricants like oil reduces friction and so improves efficiency. No devices are 100 per cent efficient as some energy is always lost through heating, light, sound, or other energy transfers.

Describing motion

Speed

Speed is a measure of how fast something is moving. It describes distance travelled over a certain amount of time. It is usually measured in metres per second (m/s), kilometres per hour (km/h), or miles per hour (mph). Unlike velocity, which tells you how fast something is moving in a particular direction, speed has no direction – it is a scalar quantity rather than a vector (see page 66).

Key facts

✓ Speed describes how far something travels in a given amount of time.

✓ Speed is a scalar quantity rather than a vector, so it has no direction.

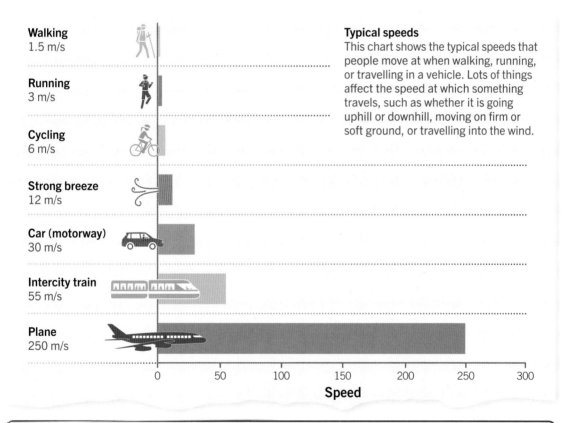

Walking
1.5 m/s

Running
3 m/s

Cycling
6 m/s

Strong breeze
12 m/s

Car (motorway)
30 m/s

Intercity train
55 m/s

Plane
250 m/s

0   50   100   150   200   250   300
Speed

Typical speeds
This chart shows the typical speeds that people move at when walking, running, or travelling in a vehicle. Lots of things affect the speed at which something travels, such as whether it is going uphill or downhill, moving on firm or soft ground, or travelling into the wind.

Measuring speed

Scientists usually measure speed in metres per second, but the speedometers in vehicles display speed in other units. Cars use kilometres per hour or miles per hour, and ships and planes usually use knots (nautical miles per hour).

This car speedometer shows speed in both miles per hour (green) and kilometres per hour (orange).

Calculating speed

To calculate the speed of a moving object, you divide the distance it travels by the time it takes to travel that distance. Average speed is the total distance divided by the total time taken, but instantaneous speed tells you how fast something is moving at a particular moment.

Average and instantaneous speed
Imagine a sprinter running a 100 m race. At the very start, she moves slowly, but she soon speeds up. Towards the end, she might get tired and slow down a little. Her instantaneous speed has changed throughout the race, but we can calculate her average speed using the formula below.

$$\text{average speed (m/s)} = \frac{\text{total distance (m)}}{\text{total time (s)}}$$

Instantaneous speed = 6 m/s Instantaneous speed = 14 m/s Instantaneous speed = 8 m/s

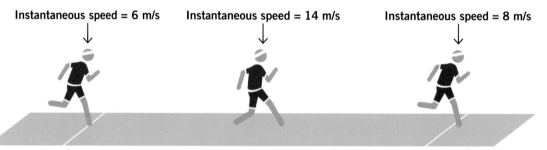

Total distance = 100 m

📑 Calculating speed

Question
A sprinter completes a 100 m race in 12.5 seconds. What is her average speed?

Answer
Average speed = $\dfrac{\text{total distance}}{\text{total time}}$

$= \dfrac{100 \text{ m}}{12.5 \text{ s}}$

$= 8 \text{ m/s}$

📑 Calculating distance

Question
A cyclist in a race rides for 25 seconds with an average speed of 12 m/s. How far does he cycle?

Answer
Rearrange the equation to work out distance rather than speed:
Total distance = average speed × total time
$= 12 \text{ m/s} \times 25 \text{ s}$
$= 300 \text{ m}$

Measuring speed

To measure speed, you have to measure the distance an object travels and the time it takes to travel that distance. Instruments used to measure distance include rulers and tape measures. Instruments used to measure time include stopwatches and light gates.

Light gates
A light gate is used to calculate the speed of fast-moving objects. It measures very brief time intervals much more accurately than a person can do with a stopwatch. In the experiment shown here, a trolley carrying a card breaks the light beam for a fraction of a second. To find the trolley's speed at that point, divide the length of the card by the time interval recorded.

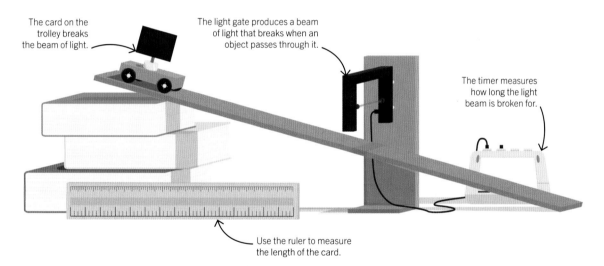

The card on the trolley breaks the beam of light.

The light gate produces a beam of light that breaks when an object passes through it.

The timer measures how long the light beam is broken for.

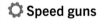

Use the ruler to measure the length of the card.

Speed guns

The radar speed guns used by police to check if drivers are speeding use radio waves. When the outgoing radio waves reflect off an approaching car, their frequency and wavelength change. The faster the car, the higher the frequency of the reflected waves. The speed gun detects the returning echoes and uses their frequency to calculate the car's speed.

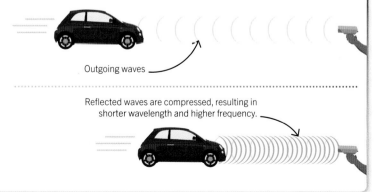

Outgoing waves

Reflected waves are compressed, resulting in shorter wavelength and higher frequency.

Distance–time graphs

A distance–time graph shows the journey of an object travelling in a straight line. The slope (gradient) of the line reveals how fast it's moving and when it speeds up, slows down, or stands still.

Understanding distance–time graphs
Each of the lines on this distance–time graph shows a different journey. The steeper the line, the faster an object is moving. A curved line has a changing gradient, which means an object is changing speed. A flat horizontal line means an object is stationary.

Key facts

✓ A distance–time graph shows how far and how fast an object has travelled at different times in its journey.

✓ The gradient shows the speed of an object – the steeper the gradient, the faster the speed.

✓ You can use a distance–time graph to calculate an object's speed at any point in the journey.

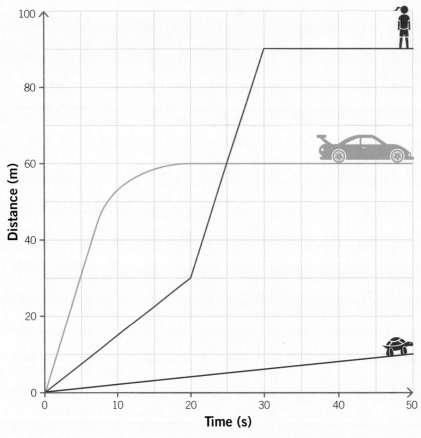

This person starts walking at a constant speed, but after 20 seconds she suddenly speeds up – she must be running. After 10 seconds of running, she comes to a stop and the line remains horizontal.

At first the car travels quickly at a constant speed, but then it gradually slows. When it reaches a distance of 60 m, its distance travelled stops changing, so the car must have stopped.

The low gradient of the tortoise's line shows that it walks slowly. The line is perfectly straight, which means that its speed is not changing.

Calculating speed from a gradient

Question
This graph shows the distance–time journey for a car. At what speed was the car travelling during the last 40 seconds of the journey?

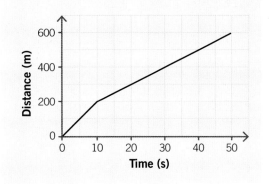

Answer
1. To find the speed you need to calculate the gradient of the straight line. Draw a right-angled triangle under any part of the line. The triangle's vertical side is the change in distance. The horizontal side is the change in time.
2. Work out both values.
   Change in distance = 400 m – 200 m = 200 m
   Change in time = 30 s – 10 s = 20 s
3. Divide the change in distance by the change in time to find the speed.

$$\text{speed} = \frac{\text{change in distance}}{\text{change in time}}$$
$$= \frac{200 \text{ m}}{20 \text{ s}}$$
$$= 10 \text{ m/s}$$

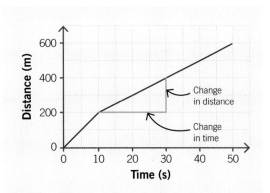

Drawing a tangent

Sometimes you might have to work out the gradient on a curved part of the line. This is easy – you do it by drawing a line called a tangent. A tangent is a straight line that touches the curve without crossing it, matching the slope at the point in question. After drawing a tangent, complete a right-angled triangle as described above and use it to work out the change in distance divided by the change in time.

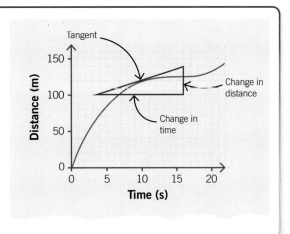

Scalars and vectors

Scientific measurements are either scalar quantities or vector quantities. Scalar quantities just have a magnitude (size), whereas vector quantities have magnitude and direction.

Distance and displacement

The map below shows the route a jogger takes around a park. How far has he travelled? One way to answer this is to measure the total distance of his winding path. This is a scalar quantity as it has no particular direction. Another is to measure his displacement – his distance and direction in a straight line from his start point. Displacement is a vector quantity because it has a direction as well as a magnitude.

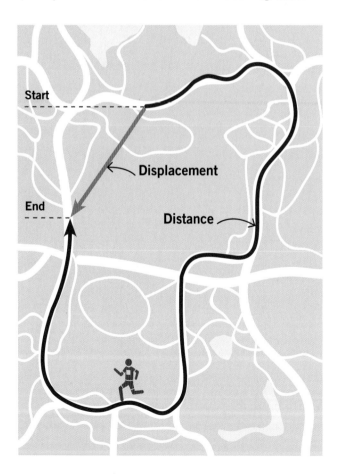

Key facts

✓ Scalar quantities have magnitude.

✓ Vector quantities have magnitude and direction.

✓ Distance is scalar, displacement is a vector.

Vector quantities

Forces always have a direction, so all forces are vectors. Your weight is a force that acts downwards towards Earth, so weight is a vector. In contrast, your mass (the amount of matter in your body) is a scalar quantity.

The velocity of an object is its speed in a particular direction. If a car is turning a corner at a steady 50 km/h, its speed is constant but its direction is changing, so its velocity is changing too.

Acceleration, in everyday language, means getting faster. However, the scientific meaning of acceleration is a change in velocity. Acceleration is a vector quantity and tells us if an object is getting faster, slower, or changing direction.

The momentum of an object is its mass multiplied by its velocity. Momentum is calculated from velocity and so is a vector quantity.

Velocity

Speed and velocity are not the same thing. Speed tells you how fast something is moving, but velocity is how fast something is moving in a particular direction. Unlike speed, which is a scalar quantity, velocity is a vector quantity – it has direction as well as magnitude.

Key facts

✓ Velocity is the speed of a moving object in a particular direction.

✓ Velocity is a vector quantity – it has direction and magnitude.

✓ Speed is a scalar quantity – it has no direction.

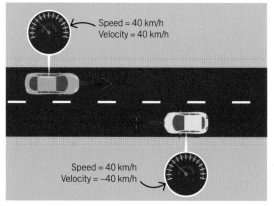

Speed = 40 km/h
Velocity = 40 km/h

Speed = 40 km/h
Velocity = –40 km/h

Speed and velocity

If two cars are travelling at the same speed but in opposite directions, they have different velocities. For example, the yellow car is travelling 40 km/h east, but the white car is travelling 40 km/h west. In physics, we can use a minus sign to show something is happening in the opposite direction. In this diagram, east is the positive direction, so the white car has a velocity of –40 km/h.

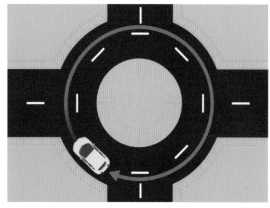

Changing velocity

When a car turns, its direction changes, which means that its velocity changes as well. The car here has driven at a constant speed all the way round a roundabout, but its velocity has been changing continually. Its average velocity going around the roundabout is 0 km/h.

⚙ **Frames of reference**

Suppose you're standing on a train moving east at 50 m/s and you throw a ball forwards at 10 m/s. What's the ball's velocity? The speed relative to you is 10 m/s, but for someone standing beside the track, the ball's velocity is 60 m/s. Likewise, if you throw the ball backwards at 10 m/s, someone beside the track will see it moving forwards at 40 m/s. All these quantities are correct, but each one depends on a different point of view. We call these different points of view "frames of reference".

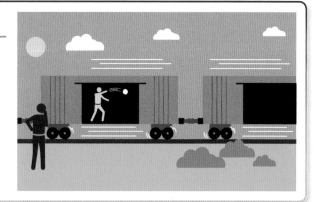

Acceleration

Acceleration is the rate at which an object's velocity is changing. It doesn't just mean speeding up. Slowing down and changing direction are forms of acceleration too.

Formula for acceleration
You can calculate acceleration using the formula below. The unit to use for acceleration is m/s² (metres per second squared).

$$\text{acceleration (m/s}^2) = \frac{\text{change in velocity (m/s)}}{\text{time taken (s)}}$$

Final velocity
Initial velocity
$$a = \frac{v - u}{t}$$

Calculating acceleration
To work out "change in velocity" in the right side of the formula, you need two figures: final velocity and initial velocity. Take care to get these the right way round. For example, a car travelling at a velocity of 13 m/s speeds up to 25 m/s in 10 seconds. What's its acceleration?

$$a = \frac{v - u}{t}$$

Put final velocity first and initial velocity second.

$$= \frac{25 \text{ m/s} - 13 \text{ m/s}}{10 \text{ s}}$$

$$= 1.2 \text{ m/s}^2$$

Acceleration is measured in metres per second squared (metres per second per second).

Key facts

✓ Acceleration is the rate at which velocity changes.

✓ The unit for acceleration is m/s².

✓ The uniform acceleration of a falling object at Earth's surface is 9.8 m/s² (g).

🔍 Acceleration due to gravity

When an object falls, the force of gravity at Earth's surface gives it a uniform acceleration of about 9.8 m/s². This means that with each passing second, its velocity increases by 9.8 m/s. This value is used so often in calculations that it has its own abbreviation, g. In real life, objects don't always accelerate uniformly at 9.8 m/s² because air resistance produces an upward force.

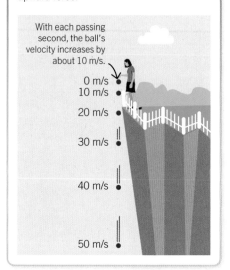

With each passing second, the ball's velocity increases by about 10 m/s.

0 m/s
10 m/s
20 m/s
30 m/s
40 m/s
50 m/s

Initial velocity (u)

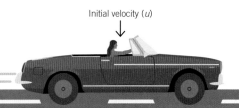

Final velocity (v)

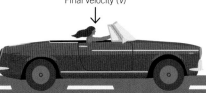

Drogue parachute

Some high-speed aircraft must slow down (decelerate) very quickly in order to land in confined spaces. One solution is to deploy a drogue parachute – a small parachute that dramatically increases the force of drag.

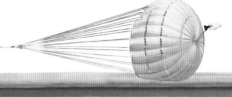

Slowing down

Question

If an object is slowing down, it has negative acceleration. A motorbike is travelling at 30 m/s on a country road. It arrives at a town and the rider slows down to 10 m/s, taking 25 seconds to do so. What was the average acceleration?

30 m/s   10 m/s

25 seconds

Answer

$$a = \frac{v - u}{t}$$

$$= \frac{10 \text{ m/s} - 30 \text{ m/s}}{25 \text{ s}}$$

$$= -0.8 \text{ m/s}^2$$

Acceleration is negative here because the motorbike was slowing down.

Using distance

Sometimes we have to calculate acceleration from a change in velocity over a certain distance rather than over a period of time. We use the equation below to do this.

Displacement (distance travelled)

$$v^2 - u^2 = 2as$$

Final velocity   Initial velocity

Finding acceleration

Question

A train pulls out from a station and accelerates uniformly for 1350 m until it reaches a velocity of 55 m/s. What is the train's acceleration?

Answer

Rearrange the formula to find a.

$$a = \frac{v^2 - u^2}{2s}$$

$$= \frac{(55 \text{ m/s})^2 - (0 \text{ m/s})^2}{2 \times 1350 \text{ m}}$$

$$= \frac{3025}{2700}$$

$$= 1.12 \text{ m/s}^2$$

Velocity–time graphs

A velocity–time graph shows how an object's velocity changes over time. The gradient (steepness) of the line represents the object's acceleration or deceleration (negative acceleration). The graph can also show whether or not an object's acceleration is uniform.

Understanding velocity–time graphs
This velocity–time graph shows two different journeys. Slopes with a straight line represent uniform acceleration, whereas curved lines represent changing acceleration. Flat horizontal lines represent constant velocity.

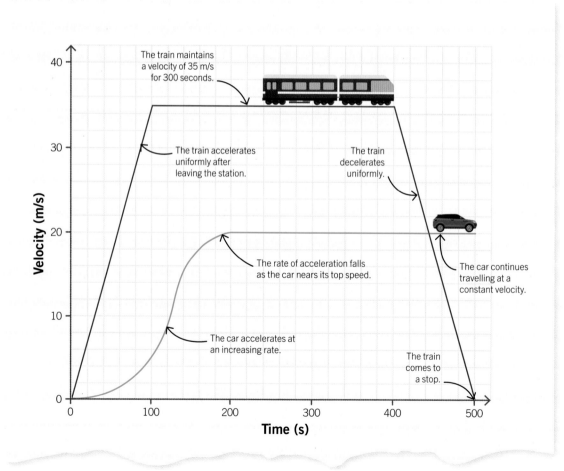

Calculating acceleration

Question
The graph below shows a car's journey. What was the car's acceleration between 10 and 30 seconds?

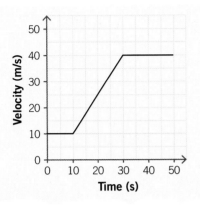

Answer
1. Acceleration is change in velocity divided by time taken, so work these out by drawing a triangle under the sloped part of the graph.

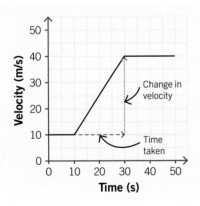

2. Change in velocity = final velocity − initial velocity
= 40 m/s − 10 m/s
= 30 m/s
3. Time taken = 30 s − 10 s
= 20 s
4. Acceleration = $\dfrac{30 \text{ m/s}}{20 \text{ s}}$
= 1.5 m/s²

Calculating displacement

You can use a velocity–time graph to work out the displacement of a moving object – the total distance it has travelled. You do this by finding the area under the graph. This works because distance travelled = velocity × time.

Question
The graph shows a 50-second train journey. How far did the train travel?

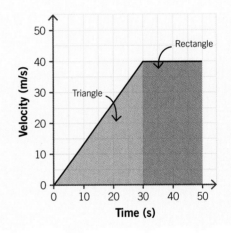

Answer
1. Start by separating the space under the line into a triangle and a rectangle.
2. Next, work out the triangle's area using the formula for the area of a triangle:
area = $\dfrac{\text{base} \times \text{height}}{2}$
= $\dfrac{30 \text{ s} \times 40 \text{ m/s}}{2}$ The units are metres because the area under the line represents distance.
= 600 m
3. Now work out the area of the rectangle:
area = base × height
= 20 s × 40 m/s
= 800 m
4. Add the two values to find the displacement:
displacement = 600 m + 800 m
= 1400 m

Forces

Forces

A force is a push or a pull that changes the motion or shape of an object. There are many types of force. Some require physical contact, such as when you kick a ball. Others, such as gravity and magnetism, are non-contact forces that work at a distance.

Forces at work

Several forces can act on an object at the same time. This picture shows the main forces acting on a climber abseiling down a cliff. Each force is represented by an arrow that shows the force's direction – forces are vector quantities (see page 66). The arrow's length here represents the size of the force.

Tension
in the rope
pulls upwards.

Friction between
the shoe and cliff
allows the climber
to grip the surface.

When a climber
pushes the cliff,
a reaction force
pushes them
back off it.

Gravity pulls
downwards.

Key facts

✓ **A force is a push or pull.**

✓ **A force can change the speed, direction of movement, or shape of an object.**

✓ **Forces can be contact or non-contact forces.**

✓ **The unit for force is the newton (N).**

✓ **Forces are vector quantities.**

Effects of forces

A force can have several effects on an object. Many forces affect the motion of an object, for instance by making it speed up, slow down, or change direction. Forces can also change an object's shape.

Gravity makes the skateboarder accelerate downhill.

Air resistance slows the skydiver's fall.

Tension bends the archer's bow.

A force applied to a stationary object can make it move.

When an object is already moving, a force in the same direction makes it move faster.

A force may also cause a moving object to change direction.

A force in the opposite direction to a moving object makes it slow down or stop.

Forces can also cause temporary or permanent changes in an object's shape.

Types of force

Contact forces

Pushes and pulls are the contact forces we use to move things, from kicking a ball to tapping a keyboard.

Friction is a force that opposes motion when objects rub or slide together. Static friction affects stationary objects and must be overcome to make them move. Kinetic friction is the force between moving objects and is weaker than static friction.

Air and water resistance are forces that objects moving through air and water have to overcome. They are caused by the push of air and water in the way. Like friction, these forces always act opposite to the direction of motion.

Non-contact forces

Gravity is a force of attraction between objects with mass. Earth's gravity makes things fall towards Earth.

Electrostatic force is the attraction or repulsion between objects with an electric charge.

An electrostatic charge on a person's hair makes the hairs repel each other, causing them to stand on end.

Magnetism is the force experienced when a magnetic material is near a magnet.

🔍 Reaction forces

Action Reaction

Reaction forces occur in response to every force but act in the opposite direction. If one skateboarder pushes the other, they will both move as the push results in a reaction force acting in the opposite direction.

🔍 Newtons

The unit for force is named the newton (N) after the English scientist Isaac Newton. One newton is about the weight of an apple. The scientific definition of a newton is the force needed to accelerate a 1 kg object by 1 m/s^2.

1 N force

Balanced and unbalanced forces

When forces acting on the same object in opposite directions are the same size, we say they are balanced. Balanced forces cancel each other out. A change in an object's motion only happens if the forces acting on it are unbalanced.

Balanced forces

These two tug-of-war teams are pulling with equal force. The forces are balanced and cancel each other out, so there is no movement.

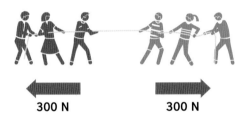

300 N   **300 N**

Unbalanced forces

When the purple team pulls harder, there is an overall force in that direction and the teams begin to move.

400 N   **300 N**

When an object is moving at a constant velocity, the forces acting on it are balanced. Here, the pulling force from the dog is balanced by friction between the sledge and the snow, which acts in the opposite direction. The dog and the sledge both move forwards at a constant velocity.

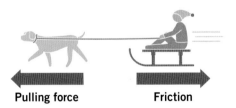

Pulling force   **Friction**

If the dog stops pulling, an unbalanced force is acting in the opposite direction to the sledge's motion, so it slows down. An unbalanced force acting sideways (such as a strong wind) would change the direction of movement.

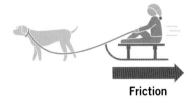

Friction

🔍 First law of motion

In the eighteenth century, the English scientist Isaac Newton described the effect of forces on motion with his first law of motion. This says that an object either remains at rest or moves in a straight line at a constant velocity unless an unbalanced force acts on it. For example, when you flick a marble it continues rolling after the force from your finger has stopped.

If there was no friction to slow down the marble, it would carry on rolling forever.

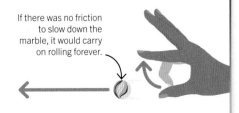

Resultant forces

When several forces act on an object at the same time, their effects combine and act as though there is a single force, called a resultant force. The resultant force can be found by drawing the forces as arrows on a diagram.

Finding resultant forces

The sledge below has several different forces acting on it. The sledge's weight pushing down on the ground is balanced by a reaction force (called a normal force) acting upwards from the ground. The dogs are creating a pulling force (called tension) through the ropes, but friction with the ground creates a force in the opposite direction. If the pulling force is greater than friction, there is a resultant force that causes a change in motion: the sledge accelerates.

Key facts

✓ When several forces act on an object, their effects combine and act as if there is a single force (a resultant force).

✓ Forces acting on an object can be shown on a free body diagram.

✓ If two forces are acting in the same direction, you can work out the resultant by adding them.

✓ If two forces are acting in opposite directions, work out the resultant by subtracting one from the other.

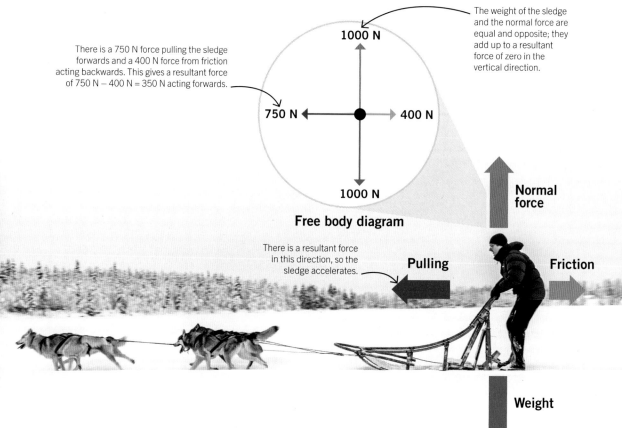

The weight of the sledge and the normal force are equal and opposite; they add up to a resultant force of zero in the vertical direction.

There is a 750 N force pulling the sledge forwards and a 400 N force from friction acting backwards. This gives a resultant force of 750 N − 400 N = 350 N acting forwards.

1000 N

750 N ← → 400 N

1000 N

Free body diagram

There is a resultant force in this direction, so the sledge accelerates.

Pulling

Normal force

Friction

Weight

🔍 Free body diagrams

A free body diagram shows the forces acting on an object. The object can be represented by a dot or a square, and the forces are represented by labelled arrows pointing away from it. Here, a book is resting on a table. The diagram only shows forces acting on the book (forces acting on the table are omitted).

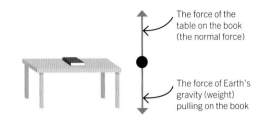

The force of the table on the book (the normal force)

The force of Earth's gravity (weight) pulling on the book

🖹 Calculating resultant forces

Question 1

One person pushes a piano with a force of 100 N, but another person pushes back the opposite way with a force of 150 N. What's the resultant force?

Answer 1

1. Draw a free body diagram showing the forces acting on the piano.

150 N   100 N

2. Find the answer by subtraction:
   Resultant force = 150 N – 100 N
   = 50 N to the left

Question 2

Two people try to push a heavy box. One person pushes with a force of 100 N. The other person pushes at right angles with a force of 120 N. What's the resultant force?

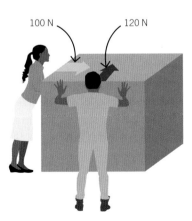

100 N   120 N

Answer 2

When forces (or any vector quantities) don't act in a straight line, you can add them by drawing a scale diagram.

1. Draw one force from the end of the other to form a triangle. In this diagram, 1 cm = 10 N.

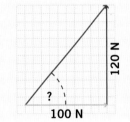

120 N

?   100 N

2. Measure the sloping side of the triangle with a ruler to find the magnitude of the force.

3. Measure the angle with a protractor to find the direction of the force.

4. Write both in your answer:
   Force = 156 N at 50°.

Resolving forces

The effects of forces are easiest to understand when they act at right angles to each other, but a force can act at any angle. To get round the problem, it can help to break down a force into two components that are at right angles but have the same combined effect as the single force. This is known as resolving forces.

Key facts

✓ A single force can be resolved into component forces acting at right angles to each other.

✓ Resolve forces by drawing a scale diagram or by using trigonometry.

Pulling power

This explorer is dragging a pack of heavy gear across a glacier, exerting a force of 50 N at an angle of 30° from the ground. Resolving this force into horizontal and vertical components is useful because we could then use the horizontal component to calculate the sledge's acceleration. To resolve the force, draw a triangle to scale. In the triangle here, 1 cm represents 10 N of force. Measure the horizontal and vertical sides of the triangle to find the two components.

The vertical force arrow measures 2.5 cm, so the vertical component is 2.5 × 10 N = 25 N.

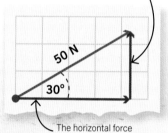

50 N

30°

The pulling force acts upwards and forwards, so it has vertical and horizontal components.

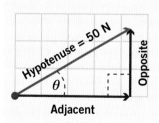

50 N Tension

Friction

The horizontal force arrow measures 4.3 cm, so the horizontal component is 4.3 × 10 N = 43 N.

🖩 Resolving forces with maths

Although forces can be resolved using scale drawings, it's faster and more accurate to use trigonometry. For instance, to find the vertical component of tension in the rope, we can use the sine formula on the right. This allows us to calculate the height of a right-angled triangle if we know the angle of the slope (θ) and the length of the slope (the hypotenuse).

Hypotenuse = 50 N

θ

Adjacent

Opposite

$$\sin \theta = \frac{\text{opposite}}{\text{hypotenuse}}$$

Rearrange the formula to make "opposite" the subject:
opposite = hypotenuse × sin θ
= 50 N × sin 30°
= 25 N

Use a calculator to find the sine of 30°.

Mass and weight

Most people know what they weigh in kilograms, but in science we use kilograms to measure mass, not weight. Mass and weight are different. Mass is the amount of matter in an object. Weight is the pull of gravity on an object. It is a force and is measured in newtons.

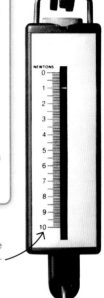

The scale shows the force in newtons.

Key facts

✓ Weight is the force that acts on an object due to gravity.

✓ Mass is measured in kilograms but weight is measured in newtons.

✓ Weight can be measured using a force meter (newton meter).

✓ Weight can be calculated using mass and the strength of gravity.

Measuring weight

You can measure the weight of an object with a force meter (newton meter), which has a spring that stretches along a scale as the force pulling the hook increases. You can also calculate weight using the formula below. The formula takes into account the strength of gravity, which varies on different planets. An object's weight depends on the strength of gravity, but its mass is the same everywhere.

$$\text{weight (N)} = \text{mass (kg)} \times \text{gravitational field strength (N/kg)}$$
$$W = m \times g$$

On Earth's surface, the gravitational field strength (g) is 10 N/kg.

An apple with a mass of 0.1 kg is pulled downwards by Earth's gravity with a force of 1 N.

📃 Calculating weight

Question

Curiosity is a car-sized rover on Mars. Its mass is 899 kg and the gravitational field strength on Mars is 3.7 N/kg. Calculate *Curiosity*'s weight on Mars. How much does it weigh on Earth?

Answer

Weight on Mars = $m \times g$
   = 899 kg × 3.7 N/kg
   = 3326 N = 3300 N (2 s.f.)

Weight on Earth = $m \times g$
   = 899 kg × 10 N/kg
   = 8990 N = 9000 N (2 s.f.)

Springs

When you stretch or squeeze a spring, the change in its length is proportional to the force you apply. This relationship is known as Hooke's law.

Hooke's law

Hang a weight on a spring and it stretches a little. Hang twice as much weight and it stretches twice as much. The extension (or compression) of springs and other elastic objects is proportional to the force applied. This relationship is summarized in the equation below. Force meters use this principle to measure forces — when you pull the hook on a force meter, it stretches a spring inside it.

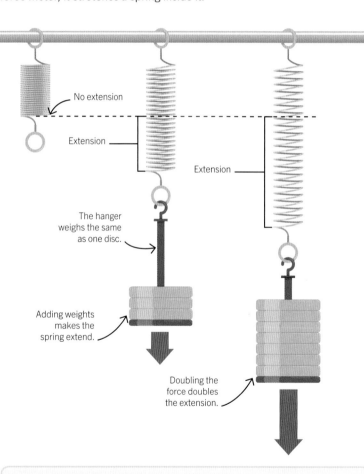

No extension

Extension

Extension

The hanger weighs the same as one disc.

Adding weights makes the spring extend.

Doubling the force doubles the extension.

force (N) = spring constant (N/m) × extension (m)

$$F = k \times e$$

Key facts

✓ Hooke's law says that the extension of a spring is directly proportional to the force applied.

✓ Elastic deformation is a reversible change in an object's shape.

✓ Inelastic deformation is an irreversible change in an object's shape.

✓ Hooke's law applies up to a point called the limit of proportionality.

✓ Work is done when a spring is deformed, storing elastic potential energy.

📑 Calculating the spring constant

The value of k, the spring constant, varies between different springs. The higher the value of k, the stiffer the spring.

Question
A spring is stretched by a force of 2 N, making it extend 5 cm. Calculate the spring constant for this spring.

Answer
First rearrange the equation to make k the subject. Remember to convert the extension to metres.

$$k = \frac{F}{e}$$

$$k = \frac{2\text{ N}}{0.05\text{ m}}$$

$$k = 40\text{ N/m}$$

⚙ Limit of proportionality

Hooke's law works only up to a certain point, called the limit of proportionality. Beyond this, the relationship is non-linear. If you stretch or squeeze an elastic object even further, it may become damaged and unable to return to its original size. The point of no return is called the elastic limit and varies with different materials.

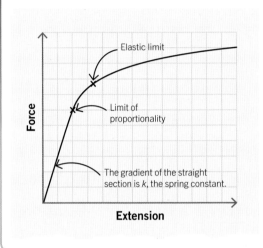

🔍 Elastic and inelastic deformation

If you stretch a spring and release it, it returns to its original shape. We call this elastic deformation. However, if you stretch it beyond its elastic limit, its shape changes permanently. We call this inelastic deformation. Different materials can sustain different amounts of elastic deformation before they reach their elastic limit.

A tennis ball can be squashed almost flat without reaching its elastic limit and will spring back into shape.

An aluminium can has a low elastic limit. If you squeeze it with enough force, it crumples and won't spring back into shape.

Glass has a high elastic limit, which is why marbles bounce, but too much force makes glass shatter.

Plasticine reaches its elastic limit almost immediately when a force is applied, making it ideal for moulding.

🗐 Elastic potential energy

A force that extends or compresses an elastic object does work, storing elastic potential energy in the object. When the object is released, it returns to its former shape and the energy is transferred to kinetic energy. That's why a stretched elastic band flies across the room when you release it and a bungee jumper is pulled back up after falling. You can calculate elastic potential energy using this equation.

$$\text{elastic potential energy (J)} = \frac{1}{2} \times \text{spring constant} \times \text{extension squared}$$

$$E = \frac{1}{2} \times k \times e^2$$

Question
A bungee cord has a spring constant of 90 N/m and extends by 8 m after a bungee jumper comes to a standstill. How much elastic potential energy is it now storing?

Answer
$E = \frac{1}{2} \times 90 \text{ N/m} \times 8 \text{ m} \times 8 \text{ m}$
$E = 2880$ J

Investigating springs

Forces can change the shape of an object, such as by stretching a spring. Investigating the effect of a pulling force on a spring shows that a spring's extension is directly proportional to the force applied.

Key facts

✓ Applying a force to a spring causes it to extend or contract.

✓ The increase in length of an object is known as its extension.

✓ The extension of a spring is directly proportional to the force applied.

Setting up the experiment

In this investigation, increasing masses are hung from a spring suspended from a clamp. The resulting spring extension – the increase from the spring's original length – is measured with a ruler and recorded. The results are plotted on a graph to investigate the relationship between force and extension.

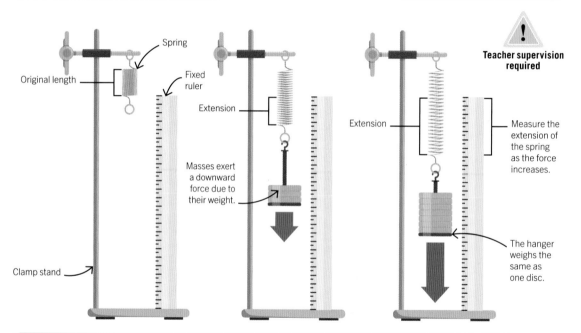

Spring

Original length

Fixed ruler

Extension

Masses exert a downward force due to their weight.

Clamp stand

Extension

Teacher supervision required

Measure the extension of the spring as the force increases.

The hanger weighs the same as one disc.

📑 Results

Plot the results on a graph with force in newtons on the y-axis and the spring's extension on the x-axis. Joining the crosses should give you a straight line, which shows that the relationship is linear. The line should also pass through the origin (0, 0), which indicates that the extension is directly proportional to the force (if you double the force, the extension doubles). However, if you add too many masses (if you overload the spring), the relationship between force and extension becomes non-linear and the line curves.

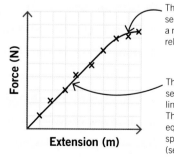

Force (N)

Extension (m)

The curved section shows a non-linear relationship.

The straight section shows a linear relationship. The gradient equals the spring constant (see page 80).

Deformations

As well as making objects move, forces can change their shape. We call these changes deformations. Changing the shape of a stationary object requires two or more forces acting in different directions.

Types of deformation
Stretching, compressing, bending, and twisting — or combinations of these deformations — are some of the ways in which objects can change shape. How an object is deformed depends on the number and direction of forces applied to it.

Key facts

✓ A change of shape caused by forces is called a deformation.

✓ Changing the shape of an object requires two or more forces acting in different directions.

✓ The type of deformation an object undergoes depends on the direction of the forces and where they act on the object.

Compression
When a pair of forces push an object in opposite directions, this creates compression and squashes the object. A bouncy toy like a space hopper undergoes an elastic compression on each bounce, before springing back to its original shape.

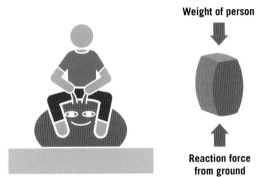

Weight of person

Reaction force from ground

Tension
When a pair of forces pull an object in opposite directions, this creates tension and causes the object to stretch. During a bungee jump, the cord experiences a downward force due to the person's weight and an upward pull from the platform it's secured to.

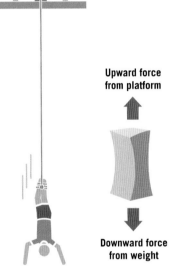

Upward force from platform

Downward force from weight

Bending
When more than two forces act on an object in different directions, they can cause bending. For instance, the bars used by gymnasts — which allow a small amount of elastic deformation — bend when the gymnast's weight acts in the middle and upward forces from the supports act at each end.

Weight

Upward force from support

Twisting
A pair of turning forces acting in opposite directions on different points of an object can cause it to twist.

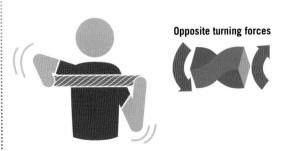

Opposite turning forces

Moments

To most people, a "moment" means a second or two, but in physics it means something completely different. A moment is the turning effect caused by a force that makes an object rotate around a fixed point called a pivot. You use moments all the time – turning a door handle, pedalling a bike, or bending an arm.

Key facts

✓ **A moment is the turning effect of a force.**

✓ **The equation for moments is moment = force × distance.**

✓ **Tools such as spanners and levers work by generating a large moment.**

How spanners work

When you use a spanner to loosen a nut, the force of your hand produces a turning effect – a moment – that turns the nut. The longer the spanner, the greater the moment and the easier it is to loosen a tight nut. The unit for moments is the newton metre (Nm). You can calculate moments with this equation.

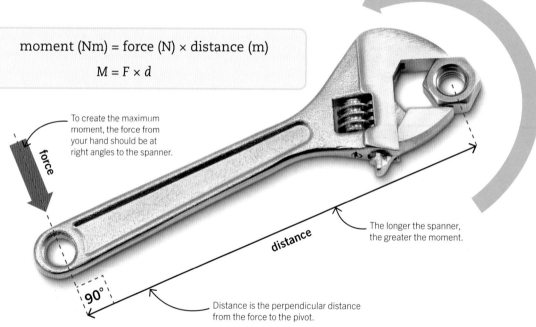

$$\text{moment (Nm)} = \text{force (N)} \times \text{distance (m)}$$
$$M = F \times d$$

To create the maximum moment, the force from your hand should be at right angles to the spanner.

force

moment

The longer the spanner, the greater the moment.

distance

90°

Distance is the perpendicular distance from the force to the pivot.

 Calculating moments

Question

A spanner 20 cm long is used to loosen a bolt. If a force of 30 N is applied at the end of the spanner, what is the size of the moment in Nm (newton metres)?

Answer

The distance must be in metres. 20 cm = 0.2 m.
$M = F \times d$
$\quad = 30\,\text{N} \times 0.2\,\text{m}$
$\quad = 6\,\text{Nm}$

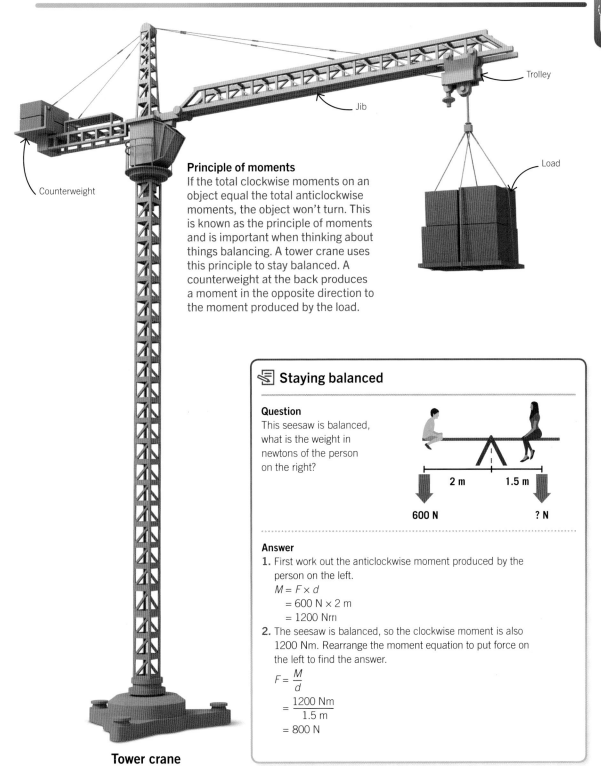

Trolley

Jib

Load

Counterweight

Principle of moments
If the total clockwise moments on an object equal the total anticlockwise moments, the object won't turn. This is known as the principle of moments and is important when thinking about things balancing. A tower crane uses this principle to stay balanced. A counterweight at the back produces a moment in the opposite direction to the moment produced by the load.

Tower crane

⬒ Staying balanced

Question
This seesaw is balanced, what is the weight in newtons of the person on the right?

2 m   1.5 m

600 N   ? N

Answer
1. First work out the anticlockwise moment produced by the person on the left.
$$M = F \times d$$
$$= 600 \text{ N} \times 2 \text{ m}$$
$$= 1200 \text{ Nm}$$
2. The seesaw is balanced, so the clockwise moment is also 1200 Nm. Rearrange the moment equation to put force on the left to find the answer.
$$F = \frac{M}{d}$$
$$= \frac{1200 \text{ Nm}}{1.5 \text{ m}}$$
$$= 800 \text{ N}$$

Centre of mass

The weight of an object (or any other force acting on it) can be thought of as acting at a single point: the centre of mass. Whether or not an object is stable depends on the position of its centre of mass.

The balancing bird

This toy bird looks like it shouldn't be able to balance on its beak. However, because its wingtips extend forwards and are weighted, the bird's centre of mass is located at the beak. The heavy wings and the rear of the body both produce moments (turning forces), but these balance each other, much like people at opposite ends of a seesaw.

Key facts

✓ The weight of an object can be thought of as acting at a single point: the centre of mass.

✓ The centre of mass can be inside or outside an object, depending on its shape.

✓ An object is stable when its centre of mass is above its base.

✓ An object will fall over if its centre of mass is outside the base.

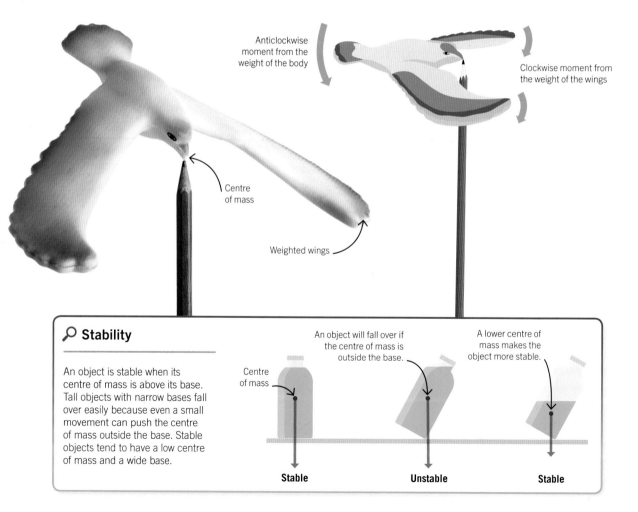

Anticlockwise moment from the weight of the body

Clockwise moment from the weight of the wings

Centre of mass

Weighted wings

🔍 Stability

An object is stable when its centre of mass is above its base. Tall objects with narrow bases fall over easily because even a small movement can push the centre of mass outside the base. Stable objects tend to have a low centre of mass and a wide base.

Centre of mass

An object will fall over if the centre of mass is outside the base.

A lower centre of mass makes the object more stable.

Stable   **Unstable**   **Stable**

⊟ Finding the centre of mass

To find the centre of mass of an irregular 2D shape (a plane lamina), hang the shape from a vertical surface with a pin so it can swing freely. After it comes to rest, hang a plumb line (a weight on a string) from the pin and use it to draw a vertical line on the object. Repeat, hanging the shape from two more pivot points. The centre of mass is the point where the lines intersect.

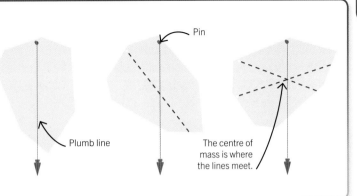

Pin

Plumb line

The centre of mass is where the lines meet.

Off-road stability

Off-road vehicles are designed to have a very low centre of mass and a wide wheelbase so they can negotiate steep or bumpy ground without becoming unstable.

Force of gravity

The car remains stable provided the centre of mass stays between the wheels.

Stable

Levers

Levers are simple machines that magnify or reduce the effects of forces. We use them all the time, often without realizing. Scissors, wheelbarrows, door handles, and even our arms and legs work as levers.

How levers work

A wheelbarrow acts as a lever to make lifting easier. Like all levers, it rotates around a point called a pivot (or fulcrum), which in this case is the wheel. When a force (called the effort) is applied at the handles to lift the wheelbarrow, it is magnified to create a larger output force that overcomes the load in the barrow. The further the effort is from the load, the greater the force is magnified.

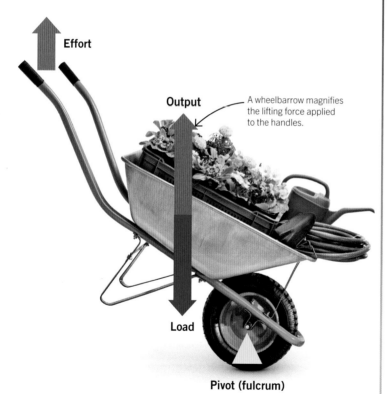

Effort

Output

A wheelbarrow magnifies the lifting force applied to the handles.

Load

Pivot (fulcrum)

📌 Key facts

✓ **A lever is a rigid object that can rotate around a fixed point called a pivot or a fulcrum.**

✓ **Levers can magnify or reduce the effect of a force.**

✓ **Levers that magnify a force reduce the distance travelled by the load.**

✓ **Levers that reduce a force increase the distance travelled by the load.**

🗐 Calculating effort

Question

A wheelbarrow is filled with soil weighing 450 N and with a centre of mass 0.5 m from the wheel. If the handles are 1.8 m from the wheel, what is the effort needed to lift the soil?

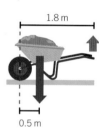

1.8 m

0.5 m

Answer

First use the equation for moments (see page 84) to calculate the moment due to the load.

moment (Nm) = force (N) × distance (m)
= 450 N × 0.5 m
= 225 Nm

Next calculate the force needed to produce a moment of the same size when applied at the handles. Rearrange the equation to make force the subject.

$$F = \frac{M}{d}$$

$$= \frac{225 \text{ Nm}}{1.8 \text{ m}}$$

$$= 125 \text{ N}$$

Lever classes

Levers come in three different classes depending on where the effort, load, and pivot are in relation to each other. If the effort is further from the pivot than the load, the lever magnifies the force. If the effort is nearer, the lever reduces the force but increases the distance moved.

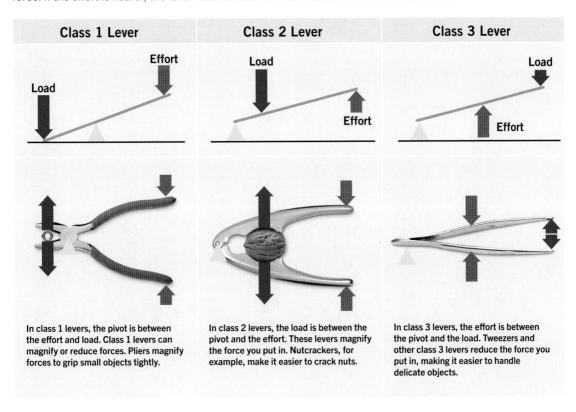

Class 1 Lever	Class 2 Lever	Class 3 Lever
In class 1 levers, the pivot is between the effort and load. Class 1 levers can magnify or reduce forces. Pliers magnify forces to grip small objects tightly.	In class 2 levers, the load is between the pivot and the effort. These levers magnify the force you put in. Nutcrackers, for example, make it easier to crack nuts.	In class 3 levers, the effort is between the pivot and the load. Tweezers and other class 3 levers reduce the force you put in, making it easier to handle delicate objects.

🔍 Machines

Mechanical devices that magnify or reduce forces (or that change the direction of forces) are known as machines. Simple machines such as levers often form parts of more complex machines with several moving parts. Here, a lever is connected via a gear to a toothed bar that moves down when the lever swings, magnifying the force from the user to squeeze oranges.

Pivot

Lever

The squeezer moves down more slowly than the lever but with much greater force.

Gears

Gears are wheels with toothed edges that interlock to transmit rotational (turning) forces. Like levers, they can magnify or reduce the turning effects (moments) of forces.

How gears work

A gear transmits rotational force when its teeth mesh with those of another gear, causing it to turn as well. The forces acting at the teeth are the same for both gears, but the moments (the turning forces exerted on the axles) are different if connected gears have different numbers of teeth.

Key facts

✓ A gear is a wheel with a toothed edge.

✓ Gears transmit rotational forces.

✓ When the driven gear is larger than the gear driving it, it rotates more slowly but with a greater moment (stronger turning force).

✓ When the driven gear is smaller than the gear driving it, it rotates more quickly but with a smaller moment (weaker turning force).

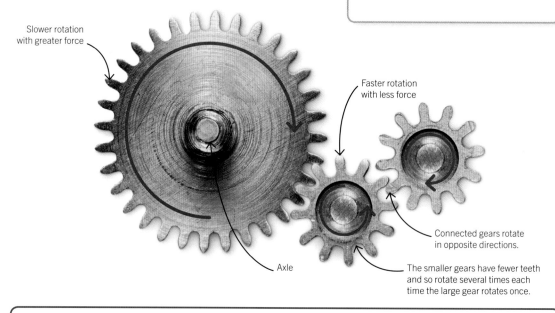

Slower rotation with greater force

Faster rotation with less force

Axle

Connected gears rotate in opposite directions.

The smaller gears have fewer teeth and so rotate several times each time the large gear rotates once.

⚙ Using gears

Gears can either magnify moments or increase the speed of rotation. Which they do depends on whether the driving gear is smaller or larger than the driven gear.

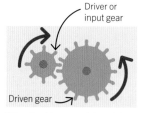

Driver or input gear

Driven gear

When the driven gear is larger than the gear driving it, the greater distance between the teeth and the axle means it produces a greater moment. This arrangement magnifies the input turning force.

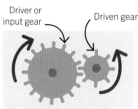

Driver or input gear

Driven gear

When the driven gear is smaller than the driver gear, it produces a smaller moment on its axle but rotates faster. This arrangement increases speed.

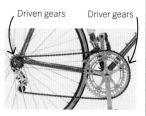

Driven gears

Driver gears

The gears on a bike are connected by a chain. Choosing a small front gear and a large rear gear increases the moment – ideal for climbing a hill. Choosing a large front gear and small rear gear increases speed.

More simple machines

Levers and gears are not the only simple machines that can magnify or reduce forces. All the simple machines on this page make jobs easier by changing forces.

Wedges
A wedge is thick at one end and thin at the other. When you apply a force downwards to the thick end, the thin end increases the force and drives it sideways, cutting or splitting an object.

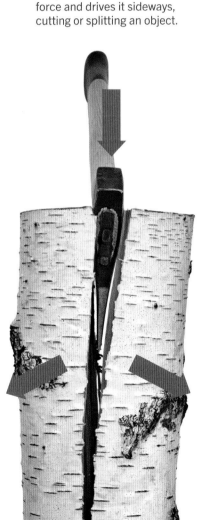

Ramps
The sloping surface of a ramp makes it easier to raise a heavy object. The shallower the slope, the lower the input force needed. However, the load has to travel a longer distance, so the work done to lift the object is the same.

Wheels and axles
A wheel and axle work like a circular lever. Like levers, they can both increase or reduce forces. When the input force is applied to the rim, as with a steering wheel, the turning force around the circumference of the axle is magnified. When the input force is applied to the axle, the force at the rim is smaller but the rim moves faster than the circumference of the axle, as with a bicycle wheel.

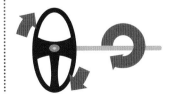

Screws
A screw is a ramp that has been coiled around a cylinder. Each twist of the screwdriver pushes the tip of the screw only a small amount forwards, but with greater force than the screwdriver exerts on the screw.

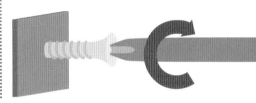

Pulleys
A pulley is a rope or cable that runs around one or more wheels. If only one wheel is used, a pulley merely changes the direction of a force. However, if two wheels are arranged as shown below, the pulley doubles the lifting force. A three-wheel pulley can triple the lifting force.

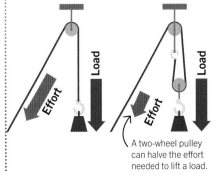

A two-wheel pulley can halve the effort needed to lift a load.

Action–reaction forces

The English scientist Isaac Newton realized that forces always come in pairs. He said that every "action" (meaning force) has an equal and opposite "reaction" (opposing force). We call this Newton's third law of motion.

Action and reaction
This dog is pulling a towel, but the towel is also exerting a pulling force on the dog. These two forces are called action–reaction forces and exist whether the dog is moving or stationary. The dog also exerts a force on the ground because of its weight. This has a reaction force too: the ground is pushing up on the dog. Action–reaction forces are not the same as balanced forces (see page 75). Balanced forces act on the same object, but action and reaction forces act between pairs of objects.

Key facts

✓ Newton's third law states that every force is accompanied by an equal force acting in the opposite direction.

✓ Pairs of action and reaction forces are always the same type of force and act between pairs of objects.

✓ Action and reaction forces shouldn't be confused with balanced forces.

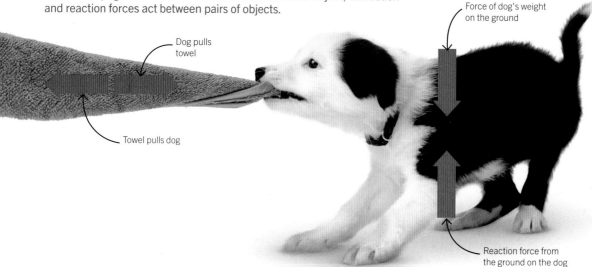

Force of dog's weight on the ground

Dog pulls towel

Towel pulls dog

Reaction force from the ground on the dog

⚙ Effects of action–reaction pairs

Both forces in an action–reaction pair are real and can cause changes in motion or shape for the objects involved. For example, when a skateboarder pushes against a wall, she exerts a force on the wall and the wall exerts an equal and opposite force on her. The wall stays still but the skateboarder gets a push in the opposite direction. If she pushes against another skateboarder, both move in opposite directions.

Reaction   Action

Skateboarder moves

Action   Reaction

Skateboarders move in opposite directions

Fields

Not all forces require physical contact. Some forces, such as gravity, act from a distance. These non-contact forces involve something called a field: a region around an object in which the object can exert forces.

Objects with more mass experience a greater gravitational pull.

0.2 N   40 000 N

Action at a distance

Gravity, magnetism, and the attraction or repulsion between charged objects are all forces that act through a field. A gravitational field surrounds all objects with mass, but the pull of gravity is only noticeable around very massive objects, such as Earth. The strength of a non-contact force on an object depends on the strength of the field, the object's position within it, and the object's properties. For instance, Earth exerts a stronger gravitational pull on objects that are closer and that have more mass.

Key facts

✓ Non-contact forces act through a field.

✓ A field is the region around an object in which the object can exert forces.

✓ The size of the force depends on the strength of the field, the object's position within it, and the object's properties.

The lines show how a mass would move if it was placed in the gravitational field.

The field strength is greater where the lines are closer together.

⚙ Newton's third law

Newton's third law says that every force has an equal and opposite reaction force. This holds true for non-contact forces exerted through fields. For instance, Earth exerts a gravitational pull on a person standing on its surface, but that person also has a gravitational field of their own and exerts an equal and opposite pull on Earth. But because Earth's mass is so vast, the effect of the reaction force on Earth is imperceptible.

Gravitational force exerted by Earth on person

Gravitational force exerted by person on Earth

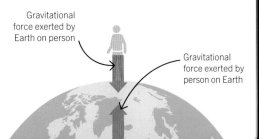

Law of gravity

All objects with mass, from galaxies to atoms, exert an attractive force on other objects with mass through their gravitational fields. The size of the force between any two objects can be worked out from Newton's law of universal gravitation, which was developed by the English scientist Isaac Newton.

Earth and Moon

Newton used observations of the Moon and planets to work out his law of gravity. He realized that the force of gravity between any two bodies is proportional to their masses multiplied together (the product of their masses). But gravity also declines as objects get further apart, falling in proportion to the square of the distance between their centres. This relationship can be written as an equation.

Key facts

✓ All objects with mass are surrounded by a gravitational field in which other objects with mass are attracted.

✓ The gravitational force between two objects is proportional to the product of their masses.

✓ The gravitational force between two objects is inversely proportional to the square of the distance between them.

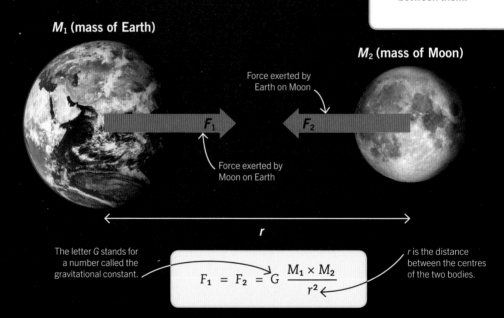

M_1 (mass of Earth)

M_2 (mass of Moon)

Force exerted by Earth on Moon

F_1 F_2

Force exerted by Moon on Earth

r

The letter G stands for a number called the gravitational constant.

$$F_1 = F_2 = G \frac{M_1 \times M_2}{r^2}$$

r is the distance between the centres of the two bodies.

⚙ The inverse square law

Newton's law of universal gravitation follows a pattern known as the inverse square law: as the distance between two objects increases, the gravitational force between them falls in proportion to the square of the distance. In nature, there are many examples of a property following this pattern, including light intensity and the electrostatic force between charged objects.

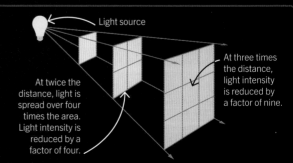

Light source

At twice the distance, light is spread over four times the area. Light intensity is reduced by a factor of four.

At three times the distance, light intensity is reduced by a factor of nine.

Force and motion

Circular motion

Many objects move along curved or circular paths, from the Moon orbiting planet Earth to the passengers on a fairground ride. The force that makes an object travel in a circle is called centripetal force.

Centripetal force

In the hammer throw, a weighted ball is swung around in circles before being released. Its velocity is changing continually as it swings, which means the ball is accelerating. All accelerations are caused by a force, and in this case the force is tension in the cable. This is an example of centripetal force. If the centripetal force suddenly stops, the object flies off in a straight line.

Key facts

✓ Circular motion occurs due to a centripetal force, which acts inwards.

✓ Without centripetal force, a moving object would travel in a straight line.

✓ Centrifugal force is a fictitious force experienced by objects travelling along a curved path.

✓ The force needed to keep an object moving in a circle increases with an object's mass and velocity but falls as the radius of the circle increases.

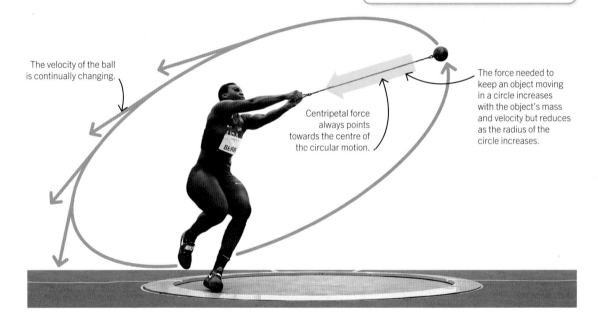

The velocity of the ball is continually changing.

Centripetal force always points towards the centre of the circular motion.

The force needed to keep an object moving in a circle increases with the object's mass and velocity but reduces as the radius of the circle increases.

⚙ Centrifugal force

On a swing ride the riders experience what feels like a real force pulling them outwards and making their seat rise. This is called centrifugal force, but it is not a real force. It only feels like a force from the point of view of the riders, so we call it a fictitious force. It is caused by centripetal force pulling them towards the centre while their mass tries to move away in a straight line due to its inertia.

Centripetal force from tension in the cables

The seats rise as though pulled by a force.

Newton's second law

When an unbalanced force acts on an object, the object accelerates. The English scientist Isaac Newton worked out a simple relationship between the size of the force, the mass of the object, and its acceleration. We call this Newton's second law.

Force, mass, and acceleration
A van with lots of luggage accelerates more slowly than a van with no luggage because it has more mass. The greater the mass, the smaller the acceleration. Cars with more powerful engines also accelerate faster because they can generate a greater pushing force. The greater the force, the greater the acceleration. The relationship between force, mass, and acceleration is shown by this equation.

$$\text{force (N)} = \text{mass (kg)} \times \text{acceleration (m/s}^2)$$
$$F = m \times a$$

The van with no luggage accelerates faster.

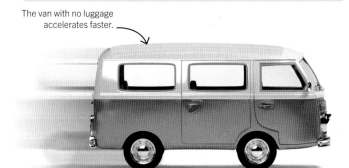

Key facts
- ✓ The larger the force on an object, the greater the acceleration.
- ✓ The greater the mass of an object, the smaller the acceleration.
- ✓ Newton's second law can be summed up by an equation: force = mass × acceleration.
- ✓ Inertial mass is a measure of how difficult it is to change an object's velocity.

🔍 Inertial mass

Massive objects are hard to get moving, and once moving they're difficult to stop. We say they have lots of "inertia". The inertial mass of an object is a measure of how difficult it is to change its velocity. It is defined as the ratio of force over acceleration:

$$m = \frac{F}{a}$$

📑 Calculating acceleration

Question
A 500 kg trolley is pushed with a force of 90 N. What is its acceleration?

Answer
Rearrange the equation to make acceleration the subject.
$$a = \frac{F}{m}$$
$$= \frac{90 \text{ N}}{500 \text{ kg}}$$
$$= 0.18 \text{ m/s}^2$$

Investigating acceleration

This experiment demonstrates the effect of force or mass on motion by using a hanging weight to pull a trolley along a ramp. It shows that acceleration is directly proportional to force (doubling the force doubles the acceleration) and inversely proportional to mass (doubling the mass halves the acceleration).

Key facts

✓ Increasing the force applied to a moving object increases its acceleration.

✓ Acceleration is directly proportional to force.

✓ Acceleration is inversely proportional to mass.

Accelerating trolley

You can use a setup like the one below for the experiment. Light gates measure the trolley's velocity at two points on a ramp, and a data logger uses the two velocities and the time between the measurements to calculate acceleration. The slope of the ramp compensates for friction.

Teacher supervision required

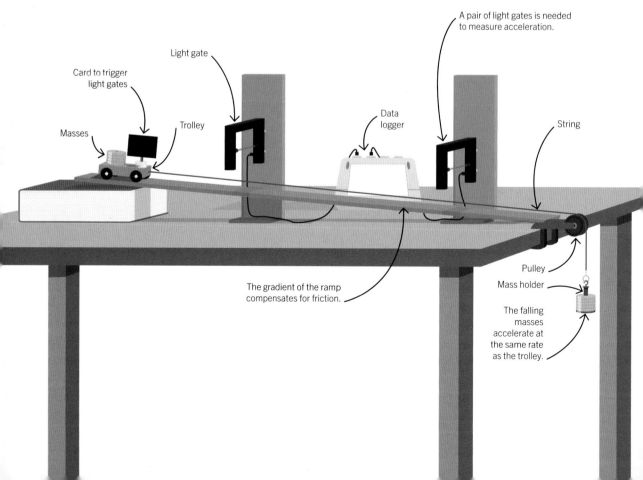

A pair of light gates is needed to measure acceleration.

Light gate

Card to trigger light gates

Data logger

String

Masses

Trolley

Pulley

Mass holder

The gradient of the ramp compensates for friction.

The falling masses accelerate at the same rate as the trolley.

🗐 Methods

Method 1: Effect of force on acceleration

1. Set up the equipment as shown and set the data logger to calculate acceleration.

2. Adjust the gradient of the ramp until an unweighted trolley rolls at a constant speed when given a gentle push.

3. Begin by placing a single mass at the end of the string and nine masses on the trolley. If you use a mass holder designed to equal one mass, use that as the first mass. Record the total mass of the system (the trolley plus all the masses).

4. Release the trolley from the top of the ramp and record the acceleration. Roll the trolley down the ramp two more times and take the average of the three measurements of acceleration.

5. Move a mass from the trolley to the string to increase the force, then repeat step 4. Keep doing this until 10 masses are on the string. Record all your data in a table.

Method 2: Effect of mass on acceleration

1. Use the same setup as above but place five masses on the end of the string and none on the trolley to begin with.

2. Roll the trolley down the ramp. Record the total mass (trolley + masses) and the acceleration. Roll the trolley two more times and take an average of the three acceleration readings.

3. Add a mass to the trolley and repeat step 2. Repeat with additional masses until the trolley has five masses.

🗐 Results

Result 1

Use the data from the first investigation to draw a graph of acceleration against force. Acceleration is the dependent variable and so should go on the y-axis. The points should form a straight line that goes through the origin (0, 0). This shows that acceleration is directly proportional to the force.

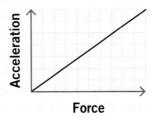

Result 2

Plotting acceleration against mass on a graph produces a downward curve showing an inversely proportional relationship (if mass doubles, acceleration halves).

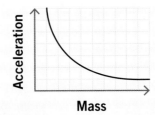

Ariel Atom

Some sports cars are designed to minimize mass so they can accelerate as fast as possible for the same engine power. The Ariel Atom has a naked chassis with no roof, doors, or windows, resulting in a mass about half that of a hatchback car.

Momentum

When objects collide, the effect one object has on another depends on a quantity called momentum. The greater the mass of a moving object, or the faster the object is moving, the greater its momentum and the greater the effect it can have.

Conservation of momentum

Newton's cradle is a device that demonstrates a law known as conservation of momentum. According to this law, when a system is not affected by external forces, the total momentum in the system is the same before and after a collision. When one of the metal balls is lifted and allowed to hit the others, its momentum passes from ball to ball, making the last ball rise and repeat the cycle.

Key facts

✓ The greater an object's mass or the faster it is moving, the more momentum it has.

✓ Momentum = mass × velocity.

✓ The law of conservation of momentum says that in a system not affected by external forces, total momentum is the same before and after a collision.

✓ Momentum is a vector, so calculations must take into account the direction the object is moving in.

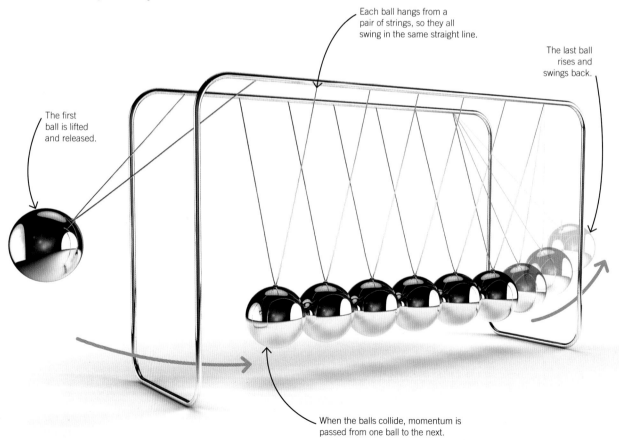

Each ball hangs from a pair of strings, so they all swing in the same straight line.

The last ball rises and swings back.

The first ball is lifted and released.

When the balls collide, momentum is passed from one ball to the next.

Formula for momentum
Both velocity and mass affect an object's momentum, as the equation below shows. Shooting stars are often no bigger than grains of sand, but they have great momentum because of their speed. Large vehicles such as freight trains have enormous momentum due to their great mass and can cause dangerous collisions even when moving slowly. Momentum is a vector, so calculations must take into account the direction in which the object is moving.

$$\text{momentum (kg m/s)} = \text{mass (kg)} \times \text{velocity (m/s)}$$
$$p = m \times v$$

Calculating momentum

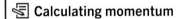

Question 1
A rhinoceros has a mass of 1000 kg and is travelling at 15 m/s. How much momentum does it have?

Answer 1
$p = m \times v$
    $= 1000 \text{ kg} \times 15 \text{ m/s}$
    $= 15\,000 \text{ kg m/s}$

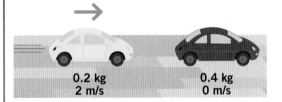

0.2 kg
2 m/s

0.4 kg
0 m/s

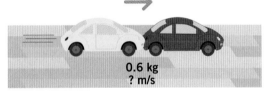

0.6 kg
? m/s

Question 2
A toy car with a mass of 0.2 kg hits another toy car with a mass of 0.4 kg while travelling at 2 m/s. The two cars stick together and continue moving in the same direction. What speed are they going at?

Answer 2
The total momentum is conserved, so use the following equation to work out the answer:

momentum before collision = momentum after collision

momentum before = (0.2 kg × 2 m/s) + (0.4 kg × 0 m/s)
                    = 0.4 kg m/s
momentum after = 0.4 kg m/s

$v = \dfrac{p}{m}$

$= \dfrac{0.4 \text{ kg m/s}}{0.2 \text{ kg} + 0.4 \text{ kg}}$

$= 0.67 \text{ m/s}$

Elastic and inelastic collisions

When objects collide, the total momentum before and after the collision is conserved (see page 100). However, kinetic energy may not be. Whether kinetic energy is conserved or not depends on whether a collision is elastic or inelastic.

Key facts

✓ Collisions can be elastic or inelastic.

✓ Kinetic energy is conserved in an elastic collision and lost in an inelastic collision.

✓ Total momentum is the same before and after a collision.

Elastic collisions

During an elastic collision, the colliding objects change shape but then spring back into their original shapes and separate. The total kinetic energy of the moving objects is the same before and after the collision. Few collisions in the real world are perfectly elastic as some kinetic energy is usually lost. For example, when a foot kicks a ball, some kinetic energy is transferred to sound.

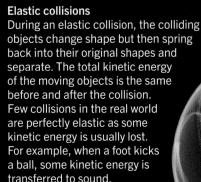

During an elastic collision, both objects change shape temporarily.

🗐 Calculating kinetic energy

Most collisions result in a loss of some kinetic energy. We can find out how much is lost by calculating the kinetic energy before and after the collision.

Question

During a game of snooker, a 0.17 kg white ball travelling at 1.5 m/s hits a stationary red ball with a mass of 0.16 kg. The red ball moves forwards at 1.2 m/s and the white ball at 0.37 m/s. How much kinetic energy was lost?

1.5 m/s		0.37 m/s	1.2 m/s
0.17 kg	0.16 kg	0.17 kg	0.16 kg

Answer

Use the equation for kinetic energy from page 52 ($E_k = \frac{1}{2} \times m \times v^2$) to work out the total kinetic energy before and after the collision.

Kinetic energy before collision $= \frac{1}{2} \times 0.17 \times 1.5^2$
$= 0.19$ J

Kinetic energy after collision
$= (\frac{1}{2} \times 0.17 \times 0.37^2) + (\frac{1}{2} \times 0.16 \times 1.2^2)$
$= 0.13$ J

The energy lost $= 0.19$ J $- 0.13$ J
$= 0.06$ J

Inelastic collisions

In an inelastic collision, the colliding objects can change shape permanently and may join together. Kinetic energy is transferred to sound, internal energy, and other energy stores. For example, the car collision shown below is inelastic. Instead of rebounding like a football off a boot, the cars lose kinetic energy and come to a halt. The shape of both cars is permanently changed.

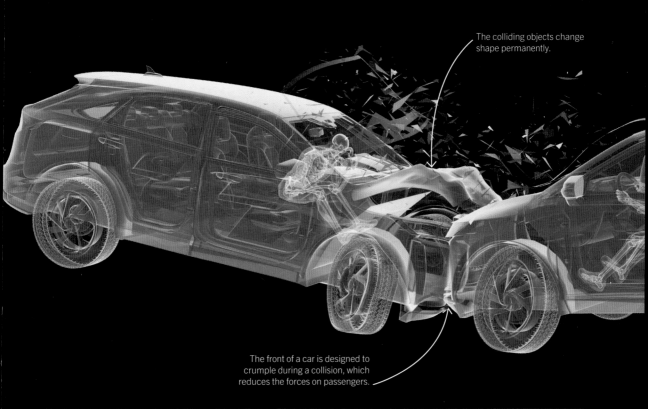

The colliding objects change shape permanently.

The front of a car is designed to crumple during a collision, which reduces the forces on passengers.

⚙ Explosions

In an explosion, momentum is conserved but kinetic energy is not. An unexploded bomb has zero kinetic energy when it's stationary, but the exploding fragments have a huge amount of kinetic energy. However, momentum stays the same. The total momentum of a stationary bomb is zero, and the total momentum of the fragments is also zero (momentum is a vector quantity, and the fragments all travel outwards in different directions).

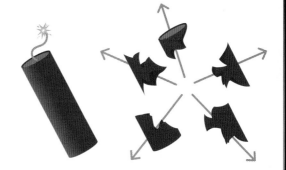

Changing momentum

Changing the momentum of a moving object – whether stopping a car or striking a tennis ball – requires a force. The greater the change in momentum, or the more quickly the momentum changes, the greater the force required. Car crashes are dangerous because the very rapid change in momentum involves huge forces.

Force and momentum
When a car comes to a halt, its momentum falls to zero. We can calculate the force needed to change the car's momentum using the equation here. As the examples below demonstrate, a far greater force is needed to stop a car suddenly than to slow it down gradually.

$$\text{force (N)} = \frac{\text{change in momentum (kg m/s)}}{\text{time (s)}}$$

Final velocity

$$F = \frac{mv - mu}{t}$$

Initial velocity

14 m/s   0 m/s

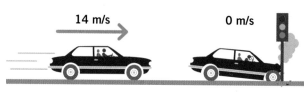

14 m/s   0 m/s

Stopping gradually
A car with a mass of 1000 kg is travelling at 14 m/s (about 50 km/h). The driver brakes for 10 seconds, bringing the car to a stop. What is the force acting on the car?

Remember to take the initial momentum away from the final momentum.

$$F = \frac{(1000 \text{ kg} \times 0 \text{ m/s}) - (1000 \text{ kg} \times 14 \text{ m/s})}{10 \text{ s}}$$

$$= \frac{0 - 14\,000 \text{ kg m/s}}{10 \text{ s}}$$

$$= -1400 \text{ N}$$

The force is negative because it acts in the opposite direction to the motion of the car.

Stopping suddenly
A car of the same mass is also travelling at 14 m/s. It hits a traffic light and decelerates to 0 m/s in 0.07 seconds. What is the force acting on this car?

$$F = \frac{(1000 \text{ kg} \times 0 \text{ m/s}) - (1000 \text{ kg} \times 14 \text{ m/s})}{0.07 \text{ s}}$$

$$= \frac{0 - 14\,000 \text{ kg m/s}}{0.07 \text{ s}}$$

$$= -200\,000 \text{ N}$$

The force that stops the car is equivalent to the weight of five elephants.

Stopping distance

In an emergency, a driver may see a hazard and have to stop the car very quickly. The distance the car travels between the driver seeing the hazard and the car coming to a stop is called the stopping distance and is affected by the car's speed, mass, and other factors.

Thinking and braking
Total stopping distance can be divided into two parts: thinking distance and braking distance. Thinking distance is the distance the car travels during the time a driver takes to react and use the brakes after seeing a hazard. Braking distance is the distance the car travels after braking begins.

Key facts

✓ Stopping distance is the distance covered between the driver seeing a hazard and the vehicle stopping.

✓ Stopping distance is the sum of thinking distance and braking distance.

✓ Factors affecting thinking distance include tiredness, use of drugs or alcohol, distractions, and the vehicle's speed.

✓ Factors affecting braking distance include the vehicle's speed, mass, condition, and road and weather conditions.

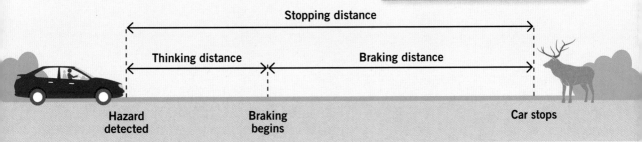

Stopping distance and speed
The most important factor affecting stopping distance is speed: the faster a car is travelling, the longer it takes to stop safely. This is because a fast car has far more kinetic energy than a slow car, so the brakes must do much more work to bring the car to a stop.

■ Thinking distance
■ Braking distance

The chart shows typical stopping distances for an average family car.

Braking distance increases in proportion to the square of speed. If the speed doubles, the braking distance increases by a factor of four.

Thinking distance increases in proportion to speed.

Speed (km/h): 40, 50, 60, 70, 80, 90, 100, 110

Total stopping distance (m): 0, 25, 50, 75, 100

🔍 Reaction time

Most drivers take about 0.7 seconds to react to a hazard, but this time can more than triple if a driver has been drinking alcohol, taking drugs, or is distracted by a mobile phone. Reaction times also vary from person to person and are affected by how tired we are. You can assess your reaction time with a simple experiment: ask a helper to drop a ruler without warning and see how quickly you can catch it.

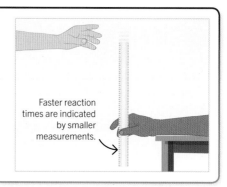

Faster reaction times are indicated by smaller measurements.

🔍 Factors affecting braking distance

Massive vehicles have more kinetic energy than smaller vehicles and so require a longer braking distance.

Fast vehicles have more kinetic energy than slow vehicles and so require a longer braking distance.

Tyre and brake condition affect braking distance. If they are worn or in poor condition, they create less friction, which means less force to reduce kinetic energy.

Wet or icy roads reduce friction, resulting in a smaller stopping force. They may also cause skids.

Supersonic stopping distance
Braking distance increases in proportion to the square of a car's speed (doubling the speed causes braking distance to increase by a factor of four). As a result, the supersonic car *Bloodhound LSR*, which is designed to break the land speed record, has a braking distance of around 7.2 km, even with the assistance of a braking parachute.

Bloodhound LSR's streamlined nose helps to reduce air resistance.

Car safety features

During a car crash, the car and everything inside it undergo a rapid change in momentum. The force on the people in the car from the collision is equal to the rate of change of their momentum. In order to minimize this large force, which can cause serious injuries, cars have safety features that slow the change in momentum.

Crash test

Simulating car crashes allows engineers to measure the forces on different parts of a passenger's body and ensure that safety features are effective. The main safety features are seatbelts, the front and rear crumple zones, and airbags. Airbags and crumple zones increase the time it takes for the person's body to come to a stop, which reduces the change in momentum and hence the forces on the passengers.

Key facts

- ✓ Car crashes involve extreme changes in momentum and large, dangerous forces.
- ✓ Slowing down the change in momentum reduces the forces in a crash.
- ✓ Car safety features include airbags, seatbelts, and crumple zones.

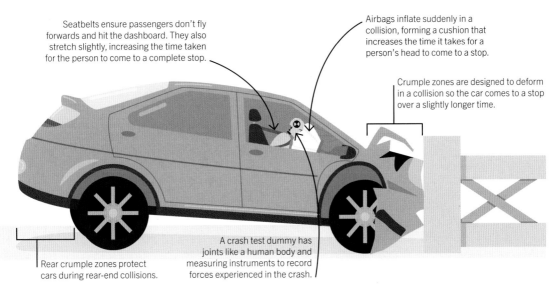

Seatbelts ensure passengers don't fly forwards and hit the dashboard. They also stretch slightly, increasing the time taken for the person to come to a complete stop.

Airbags inflate suddenly in a collision, forming a cushion that increases the time it takes for a person's head to come to a stop.

Crumple zones are designed to deform in a collision so the car comes to a stop over a slightly longer time.

Rear crumple zones protect cars during rear-end collisions.

A crash test dummy has joints like a human body and measuring instruments to record forces experienced in the crash.

⚙ Safety cage

Many parts of a modern car are designed to deform safely during a collision, reducing the forces on the passengers. However, some parts must be protected from crumpling, including the cabin containing the occupants and the fuel tank or battery. These areas are enclosed by a rigid steel frame called a safety cage, which can withstand huge forces without significant deformation.

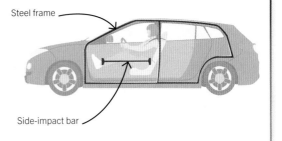

Steel frame

Side-impact bar

Braking distance and energy

To stop a car, its kinetic energy must be transferred to other energy stores. The faster a car is moving, the more kinetic energy it has to transfer away and the greater its braking distance.

Kinetic energy

A moving car has a store of kinetic energy. We can calculate how much by using the equation from page 52: kinetic energy = ½ × m × v^2. When the brakes are used to slow down the car, they exert a force and do work. Since the work done braking is equal to the change in kinetic energy, we can combine the equation for work (see page 55) with the equation for kinetic energy to make a new equation:

Key facts

✓ A braking force does work on a vehicle to change its motion.

✓ The work done braking is equal to the change in kinetic energy.

✓ The braking distance required to stop a car safely increases in proportion to the square of the car's speed.

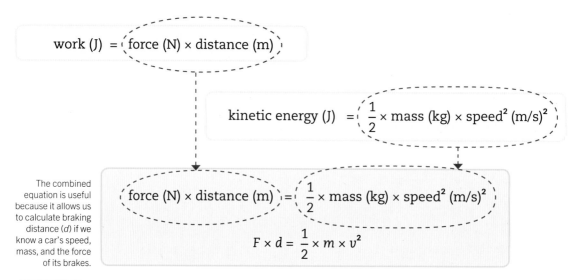

$$\text{work (J)} = \text{force (N)} \times \text{distance (m)}$$

$$\text{kinetic energy (J)} = \frac{1}{2} \times \text{mass (kg)} \times \text{speed}^2 \text{ (m/s)}^2$$

The combined equation is useful because it allows us to calculate braking distance (d) if we know a car's speed, mass, and the force of its brakes.

$$\text{force (N)} \times \text{distance (m)} = \frac{1}{2} \times \text{mass (kg)} \times \text{speed}^2 \text{ (m/s)}^2$$

$$F \times d = \frac{1}{2} \times m \times v^2$$

📑 Calculating braking distance

Question

A uniform braking force of 2000 N is applied to the wheels of a 1100 kg car travelling at 13 m/s (about 47 km/h). What is its braking distance? What would the braking distance be at twice that speed?

Answer 1

Rearrange the equation to make braking distance the subject.

$$d = \frac{\frac{1}{2} \times m \times v^2}{F}$$

$$= \frac{\frac{1}{2} \times 1100 \text{ kg} \times 13 \text{ m/s} \times 13 \text{ m/s}}{2000 \text{ N}}$$

$$= 46 \text{ m}$$

Answer 2

$$d = \frac{\frac{1}{2} \times 1100 \text{ kg} \times 26 \text{ m/s} \times 26 \text{ m/s}}{2000 \text{ N}}$$

$$= 186 \text{ m}$$

At twice the speed, braking distance is four times greater. Braking distance is proportional to the square of the speed.

Speed and safety

The combined equation shows that braking distance increases in proportion to the square of a car's speed. In other words, if you double the speed, the braking distance is four times greater; if you triple the speed, the braking distance is nine times greater. This is one of the reasons that driving at high speeds is dangerous – a faster car not only has a lot more momentum than a slow car but also needs far more room to stop.

Brake discs

When a car brakes, energy is transferred from its store of kinetic energy to thermal energy stores, making the brakes hot. Formula 1 cars are built to accelerate and decelerate incredibly quickly. Huge amounts of energy are transferred while braking, causing the brake discs to glow red hot.

The disc brakes in the wheels glow red-hot when braking.

Terminal velocity

Falling objects accelerate due to the pull of Earth's gravity. However, a falling object stops accelerating when it reaches terminal velocity. At this point, the downward force of its weight is balanced by the upward force of air resistance.

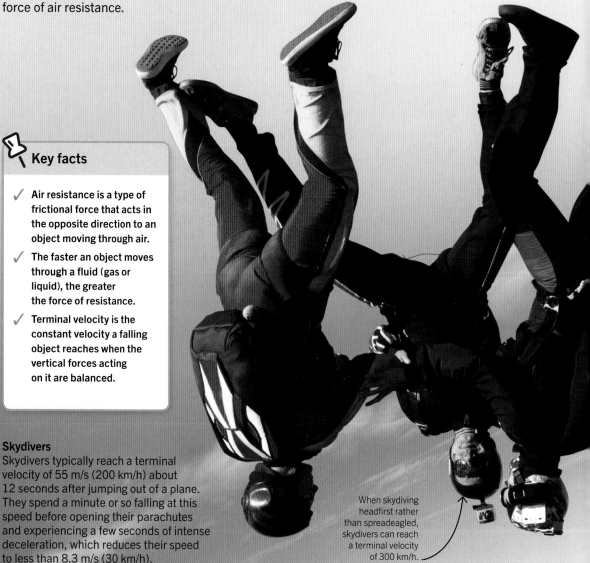

Key facts

✓ Air resistance is a type of frictional force that acts in the opposite direction to an object moving through air.

✓ The faster an object moves through a fluid (gas or liquid), the greater the force of resistance.

✓ Terminal velocity is the constant velocity a falling object reaches when the vertical forces acting on it are balanced.

Skydivers

Skydivers typically reach a terminal velocity of 55 m/s (200 km/h) about 12 seconds after jumping out of a plane. They spend a minute or so falling at this speed before opening their parachutes and experiencing a few seconds of intense deceleration, which reduces their speed to less than 8.3 m/s (30 km/h).

When skydiving headfirst rather than spreadeagled, skydivers can reach a terminal velocity of 300 km/h.

⚙ Using air resistance

Air resistance acts in the opposite direction to an object's motion. Planes and birds are streamlined to minimize air resistance, but parachutes work the opposite way: their large area creates maximum air resistance, allowing a person to fall to Earth at a very low terminal velocity.

1. When a skydiver leaps from a plane, air resistance is small to begin with. The skydiver's weight is greater than the force of air resistance, so the resultant force is downwards. As a result, the skydiver accelerates.

2. As the skydiver speeds up, air resistance increases until it equals the skydiver's weight. The forces are now balanced, so the skydiver stops accelerating and falls at a constant speed: terminal velocity.

3. When the skydiver opens the parachute, air resistance increases dramatically. It is now much greater than the skydiver's weight, causing a resultant upward force. The skydiver decelerates (but continues to fall).

4. As the skydiver slows down, air resistance falls. Eventually it matches weight again, and the skydiver reaches a new, lower terminal velocity that makes it safe to land.

■ Air resistance
■ Weight

▤ Velocity–time graph

A skydiver's journey from plane to ground can be shown on a velocity–time graph. The two horizontal sections represent terminal velocity, and the sudden drop in velocity marks the sudden deceleration after the parachute opens.

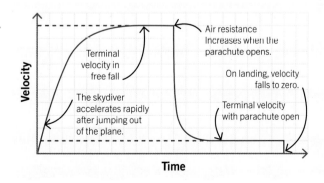

Air resistance increases when the parachute opens.

Terminal velocity in free fall

On landing, velocity falls to zero.

The skydiver accelerates rapidly after jumping out of the plane.

Terminal velocity with parachute open

Velocity

Time

Waves

Waves

Waves are vibrations that transfer energy from place to place without transferring matter at the same time. Some waves, such as ripples in a pond or sound waves in air, can only travel through matter. Other kinds of wave, such as light, can travel through empty space.

Waves in water

When you throw a stone in a pond, it creates circular waves that spread outwards. It might look like the water is travelling outwards, but it is actually only rising and falling as the energy of the waves travels through it. An object floating on the water bobs up and down as the waves pass.

Key facts

✓ Waves are vibrations that transfer energy without transferring matter.

✓ The wavelength of a wave is the distance from one wave peak to the next.

✓ The amplitude of a wave is the height of its peak above the midline.

✓ The frequency of a wave is the number of waves passing a fixed point each second.

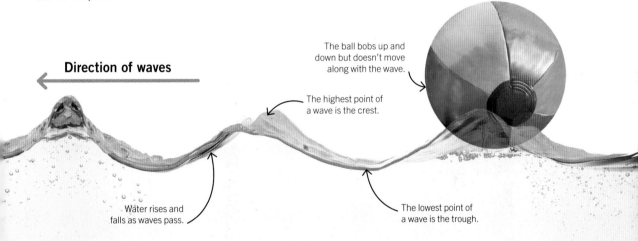

Direction of waves

The ball bobs up and down but doesn't move along with the wave.

The highest point of a wave is the crest.

Water rises and falls as waves pass.

The lowest point of a wave is the trough.

🔍 Describing waves

All types of wave can be described using three different measurements. Wavelength is the length of one wave, and frequency is the number of waves that pass a fixed point each second. The longer the wavelength, the lower the frequency. Amplitude is the height of a wave's peak above the midline. The greater the amplitude, the greater the energy the wave transfers.

Long wavelength, low frequency

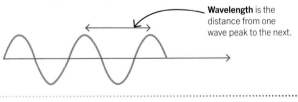

Wavelength is the distance from one wave peak to the next.

Short wavelength, high frequency

Rest position

Amplitude is the height of a wave's peak above the midline.

Sound

Sound consists of invisible waves that travel through matter (including air, water, and solid objects). They are created when objects vibrate. Plucking a guitar string or beating a drum, for instance, causes vibrations that pass into the air, producing waves that travel outwards in all directions.

Sound waves

When a loudspeaker plays music, its surface moves very rapidly back and forth — it vibrates. As it does so, particles in the air are alternately pushed together and pulled apart. The moving particles collide with neighbouring particles, causing waves of compression to travel outwards. These are sound waves. Sound travels through liquids and solids in the same way.

Key facts

✓ Sound consists of waves that travel through matter.

✓ Sound waves are created when objects vibrate.

✓ Sound waves are longitudinal waves: the vibration is forwards and backwards relative to the direction in which the wave travels.

✓ In transverse waves such as light, the vibration is at right angles to the direction in which the wave travels.

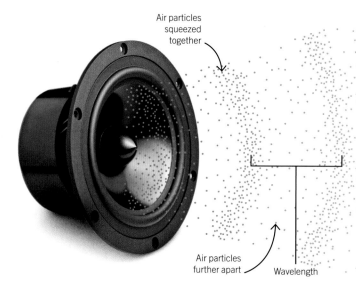

Air particles squeezed together

Direction of travel

Vibration of particles forwards and backwards along the direction of travel of the wave

Air particles further apart

Wavelength

🔍 Longitudinal and transverse waves

All waves involve some form of vibration. In sound waves, the vibration is forwards and backwards along the direction of travel of the wave. We call these longitudinal waves. In water waves and light waves, the vibration is sideways relative to the direction in which the wave travels. We call these transverse waves.

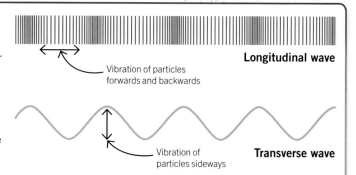

Vibration of particles forwards and backwards

Longitudinal wave

Vibration of particles sideways

Transverse wave

Oscilloscopes

Sounds can vary from quiet to loud and from low-pitched to high-pitched. The loudness of a sound depends on the amplitude of the sound waves, and the pitch depends on their frequency. We can study these properties using an oscilloscope — a device that displays waves as a moving graph on a screen.

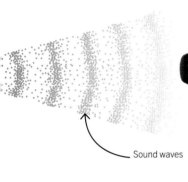

A microphone detects sounds and converts the waves into electrical signals.

Sound waves

The oscilloscope displays the signals as a moving graph, forming a pattern called a waveform.

Seeing sound
Although sound waves are longitudinal, the waveform on an oscilloscope is a transverse wave, which makes it easy to interpret. The x-axis on the display represents time and the y-axis can be used to measure amplitude.

Waveform

Different sounds
Different sounds produce distinct patterns on an oscilloscope, allowing us to see the wave's amplitude, frequency, and complexity.

Complex waveforms are typical of musical instruments and give each type of instrument a distinct timbre (sound quality).

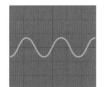

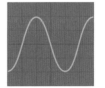

Loud sounds have a large amplitude, resulting in a tall waveform.

Quiet sounds have a low amplitude, resulting in a shallow waveform.

High-pitched sounds have a high frequency, resulting in a waveform with many peaks close together.

Low-pitched sounds have a low frequency, resulting in a longer waveform with fewer peaks.

Most sources of sound produce multiple waves. They combine to create a complex waveform.

Wave equations

The speed at which waves travel and their wavelength, frequency, and period (the time for one wavelength to pass) are all related. The equations on these pages show you how.

Key facts

✓ The time it takes for one wavelength to pass is the wave's period.

✓ The frequency of a wave equals 1 divided by the wave's period.

✓ The speed of a wave = frequency × wavelength.

Frequency and period
Unlike most wave diagrams in this book, the graph below shows how a wave varies over a period of time. Each complete wavelength lasts a quarter of a second, which we call the wave's period. Every second, four complete waves pass – this is the wave's frequency, which we measure in units called hertz (Hz). One Hz means one cycle per second.

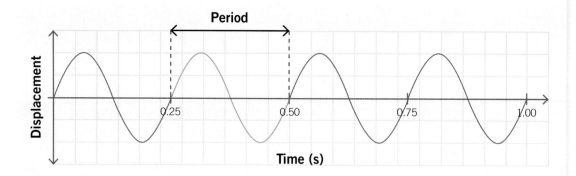

Frequency equation
The equation below shows how period and frequency are related. We say they are inversely related – as one halves, the other doubles.

$$\text{frequency (Hz)} = \frac{1}{\text{period (s)}}$$

$$f = \frac{1}{T}$$

Calculating frequency

Question
The piano key known as middle C plays a musical note with a period of 0.00382 seconds. What is the note's frequency?

Answer
$f = \dfrac{1}{T}$

$= \dfrac{1}{0.00382 \text{ s}}$

$= 262$ Hz

Speed of waves
The equation here shows how the speed, frequency, and wavelength of any wave are related. The symbol for wavelength is the Greek letter lambda λ.

$$\text{speed (m/s)} = \text{frequency (Hz)} \times \text{wavelength (m)}$$
$$v = f \times \lambda$$

Speed of sound
Sound travels through air at around 343 m/s, but it moves faster in water (1480 m/s) and can pass through solids faster still (5000 m/s in steel). However, light travels about a million times faster than the speed of sound in air. As a result, when you watch fireworks or see a lightning storm, the flash of light reaches you faster than the sound.

Calculating wavelength

Question
A violinist plays a note with a frequency of 880 Hz. If the speed of sound in air is 343 m/s, what is the note's wavelength?

Answer
First rearrange the equation to make lambda the subject.
$$v = f \times \lambda$$
$$\lambda = \frac{v}{f}$$
$$\lambda = \frac{343 \text{ m/s}}{880 \text{ Hz}}$$
$$= 0.390 \text{ m}$$

If you count the seconds between the light and sound, you can calculate how far away the firework or bolt of lightning is by using the speed of sound in air (the number of seconds divided by three gives the approximate distance in km).

Hearing sound

The human ear converts the energy transferred by sound waves into electrical impulses that are transmitted to the brain, where they are interpreted as sounds.

Inside the ear

Sound enters the ear as waves in the air but is converted into vibrations in solid materials by the eardrum. The way a solid vibrates when sound waves hit it depends on properties such as its stiffness. The eardrum and other structures in the ear vibrate only within a certain range of frequencies, which is why some sounds are too low or high for us to hear. As people age, the ear loses the ability to detect high-frequency sounds. Listening to very loud music can also damage our ears' sensitivity to certain sounds.

Key facts

✓ The ear converts sound waves into electrical impulses that are sent to the brain, giving people the sense of hearing.

✓ Some sounds are too high or too low in pitch for humans to hear.

✓ Both ageing and damage to the ears impair the sense of hearing.

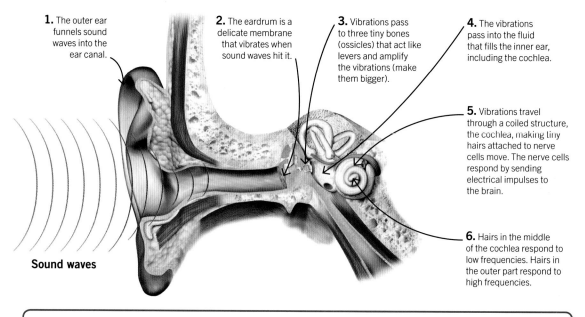

1. The outer ear funnels sound waves into the ear canal.

2. The eardrum is a delicate membrane that vibrates when sound waves hit it.

3. Vibrations pass to three tiny bones (ossicles) that act like levers and amplify the vibrations (make them bigger).

4. The vibrations pass into the fluid that fills the inner ear, including the cochlea.

5. Vibrations travel through a coiled structure, the cochlea, making tiny hairs attached to nerve cells move. The nerve cells respond by sending electrical impulses to the brain.

6. Hairs in the middle of the cochlea respond to low frequencies. Hairs in the outer part respond to high frequencies.

Sound waves

🔍 Highs and lows

Humans can hear sound within a frequency range, or pitch, of between roughly 20 Hz and 20 000 Hz. Frequencies too high for humans to hear are called ultrasound, and those too low are infrasound. Other animals have different ranges. Dolphins and bats, for example, can hear much higher ultrasound frequencies, and elephants can detect lower infrasound frequencies.

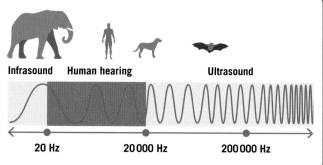

Infrasound   Human hearing   Ultrasound

20 Hz   20 000 Hz   200 000 Hz

Investigating the speed of waves

This practical shows you how to find the speed of waves in water using a ripple tank. First use the tank to measure the wavelength and frequency of waves. Then use the formula for wave speed to calculate the answer.

Ripple tank

A ripple tank consists of a shallow tray of water with a transparent base. A motorized paddle creates waves, and a light above the tank casts shadows of the waves onto a sheet of white paper beneath, making the waves easier to see.

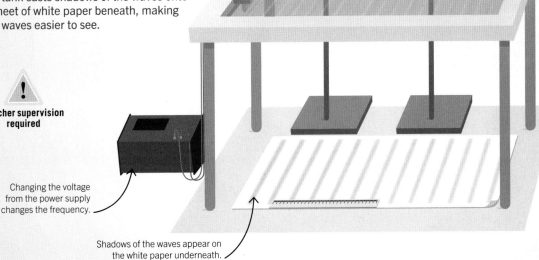

A motor moves the paddle up and down, creating waves.

Lamp

Water

Transparent base

Teacher supervision required

Changing the voltage from the power supply changes the frequency.

Shadows of the waves appear on the white paper underneath.

🗐 Method

1. Set up the tank and adjust the voltage on the power supply so the paddle creates waves with wavelengths about half as long as the tank.

2. Place a ruler on the white paper and take a photograph of the waves' shadows to freeze their motion. Use the image of the ruler to measure the wavelength (the distance between two waves).

3. Next measure the frequency. Mark a point on the white paper and use a timer to count how many waves pass it in 10 seconds. Divide the result by 10 to find the frequency in waves per second (Hz).

4. Use the formula for the speed of waves to find the answer:

   speed (m/s) = frequency (Hz) × wavelength (m)

5. To check the result, you can time how long one wave takes to pass between two points a measured distance apart on the paper. Then use this formula to calculate the speed again:

   $$\text{speed (m/s)} = \frac{\text{distance (m)}}{\text{time (s)}}$$

Measuring the speed of sound

Sound can travel through solids, liquids, and gases. The practicals here show two ways of measuring the speed of sound: one in air, and one in a solid.

Key facts

✓ Sound can travel in solids, liquids, and gases.

✓ The speed of sound in air can be measured using a stopwatch.

✓ The speed of sound in a solid object can be calculated from the sound's frequency and the object's size.

Speed of sound in air

Two people stand at opposite ends of a field a measured distance apart. One person hits two cymbals to make a noise. The second person starts a timer when they see the cymbals hit and stops it when they hear the sound. The formula below reveals the sound's speed. This method isn't very accurate as it involves human reaction time. To improve it, the second person could film the first person and use the recording to calculate the time interval.

0.29

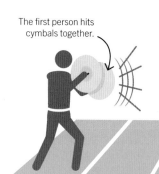

The first person hits cymbals together.

The second person times how long the sound takes to travel.

$$\text{speed (m/s)} = \frac{\text{distance (m)}}{\text{time (s)}}$$

100 m

Speed of sound in a solid

To measure the speed of sound in a solid, suspend a metal bar loosely from a stand using thin rubber bands. Strike the bar with a hammer, and use a smartphone app to measure the frequency of the loudest sound detected when the phone is next to the bar. Vibration of the bar causes a "standing wave", the wavelength of which is twice the length of the bar. Use the formula below to calculate the wave's speed.

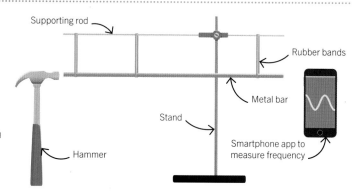

Supporting rod

Rubber bands

Metal bar

Stand

Smartphone app to measure frequency

Hammer

$$\text{wave speed (m/s)} = \text{frequency (Hz)} \times \text{wavelength (m)}$$

Using ultrasound

Sound that is too high in frequency for humans to hear is called ultrasound. Ultrasound has many uses: it can be used to look inside the human body, dislodge dirt from delicate jewellery, or find cracks in pipelines and railway tracks.

Ultrasound scans

Ultrasound scanning machines allow doctors to obtain images of babies developing inside a mother's body. A typical scanner uses frequencies of 2–18 megahertz (2–18 million hertz) – hundreds of times higher than the upper limit of human hearing.

Key facts

✓ Ultrasonic cleaning uses ultrasound vibrations to dislodge dirt.

✓ Ultrasound scanners allow doctors to obtain images of babies inside their mothers' bodies.

✓ Ultrasound can be used to detect hidden flaws in metal components.

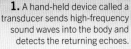

1. A hand-held device called a transducer sends high-frequency sound waves into the body and detects the returning echoes.

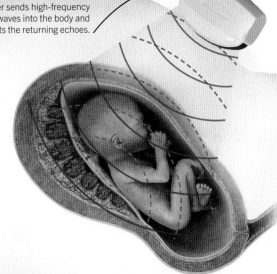

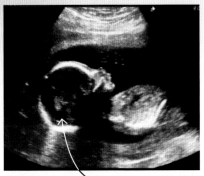

2. A computer processes the information and produces a real-time, moving image called a sonogram, which appears on a screen.

⚙ Scanning machinery

Ultrasound can be used to detect cracks in machinery, pipelines, and railway tracks that would otherwise remain hidden. When ultrasound waves hit a boundary between two materials, part of the wave reflects off the boundary, and part of it passes through. Cracks produce additional boundaries between materials, creating additional reflections, which are revealed as spikes on a graph.

Sonar

Sound waves can travel great distances underwater. This ability is exploited by sonar, a technology that uses ultrasound echoes to detect objects in the sea, such as submarines.

Searching for the sound

Sonar was invented during World War I to search for submarines, but today it is also used for locating shoals of fish or mapping the seabed. It relies on measuring how long it takes for a sound to be reflected by an object and return to the ship. Sound travels at roughly 1500 m/s through sea water, so if it takes one second for an echo to return, the reflecting object must be 750 m away.

Key facts

✓ Sonar uses ultrasound pulses to detect objects underwater.

✓ Sound travels through sea water at roughly 1500 m/s.

✓ Bats use echolocation to navigate and find their prey.

1. Pulses of ultrasound are emitted by a transmitter.

3. A receiver on the ship detects the echoes and calculates the object's distance.

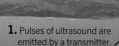

2. Objects underwater reflect the sound waves.

⚙ Echolocation

Some animals, including bats and dolphins, use a system like sonar to navigate and find food in the dark. Bats send out ultrasound waves from their mouth and use the echoes to locate and catch moths in mid-flight. The time it takes for echoes to return reveals a moth's distance, and the frequency of the echoes reveals whether the moth is flying towards or away from the bat.

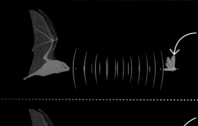

A moth flying away from the bat produces lower-frequency echoes.

A moth flying towards the bat produces higher-frequency echoes.

Investigating Earth's interior

Earthquakes cause vibrations that send powerful seismic waves travelling through Earth's interior. Studying the behaviour of these waves has allowed us to build up a picture of the inside of our planet.

Key facts

✓ Earthquakes generate seismic waves that travel through Earth's interior.

✓ P-waves travel through both solids and liquids.

✓ S-waves only travel through solids.

✓ Shadow zones where P- and S-waves are not detected helped scientists discover Earth's inner structure.

Earth's interior

There are two types of seismic wave that help us investigate Earth's structure: primary waves (P-waves) and secondary waves (S-waves).

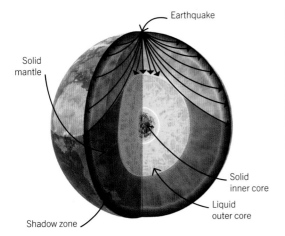

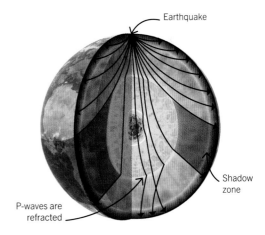

S-waves are only detected on the same side of Earth as the earthquake. These waves travel slowly and can only pass through solids, so their absence on the far side of the planet shows that Earth has a partly liquid interior.

P-waves are detected on the far side of Earth after an earthquake, but there are shadow zones where they are missing. These fast-moving waves can pass through liquids but are refracted when they pass between different kinds of material. The pattern of shadow zones reveals the size of Earth's liquid outer core and solid inner core.

🔍 P-waves and S-waves

P-waves and S-waves differ in the way they travel. P-waves, like sound waves, are longitudinal waves of pressure that can move through solids and liquids. S-waves, however, are transverse waves and can only travel through rigid materials such as solid rock. When they reach the molten rock of the outer core, they dissipate.

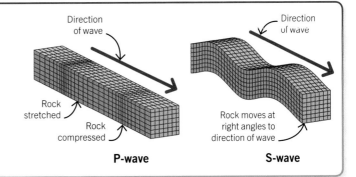

Interference

When waves meet, they interfere with each other. Interference can affect all kinds of wave. The shimmering colours on soap bubbles, for instance, are caused by interference in light waves.

Interference patterns

Interference patterns exist only where waves meet. After passing the meeting point, waves carry on with the same amplitude as they had before. You can produce interference patterns in a ripple tank by vibrating two balls touching the water surface. Where two peaks meet, the waves reinforce each other and produce higher peaks (constructive interference). Where peaks meet with troughs, they cancel each other out (destructive interference).

 Key facts

✓ Constructive interference occurs when waves are in step and results in a higher amplitude.

✓ Destructive interference occurs when waves cancel each other out, resulting in a lower amplitude.

✓ Waves remain unchanged after they have passed through each other.

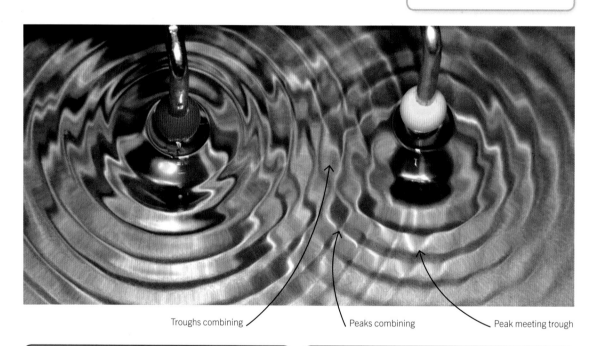

Troughs combining / Peaks combining / Peak meeting trough

✪ Constructive interference

When waves meet, their amplitudes add together. If the waves are in step, the combined wave has a larger amplitude.

Combined wave

✪ Destructive interference

If the waves are out of step, the amplitude is reduced. Noise-cancelling headphones use this principle to block out background sound.

The waves cancel each other out.

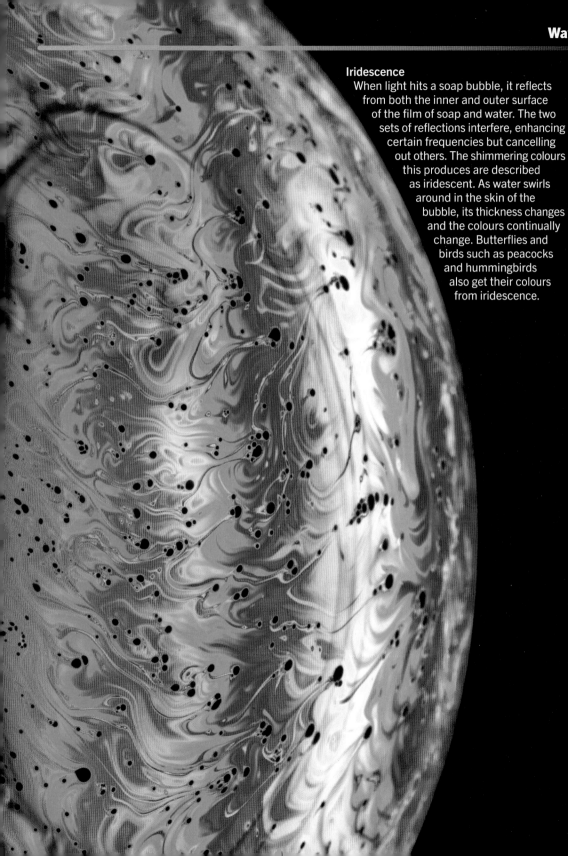

Iridescence

When light hits a soap bubble, it reflects from both the inner and outer surface of the film of soap and water. The two sets of reflections interfere, enhancing certain frequencies but cancelling out others. The shimmering colours this produces are described as iridescent. As water swirls around in the skin of the bubble, its thickness changes and the colours continually change. Butterflies and birds such as peacocks and hummingbirds also get their colours from iridescence.

Light

Light and seeing

Luminous (glowing) objects, such as the Sun or electric lights, emit light energy. Light travels as a wave and passes through anything transparent, including air, water, glass, and the vacuum of space. Light travelling in a vacuum is the fastest thing in the Universe. It takes just 8 minutes and 19 seconds for light from the Sun to travel 150 million km to Earth.

Key facts

✓ Light travels as waves.

✓ Luminous (glowing) objects, such as the Sun, emit light.

✓ Non-luminous objects can only be seen by reflected light.

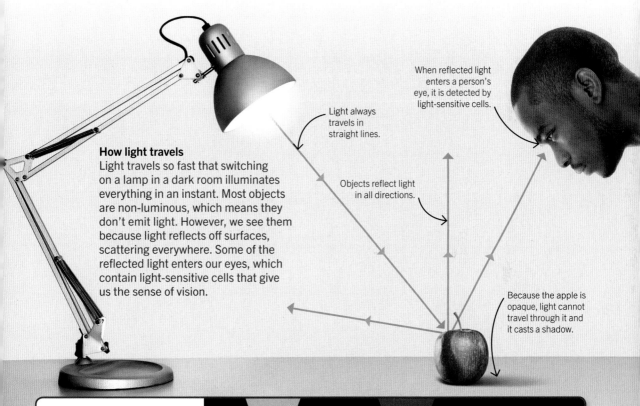

When reflected light enters a person's eye, it is detected by light-sensitive cells.

Light always travels in straight lines.

Objects reflect light in all directions.

How light travels
Light travels so fast that switching on a lamp in a dark room illuminates everything in an instant. Most objects are non-luminous, which means they don't emit light. However, we see them because light reflects off surfaces, scattering everywhere. Some of the reflected light enters our eyes, which contain light-sensitive cells that give us the sense of vision.

Because the apple is opaque, light cannot travel through it and it casts a shadow.

🔍 Transparent, translucent, and opaque

Most solid objects block light, but some materials let light waves pass through.

Transparent materials, such as glass, let light pass through. However, they also reflect a small amount of light, which is why we can see them.

Translucent materials, such as frosted glass, let some light through but scatter it.

Opaque materials let no light through and so cast a strong shadow.

Comparing sound and light

Sound and light both travel as waves and they both transfer energy. They have certain features in common, but there are also important differences between them.

Sound	Light
Sound waves travel as vibrations of particles of matter, so they cannot travel through empty space. Sound can travel through solids, liquids, and gases.	Light waves travel as vibrations in electric and magnetic fields and can cross empty space. They can pass through air and water, but most solid materials block their path.
Sound is a longitudinal wave. The particles move forwards and backwards in the same direction as the wave travels in.	Light is a transverse wave caused by vibrations in the electromagnetic field. The vibrations are at right angles to the wave's direction of travel.
The amplitude of a sound wave determines its volume. The greater the amplitude, the louder the sound.	The amplitude of a light wave determines its brightness. The greater the amplitude, the brighter the light.
The frequency of a sound wave determines its pitch. The higher the frequency, the higher the pitch.	The frequency of a visible light wave determines its colour. Low-frequency visible light is red; high-frequency visible light is violet.
Sound travels at around 343 m/s through air. Some jet aircraft can fly faster than this.	Light travels at around 300 million m/s through air (almost 1 million times faster than sound). That's why you see lightning flash before you hear thunder.
Sound waves can be reflected, refracted, and absorbed. A reflected sound is called an echo.	Light waves can be reflected, refracted, and absorbed. The image we see in a mirror is a reflection.

(Diagram labels, Sound column: "Direction of travel", "Vibration of particles"; "Low-frequency wave", "High-frequency wave"; "Echo")

(Diagram labels, Light column: "Vibration", "Direction of wave"; "Low-frequency wave", "High-frequency wave"; "Object", "Reflected image", "Light appears to come from behind the mirror.")

Pinhole cameras

A pinhole camera is a box with a tiny hole in the front and a screen at the back. When you point it towards a brightly lit scene, a faint image appears on the screen. This simple setup was the ancestor of today's cameras.

Ray diagram

We can explain how a pinhole camera works by drawing a diagram that shows light travelling in straight lines — a ray diagram. Ray diagrams include just a few rays of light as straight lines with arrows showing the direction light travels. This ray diagram shows that light rays cross as they pass through the small hole, resulting in an upside-down image. Ray diagrams are also very useful to show what happens when light is reflected, refracted, or focused by lenses.

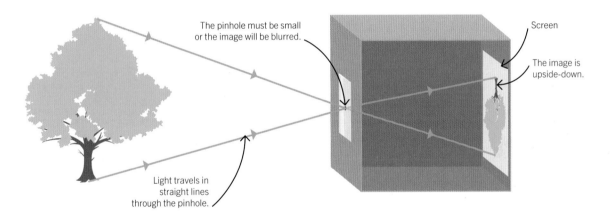

The pinhole must be small or the image will be blurred.

Screen

The image is upside-down.

Light travels in straight lines through the pinhole.

⚙ Real and virtual images

The image produced by a pinhole camera is called a real image because it can be captured on a screen, allowing people to see it from anywhere. In contrast, the enlarged image you see through a magnifying glass is a virtual image that can only be seen from a certain position. Unlike a real image, a virtual image cannot be captured on a screen.

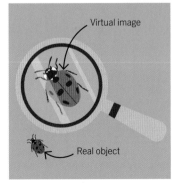

Virtual image

Real object

Magnified ladybird

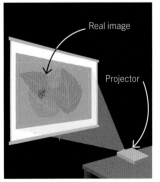

Real image

Projector

Projection on a screen

Reflection

When light strikes a surface, some of it bounces off – it is reflected. Luminous objects emit light, but we see everything else by reflected light. Most objects have a rough surface that reflects light in many directions (diffuse reflection). However, very smooth objects, such as mirrors, reflect light regularly (specular reflection).

The law of reflection

The picture below shows what happens when light is reflected by a mirror. The angle of the incoming ray (angle of incidence) is always the same as the angle of the reflected ray (angle of reflection). This is the law of reflection. Both angles are measured from a line called the normal, which is at right angles to the object's surface.

Key facts

✓ Specular reflection is the even reflection of light from a smooth surface such as a mirror.

✓ Diffuse reflection is the irregular reflection of light from a rough surface.

✓ When light is reflected by a mirror, the angle of incidence equals the angle of reflection.

angle of incidence = angle of reflection

Normal

Incident ray

Reflected ray

Mirror

Angle of incidence

Angle of reflection

✿ Mirror images

When you look in a flat mirror, you see a virtual image (see page 129) that appears to be behind the mirror. The ray diagram here shows how a mirror produces a virtual image. The dashed lines show where the light appears to come from. Mirrors don't reverse things left to right. Writing looks reversed in a mirror because we have to flip a book around to face the glass. Mirrors actually reverse images from front to back, along a line through the mirror.

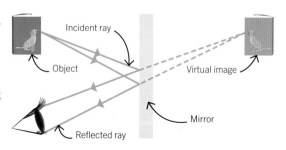

Incident ray

Object

Virtual image

Mirror

Reflected ray

Refraction

When light waves pass from one medium to another — such as from air to water — they change direction. This is known as refraction. Lenses use refraction to bend and focus light.

Refraction of light
Place a straw in a glass of water and it will appear bent or broken. This happens because light from the straw is refracted as it passes between the water, glass, and air on the way to our eyes. Our brains assume the light has travelled in a straight line, so the image of the straw in the water is distorted.

The straw looks crooked because light from the straw refracts as it passes from water and glass to air.

 Key facts

✓ Refraction is a change in the direction of waves as they pass from one medium to another.

✓ Waves bend towards the normal when they slow down and bend away from the normal when they speed up.

⚙ Refraction ray diagram

A ray diagram helps explain what happens when light is refracted. The diagram includes a line called the normal, which is drawn at right angles to the boundary. When light crosses the boundary from air to water or glass, it slows down and bends towards the normal. When the light returns to the air, it speeds up and bends away from the normal.

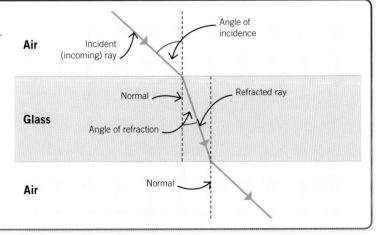

Air
Incident (incoming) ray
Angle of incidence
Normal
Refracted ray
Glass
Angle of refraction
Air
Normal

Investigating light

A ray box allows you to create ray diagrams using real rays of light. Follow the instructions here to investigate reflection and refraction.

Investigating reflection

1. Draw a straight line across a large piece of paper.

2. Draw a second line at right angles to the first line. This will be the normal in your ray diagram.

3. Place a mirror along the first line and use the ray box to shine a ray of light at the point where the two lines meet. Darkening the room may help make the rays easier to see.

4. Trace the incident ray and any reflected ray with a pencil.

5. Use a protractor to measure the angle of incidence and angle of reflection.

6. Repeat with different angles of incidence. You'll find that the angle of incidence always equals the angle of reflection.

Mirror

Incident ray

Reflected ray

Normal

Ray box

Paper

Law of reflection

Wherever you position the ray box, the angle of incidence (the angle between the incident ray and the normal) will always be the same as the angle of reflection (the angle between the reflected ray and the normal). This is called the law of reflection.

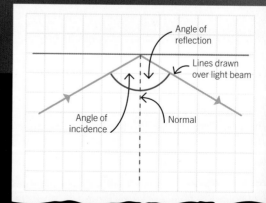

Angle of reflection

Lines drawn over light beam

Angle of incidence

Normal

Investigating refraction

1. Place a glass block on a large sheet of paper and trace around it.

2. Draw a line at right angles to the long side of the block. This will be the normal in your ray diagram.

3. Darken the room and use a ray box to shine a ray of light diagonally into the block.

4. Use a pencil to mark the ray's path up to and beyond the block by drawing small crosses.

5. Remove the block, then use a pencil and ruler to connect the crosses and to draw the ray's path through the block.

6. Measure the angles of incidence and refraction.

7. Repeat with different angles of incidence. Light bends towards the normal when it passes from air to glass, so you'll find the angle of refraction from air to glass is always less than the angle of incidence.

8. Measure the angles of incidence and refraction at the point where the light leaves the block. Light bends away from the normal as it passes from glass to air, so in this case the angle of refraction will be larger than the angle of incidence.

Investigating internal reflection

1. Place a semicircular glass block on a large sheet of paper and draw around it.

2. Remove the block. Using a ruler and pencil, find and mark the centre of the straight side. Draw a normal line through this point, perpendicular to the straight side, then replace the block.

3. Shine a ray of light from a ray box through the curved surface of the block to the point you marked.

4. The ray will bend away from the normal as it leaves the glass. Note that some light is also reflected by the straight surface of the glass block.

5. Move the ray to increase the angle of incidence. Note that the angle of refraction also increases. Continue increasing the angle of incidence until the refracted ray lines up with the flat surface of the block.

6. Increase the angle of incidence again. The light is now reflected completely, with no light escaping by refraction. This is known as total internal reflection (TIR). The angle of incidence at which TIR begins is called the critical angle.

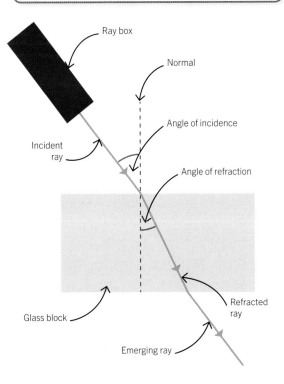

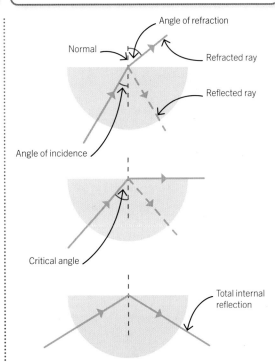

Total internal reflection

Light is refracted when it passes from one medium to another, such as from glass to air or air to water. However, if light going from glass or water to air hits the boundary at a shallow angle, all of it is reflected instead. This is called total internal reflection.

Key facts

✓ Total internal reflection takes place when the angle of incidence exceeds the critical angle.

✓ Optical fibres use total internal reflection to transmit digital data.

Optical fibres

An optical fibre is a strand of solid glass about as thin as a human hair. It uses total internal reflection to trap and transmit pulses of light carrying digital information, such as internet data. Laser light is directed into one end at a shallow angle so that the light cannot escape until it reaches the other end.

Total internal reflection

Light ray

Glass

⚙ The critical angle

Total internal reflection occurs when the angle of incidence (the angle between the light and the normal) is more than a certain angle: the "critical angle". The critical angle varies with different materials, such as glass, water, or perspex. The critical angle for light travelling from water to air is 49°. If a beam of light hits the water surface at less than 49° with the normal, it will pass through, though a small amount is reflected. If the angle is greater than 49°, it is all reflected.

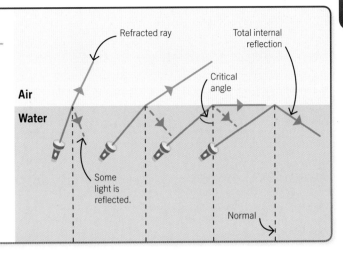

Refracted ray

Total internal reflection

Critical angle

Air

Water

Some light is reflected.

Normal

Underwater reflection

When viewed from underwater, the water surface acts like a mirror due to total internal reflection. Here, a dolphin is reflected twice off the underside of two different waves.

Lenses

A lens is a piece of transparent material with curved surfaces. Its special shape makes light refract in a way that can form images. Eyes and cameras contain converging (convex) lenses – lenses that bulge outwards in the middle and make rays of light converge to a point.

Inside an eye

The lens inside a human eye bends light rays so that they come together and form an image. This is called focusing. Diverging rays of light from the same point on a distant object are focused on the retina – a layer of light-sensitive cells that lines the back of the eyeball. The retina then sends nerve impulses to the brain, which creates the sense of sight.

Key facts

✓ A lens is a piece of transparent material with curved surfaces that refract light.

✓ Eyes and cameras contain converging (convex) lenses, which focus light rays to form an image.

✓ The human eye adjusts focus by changing the shape of the lens.

✓ A camera adjusts focus by changing the position of the lens.

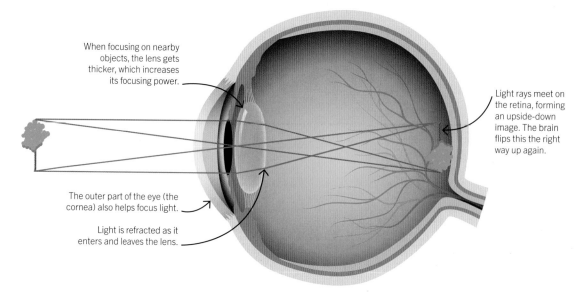

When focusing on nearby objects, the lens gets thicker, which increases its focusing power.

Light rays meet on the retina, forming an upside-down image. The brain flips this the right way up again.

The outer part of the eye (the cornea) also helps focus light.

Light is refracted as it enters and leaves the lens.

⚙ Cameras

Cameras work in a similar way to the human eye. Incoming light is focused by a converging lens to form an image on a light-sensitive sensor in the back of the camera. Images are then stored in a memory chip. Unlike a human eye, a camera contains a glass lens that cannot change shape to adjust its focusing power. Instead, cameras with adjustable focus move the lens forwards or backwards.

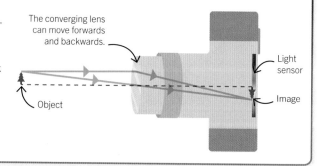

The converging lens can move forwards and backwards.

Light sensor

Image

Object

Waves and refraction

Refraction is a change in the direction of waves when they slow down or speed up. Light waves refract when they pass from one medium to another, and water waves refract when they move between deep and shallow water.

Key facts

✓ Refraction is caused by a change in the speed of waves.

✓ The frequency of waves is unchanged after refraction, but the wavelength and speed change.

✓ If a wave slows down, it bends towards the normal.

✓ If a wave speeds up, it bends away from the normal.

Refraction in water

We can see refraction in action by using a ripple tank – a tank of water through which light is shone to make the ripples visible. A glass block placed at an angle on the bottom of the tank creates a zone of shallow water, which slows down the waves. When waves slow down, they bend towards the normal. When they speed up, they bend away from the normal. The frequency of the waves remains the same after refraction, but the slower waves have a shorter wavelength.

Teacher supervision required

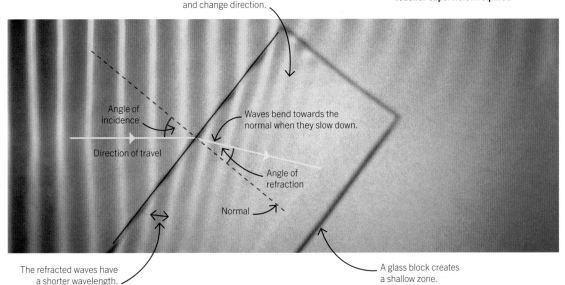

The waves slow down and change direction.

Angle of incidence

Direction of travel

Waves bend towards the normal when they slow down.

Angle of refraction

Normal

The refracted waves have a shorter wavelength.

A glass block creates a shallow zone.

⚙ Why refraction happens

To understand why a change in speed causes waves to change direction, imagine a marching band trying to stay in regular rows as they march from firm ground to muddy ground, where they slow down. If the band meets the boundary at an angle, one side slows down earlier than the other side. The faster marchers catch up a little until they reach the mud, so the whole band changes direction.

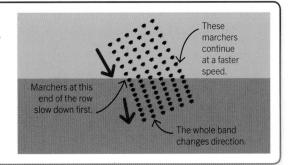

These marchers continue at a faster speed.

Marchers at this end of the row slow down first.

The whole band changes direction.

Refractive index

Light travels incredibly fast through a vacuum: 3×10^8 m/s (300 million metres per second). It travels almost as fast in air, but it slows significantly in water, glass, or other transparent materials. The refractive index of a material is a measure of how much the material slows down light.

Key facts

✓ The refractive index of a material is a measure of how much that material slows down light.

✓ Refractive index equals the speed of light in a vacuum divided by the speed of light in the material.

✓ Snell's law allows us to calculate refractive index from the angles of incidence and refraction.

Calculating refractive index

Light travels at different speeds in different materials, so each material has a different refractive index. The greater a material's refractive index, the more it slows down light and the more the light is refracted (bent). This equation shows how refractive index can be calculated from the change in the light's speed.

$$\text{refractive index } (n) = \frac{\text{speed of light in a vacuum}}{\text{speed of light in the material}}$$

Refractive index is a ratio of two speeds and so has no units.

Material	Speed of light (m/s)	Refractive index
Air	2.997×10^8	1.0003
Perspex	2×10^8	1.5
Glass	$(1.8–2.0) \times 10^8$	1.5–1.7
Diamond	1.25×10^8	2.4

Refractive index of water

Question
The speed of light in a vacuum is 3×10^8 m/s, and the speed of light in water is 2.3×10^8 m/s. What is the refractive index of water?

Answer
$$n = \frac{3 \times 10^8 \text{ m/s}}{2.3 \times 10^8 \text{ m/s}}$$
$$= 1.3$$

Snell's law

When light passes from air to a material with a higher refractive index, such as glass, it bends towards the normal. As a result, the angle of refraction is smaller than the angle of incidence. The equation here, called Snell's law, shows the relationship between the refractive index and the angles of incidence and refraction.

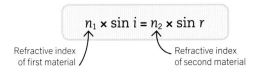

$$n_1 \times \sin i = n_2 \times \sin r$$

Refractive index of first material

Refractive index of second material

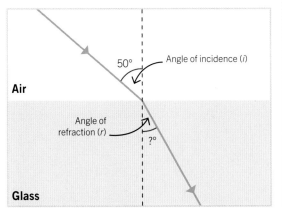

50°

Angle of incidence (i)

Air

Angle of refraction (r)

?°

Glass

Total internal reflection

When light passes from a material with a high refractive index to a material with a lower one, such as from glass to air, it bends away from the normal. If the angle of incidence is more than a certain amount – the critical angle – the light is reflected internally. This equation shows how the critical angle and refractive index are related.

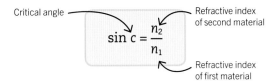

Critical angle

Refractive index of second material

$$\sin c = \frac{n_2}{n_1}$$

Refractive index of first material

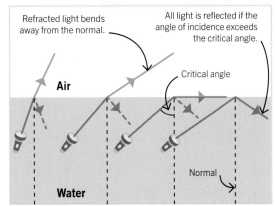

Refracted light bends away from the normal.

All light is reflected if the angle of incidence exceeds the critical angle.

Critical angle

Air

Water

Normal

📑 Calculating the angle of refraction

Question

Light enters a block of glass at an angle of incidence of 50°. If the refractive index of air is 1 and the refractive index of glass is 1.6, what is the angle of refraction?

....

Answer

1. First rearrange Snell's law to make sin r the subject.

$$\sin r = \frac{n_1 \times \sin i}{n_2}$$

2. Put in the numbers and use a calculator to find the sine of 50°.

$$\sin r = \frac{1 \times \sin 50°}{1.6}$$

$$= 0.479$$

3. Use the $\sin^{-1}$ function on a calculator to find the answer.

$$r = 29°$$

📑 Calculating the critical angle

Question

Diamonds get their sparkle from their high refractive index and small critical angle, which cause a lot of internal reflection off a diamond's faces before light escapes and reaches our eyes. If the refractive index of diamond is 2.4, what is the critical angle?

....

Answer

$$\sin c = \frac{1}{2.4}$$

Refractive index of air

$$\sin c = 0.42$$

$$c = 25°$$

Converging and diverging lenses

Lenses are shaped to change the direction of light by refraction. Converging lenses are lenses that bulge outwards in the middle. They bend light rays so that they come together (converge). Diverging lenses are thinner in the middle. They make light rays spread out (diverge).

Converging lenses
Converging lenses are also called convex lenses. When parallel rays of light pass through a converging lens, they meet at a place called the focal point (principal focus). The greater the curvature of the lens, the more powerfully it focuses light and the closer the focal point is to the lens.

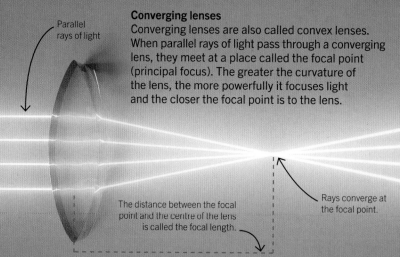

Parallel rays of light

The distance between the focal point and the centre of the lens is called the focal length.

Rays converge at the focal point.

Diverging lenses
Diverging lenses are also called concave lenses. When parallel rays of light pass through a diverging lens, they spread out (diverge). The focal point of a diverging lens is the point which the diverging rays appear to come from. The greater the curvature of the lens, the more powerfully it focuses light and the closer the focal point is to the lens.

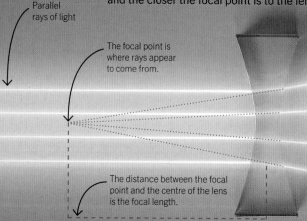

Parallel rays of light

The focal point is where rays appear to come from.

The distance between the focal point and the centre of the lens is the focal length.

Correcting vision

Converging and diverging lenses are used in glasses and contact lenses to correct two of the most common causes of blurred vision: long-sightedness and short-sightedness.

Long-sightedness

In a long-sighted eye, light rays from nearby objects are focused towards a point behind the retina, making nearby objects look blurred. This happens because the eye's focusing power is not strong enough or the eyeball is too short. A converging (convex) lens corrects vision by making light rays converge before they enter the eye.

A convex lens (a lens that curves outwards) corrects long-sightedness.

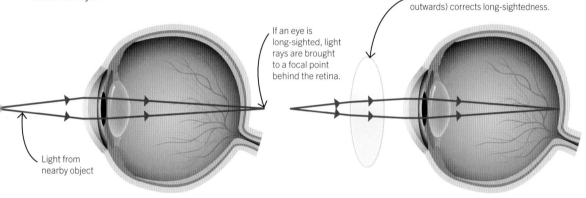

If an eye is long-sighted, light rays are brought to a focal point behind the retina.

Light from nearby object

Long-sighted eye

Corrected vision

Short-sightedness

In a short-sighted eye, light rays from distant objects are brought into focus before they reach the retina, making distant objects look blurred. This happens either because the eye's focusing power is too strong or the eyeball is too long. A diverging (concave) lens corrects vision by making light rays diverge before they enter the eye.

A concave lens (a lens that curves inwards in the middle) corrects short-sightedness.

If an eye is short-sighted, light rays are brought into focus before they reach the retina.

Light from distant object

Retina

Short-sighted eye

Corrected vision

Converging lens ray diagram

We can use ray diagrams to find out where the image produced by a converging lens appears. This diagram shows what happens when an object is further from the lens than the lens's focal point. The lens produces a real image (see page 129) that is inverted (upside down) and diminished (smaller).

Key facts

✓ A ray diagram can be used to work out where the image produced by a lens appears.

✓ Incident rays that travel parallel to the axis are refracted through the focal point.

✓ Incident rays that travel through the focal point before reaching the lens are refracted to become parallel with the axis.

✓ An incident ray travelling through the centre of the lens does not change direction.

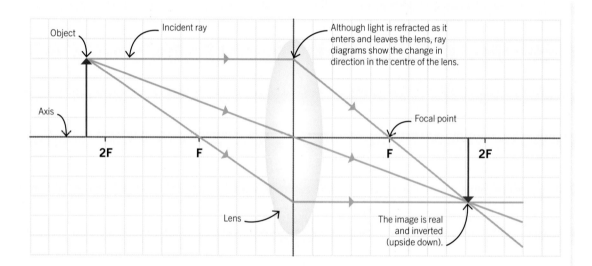

How to draw a ray diagram for a converging lens

1. Draw a horizontal axis with a lens in the middle.

2. Mark the focal point (F) on both sides of the lens.

3. Draw the object as an arrow pointing upwards.

4. Draw an incident ray from the top of the object to the lens, travelling parallel with the axis. Draw the refracted ray from the lens through the focal point.

5. For the second ray, draw a straight line from the top of the object through the centre of the lens. This ray doesn't bend.

6. Where the lines cross is the bottom of the inverted image. (The image does not necessarily form at the focal point.)

7. To check, draw a third ray from the top of the object and through the left focal point to the lens. This ray refracts and continues in parallel with the axis.

Magnifying glass ray diagram

A converging lens works as a magnifying glass if the object is closer to the lens than the focal point. The image is enlarged, upright, and virtual (see page 129), so only someone looking through the magnifying glass can see it.

> **Key facts**
>
> ✓ A magnifying glass is a converging (convex) lens.
>
> ✓ The magnifying glass produces an enlarged, upright, virtual image.
>
> ✓ The object must be within one focal length to produce the magnified image.

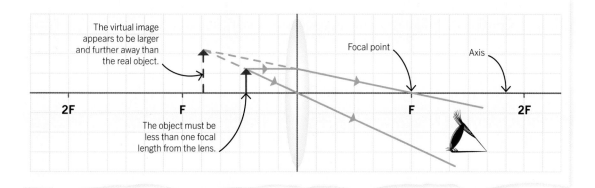

How to draw a ray diagram for a magnifying glass

1. Draw a horizontal axis with a lens in the middle.

2. Mark the focal point (F) on both sides of the lens.

3. Draw the object as an upward arrow closer to the lens than the focal point.

4. Draw an incident ray from the top of the object to the lens, travelling parallel with the axis. Then draw the refracted ray from the lens through the focal point

5. Draw a second ray from the top of the object through the centre of the lens. This ray doesn't bend.

6. Using a ruler, extend both rays backwards as dotted lines. The point where they cross is the top of the virtual image. The bottom of the virtual image is on the axis.

Calculating magnification

Use this formula to work out the magnification of an image.

$$\text{magnification} = \frac{\text{image height}}{\text{object height}}$$

Question
A beetle measuring 9 mm long is viewed through a magnifying glass, producing a 28 mm virtual image. What is the magnification?

Answer

$$\text{magnification} = \frac{28 \text{ mm}}{9 \text{ mm}}$$

magnification = 3.1

Magnification is a ratio so the answer has no units.

Diverging lens ray diagram

If you look through a diverging lens, it makes things look smaller. A diverging lens produces a virtual image that is upright but diminished (smaller). Drawing a ray diagram allows you to work out where the image will appear and how small it is.

Key facts

✓ A ray diagram shows where the image produced by a lens appears.

✓ Incident rays that travel parallel to the axis are refracted outwards by a diverging lens as though they came from the focal point.

✓ An incident ray travelling through the centre of the lens does not bend.

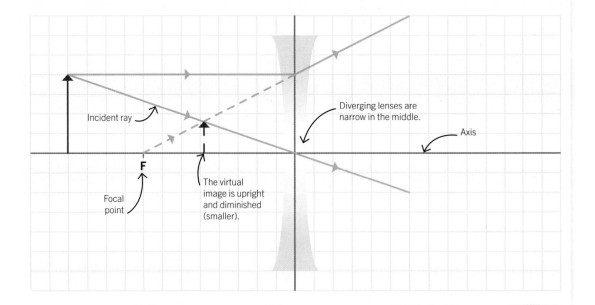

How to draw a ray diagram for a diverging lens

1. Draw a horizontal axis with a lens in the middle.

2. Mark the focal point (F) on the left of the lens.

3. Draw the object as an arrow pointing upwards.

4. Draw an incident ray from the top of the object to the lens, travelling parallel with the axis.

5. The refracted ray will travel as though it came from the focal point on the left of the lens. Use your ruler to draw a dotted line from the focal point to the lens, and continue this as a solid line travelling away.

6. Draw a second ray travelling straight through the centre of the lens. This ray doesn't refract.

7. Where the dotted line and the second ray meet is the top of the virtual image.

Light and colour

Light from the Sun is made up of a wide range, or spectrum, of different frequencies. The range of frequencies we can see – the visible spectrum – is just a tiny part of this. Different frequencies of visible light appear to our eyes as different colours. When all the visible frequencies are mixed together, they make white light.

Key facts

✓ Different frequencies of visible light appear to our eyes as colours.

✓ White light is a mixture of different frequencies.

✓ A glass prism can refract white light and split it into its component colours.

Visible light spectrum
We can split white light into its component colours by shining it through a triangular block of glass called a prism. The glass refracts each frequency differently. Colours with higher frequencies, such as violet, refract more than colours with lower frequencies, such as red. As a result, a beam of white light spreads out to produce a colourful spectrum. Although the visible spectrum is traditionally shown with seven colours, most people can't distinguish indigo and blue and so can only see six.

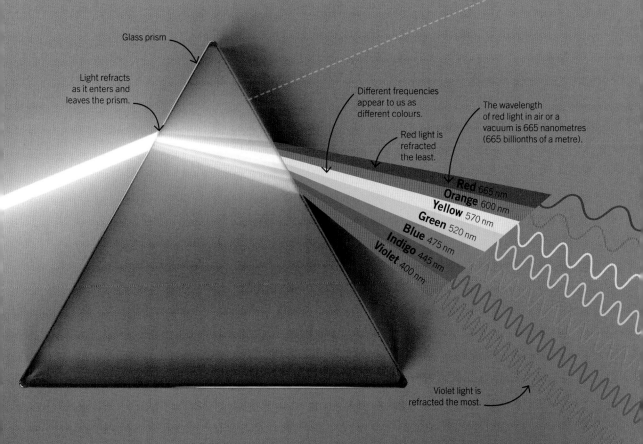

Glass prism

Light refracts as it enters and leaves the prism.

Different frequencies appear to us as different colours.

Red light is refracted the least.

The wavelength of red light in air or a vacuum is 665 nanometres (665 billionths of a metre).

Red 665 nm
Orange 600 nm
Yellow 570 nm
Green 520 nm
Blue 475 nm
Indigo 445 nm
Violet 400 nm

Violet light is refracted the most.

🔍 Rainbows

The beauty of a rainbow results from a combination of refraction and reflection. If sunlight strikes a raindrop at just the right angle, the light is refracted as it enters the raindrop, reflected inside it, and refracted again as it exits the raindrop. If you're standing in the right place, you see the refracted light as a rainbow.

A secondary rainbow, with colours in reverse order, can sometimes be seen outside the main rainbow. It is caused by light reflecting twice inside each raindrop instead of just once.

Light from the Sun

Refraction

Internal reflection

Raindrop

Refraction

Reflecting and absorbing

White light is a mixture of all the colours of the visible spectrum. When light strikes an object, some wavelengths are absorbed and others are reflected. The colour of an object depends on which wavelengths are reflected.

Key facts

✓ White light is a mixture of all the colours of the visible spectrum.

✓ Objects appear coloured because they absorb some wavelengths and reflect others.

✓ Coloured filters absorb most colours but allow some colours to pass through.

Absorption and reflection

These snooker balls are different colours because they each absorb a different range of wavelengths. Wavelengths that aren't absorbed are reflected, giving the objects their colours.

A red snooker ball looks red because its surface absorbs all wavelengths of visible light except red, which is reflected.

A black ball looks black because it absorbs every colour and reflects little light.

A white ball looks white because it reflects all the different wavelengths of visible light.

⚙ Colour filters

The colour of transparent materials depends on which wavelengths are absorbed and which are transmitted (let through). Coloured filters, such as stained glass, don't add colours to light – they subtract them. A red filter absorbs all wavelengths except red, for example.

A red filter absorbs all colours apart from red light.

A green filter absorbs all colours apart from green light.

A blue filter absorbs all colours apart from blue light.

Electromagnetic radiation

The light we can see is just a small part of a much larger electromagnetic spectrum. Electromagnetic waves transfer energy from atoms that emit them to atoms that absorb them. They don't require a medium to travel through and can cross the vacuum of space. All types of electromagnetic wave travel at the speed of light: about 300 million m/s in air or space.

Key facts

✓ Visible light is a small part of the electromagnetic spectrum.

✓ Electromagnetic waves are generated by changes in atoms.

✓ Electromagnetic waves travel at the speed of light and do not require a medium.

The electromagnetic spectrum
Electromagnetic waves range from radio waves (with wavelengths from millimetres to thousands of kilometres long) to gamma rays, (which have wavelengths smaller than atoms). The shorter the wavelength of electromagnetic radiation, the higher its frequency and the greater the amount of energy it transfers.

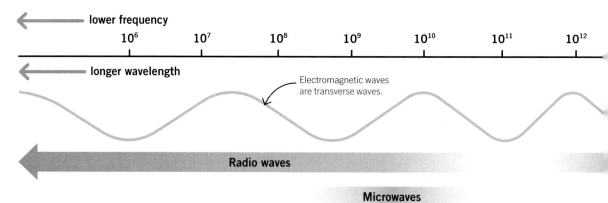

← lower frequency

10^6 10^7 10^8 10^9 10^{10} 10^{11} 10^{12}

← longer wavelength

Electromagnetic waves are transverse waves.

Radio waves

Microwaves

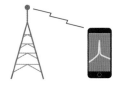

Radio waves are used for communication, such as transmitting phone calls, TV programmes, and internet data. Long-wave radio waves can bend around hills and around Earth's curved surface.

Microwaves are short wavelength radio waves and are used for communication. Certain frequencies of microwave radiation are absorbed by water molecules in food and are used for heating in microwave ovens.

Infrared is the heat you can feel when you warm your hands by a fire or stand in the Sun. TV remote controls use infrared beams to send signals to the TV, and night-vision goggles that detect infrared radiation allow people to see in the dark.

🔍 Electromagnetic waves

Electromagnetic waves can be generated by changes in atoms. For instance, light is emitted when electrons move from high-energy levels to lower levels. The frequency and wavelength of the light depend on how far the electron moves. Near Earth's poles, oxygen atoms in the atmosphere emit a greenish light when they release energy after being struck by high-speed particles from the Sun. The light causes the aurora borealis (northern lights).

An electron emits a packet of electromagnetic energy when it drops to a lower level.

Oxygen atom

Frequency (waves per second)

higher frequency ⟶

10^{13} 10^{14} 10^{15} 10^{16} 10^{17} 10^{18} 10^{19} 10^{20}

shorter wavelength ⟶

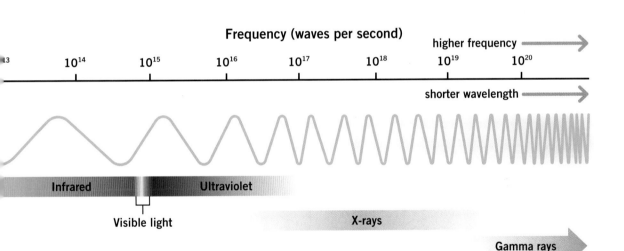

Infrared

Ultraviolet

Visible light

X-rays

Gamma rays

Visible light is the small part of the electromagnetic spectrum we can see. We use it to illuminate our surroundings and to generate images on TVs and phone screens.

Ultraviolet (UV) rays cause tanning and sunburn. UV lamps are used to kill bacteria and viruses, to detect forged banknotes, and to make fluorescent objects glow in discos.

X-rays are high-energy electromagnetic waves that pass through soft body tissues but not bones or teeth. They are used for medical imaging and to check the contents of luggage in airport security.

Gamma rays emitted by radioactive materials (see pages 240–241) are used to sterilize medical instruments, create medical images, and kill cancer cells.

Radio waves

Electromagnetic waves can be generated by the acceleration of electrons – the negatively charged particles that form the outside of atoms. When electrons oscillate back and forth at certain frequencies, they emit radio waves. These waves are used for communication.

Key facts

✓ Radio waves are produced by alternating electrical currents.

✓ Radio waves induce alternating currents in antennae (aerials).

✓ The frequency of a radio wave is the same as the frequency of the alternating current that generated it.

How radio communication works

Radio waves are produced by alternating currents, which cause electrons to oscillate back and forth in an antenna (aerial). The radio waves have the same frequency as the alternating current and trigger a current with a matching frequency in the receiving antenna. Data is transmitted as variations in the frequency (or amplitude) of the waves.

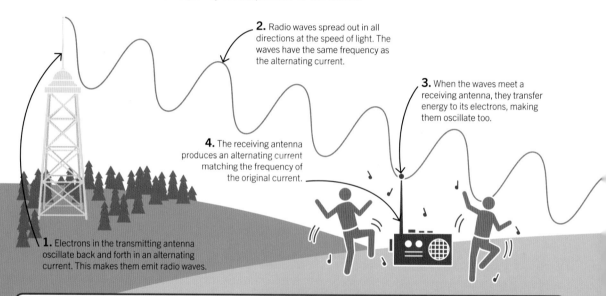

2. Radio waves spread out in all directions at the speed of light. The waves have the same frequency as the alternating current.

3. When the waves meet a receiving antenna, they transfer energy to its electrons, making them oscillate too.

4. The receiving antenna produces an alternating current matching the frequency of the original current.

1. Electrons in the transmitting antenna oscillate back and forth in an alternating current. This makes them emit radio waves.

⚙ How radio waves travel

Radio frequencies used for communication vary from low frequencies (with wavelengths kilometres in length) to high frequencies (with wavelengths just centimetres long). High-frequency waves can only travel in straight lines but can be relayed by satellites. Lower-frequency radio waves are reflected by the ionosphere (an electrically charged layer in Earth's upper atmosphere), allowing them to travel beyond the horizon.

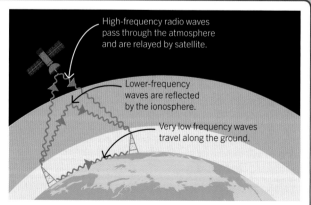

High-frequency radio waves pass through the atmosphere and are relayed by satellite.

Lower-frequency waves are reflected by the ionosphere.

Very low frequency waves travel along the ground.

Hazardous radiation

Exposure to high-energy electromagnetic radiation can be harmful to living things. The higher the frequency of the waves, the more energy they transfer and the more likely they are to do harm.

Effects on the body

Low-frequency waves, such as radio waves, pass through living tissue without being absorbed and are not dangerous. However, gamma rays, X-rays, and high-frequency ultraviolet rays are all types of ionizing radiation – they have enough energy to remove electrons from atoms and break chemical bonds, which can damage the molecules in living cells.

Key facts

✓ Electromagnetic radiation is divided into non-ionizing and ionizing radiation.

✓ Non-ionizing radiation does not have enough energy to remove electrons from atoms.

✓ Ionizing radiation is energetic enough to remove electrons from atoms and break chemical bonds.

✓ Exposure to ionizing radiation may result in tissue damage and cancer.

Ultraviolet radiation cannot penetrate the body but it can harm skin cells, leading to sunburn and an increased risk of cancer. It can also damage parts of the human eye, leading to visual defects or blindness.

X-rays penetrate the body and can damage the DNA in cells, leading to mutations that cause cancer. The risk depends on the dose, which is measured in units called sieverts. The X-ray machines in hospitals expose the body to very small doses of X-ray radiation.

Gamma rays penetrate the body and are the most dangerous form of electromagnetic radiation. They damage DNA and increase the risk of cancer. Large doses cause radiation sickness, which can be fatal.

Benefits and risks

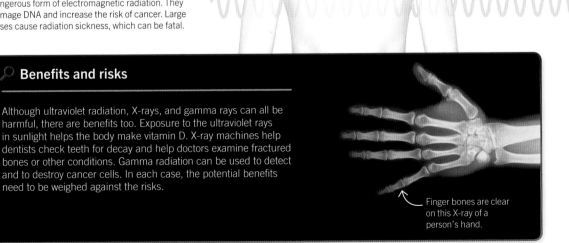

Although ultraviolet radiation, X-rays, and gamma rays can all be harmful, there are benefits too. Exposure to the ultraviolet rays in sunlight helps the body make vitamin D. X-ray machines help dentists check teeth for decay and help doctors examine fractured bones or other conditions. Gamma radiation can be used to detect and to destroy cancer cells. In each case, the potential benefits need to be weighed against the risks.

Finger bones are clear on this X-ray of a person's hand.

Electrical circuits

Current electricity

Unlike static electricity, which can stay in one place, current electricity is always moving. All the electric devices we use rely on flowing electric current. Some, such as headphones and mobile phones, use only a small current, but appliances such as cookers and electric heaters use a much larger current.

Moving electrons

Current electricity depends on the movement of electrons – the tiny, negatively charged particles that form the outer parts of atoms. In metals some of the electrons are free to move around. These free electrons normally move about randomly, but when a circuit is switched on they all move in the same direction. The electrons themselves move slowly, but all the electrons in a wire are affected at once, causing electromagnetic energy to flow through a circuit at close to the speed of light.

> **Key facts**
>
> ✓ Current electricity depends on the movement of free electrons in materials such as metals.
>
> ✓ When pushed by an electrical voltage, free electrons move in one direction. This is an electric current.
>
> ✓ Materials that let electricity flow through them are called conductors.
>
> ✓ Materials that block the flow of electricity are called insulators.

Current not flowing

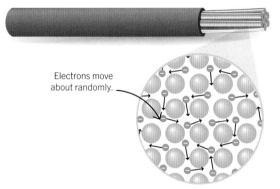

Electrons move about randomly.

Current flowing

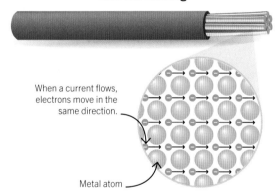

When a current flows, electrons move in the same direction.

Metal atom

🔍 Conductors and insulators

Materials that allow electricity to flow through them are called conductors. Metals are good conductors because their atoms have outer electrons that can separate from the atoms and move freely. Solutions containing dissolved ions (charged particles) can also conduct electricity. Materials with no free charged particles are called insulators because they block the flow of electricity.

Conductors

Copper

Gold

Silver

Lemon juice

Insulators

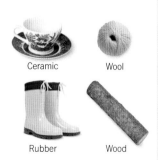
Ceramic

Wool

Rubber

Wood

Electrical circuits

Much of modern life is dependent on electricity and electrical circuits. Some circuits are simple, like the one shown below. Others are much more complex, like those in mobile phones, computers, and many other gadgets.

Key facts

✓ **All electrical circuits need a source of energy, such as a cell.**

✓ **Two or more cells used together make up a battery.**

✓ **Electric current will only flow through a circuit if there is an unbroken conducting path.**

✓ **Many electrical circuits have components such as bulbs or motors, which transfer energy to do useful jobs.**

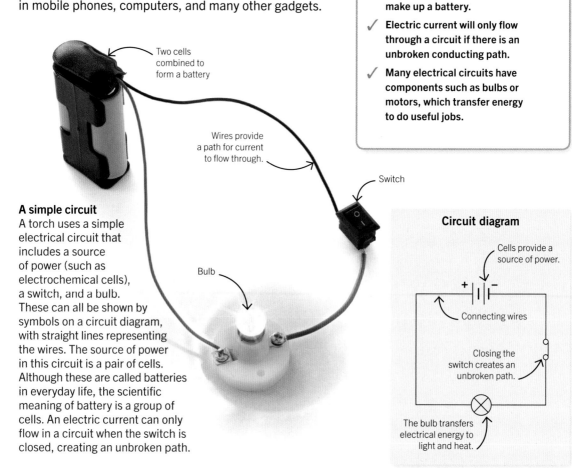

Two cells combined to form a battery

Wires provide a path for current to flow through.

Switch

Bulb

A simple circuit
A torch uses a simple electrical circuit that includes a source of power (such as electrochemical cells), a switch, and a bulb. These can all be shown by symbols on a circuit diagram, with straight lines representing the wires. The source of power in this circuit is a pair of cells. Although these are called batteries in everyday life, the scientific meaning of battery is a group of cells. An electric current can only flow in a circuit when the switch is closed, creating an unbroken path.

Circuit diagram

Cells provide a source of power.

Connecting wires

Closing the switch creates an unbroken path.

The bulb transfers electrical energy to light and heat.

Voltage

The voltage of a cell is a measure of how powerfully it pushes current around a circuit. Adding an extra cell creates twice the voltage, making twice as much current flow. As a result, the bulb glows brighter.

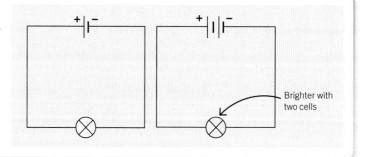

Brighter with two cells

Series and parallel circuits

Circuits can be connected in two basic ways. If all the components are connected in a single loop, they are said to be connected in series. If the circuit splits into branches, they are said to be connected in parallel.

Key facts

✓ Electrical circuits can be connected in series or in parallel.

✓ In a series circuit, the components are connected in a single loop and can all be switched on or off together.

✓ In a parallel circuit, the circuit divides so that components are on different branches. If one branch breaks, the other can continue working.

Series circuit

In a series circuit, the components are connected one after another in a single loop. The two bulbs here are connected in series. If one bulb breaks, the current cannot flow through and the other bulb stops working too. If extra bulbs are added, they will all be dimmer because each bulb reduces the flow of current through the circuit.

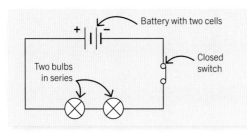

Battery with two cells

Two bulbs in series

Closed switch

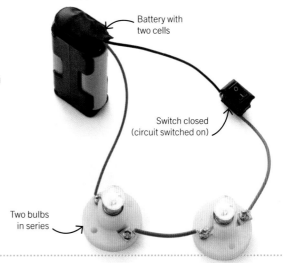

Battery with two cells

Switch closed (circuit switched on)

Two bulbs in series

Parallel circuit

In a parallel circuit, the components are on separate branches. There's more than one path for the current to take, so if one bulb breaks, the other continues working. In each branch, the electric current only has to flow through a single bulb, which means more current can flow than in the series circuit. As a result, the bulbs are brighter. The wiring in homes is arranged as parallel circuits.

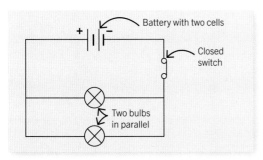

Battery with two cells

Closed switch

Two bulbs in parallel

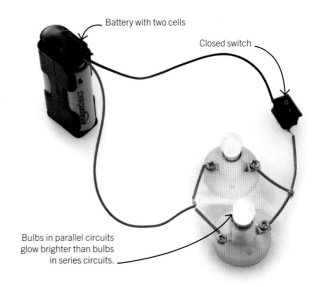

Battery with two cells

Closed switch

Bulbs in parallel circuits glow brighter than bulbs in series circuits.

Measuring electricity

Measuring electricity is a bit like measuring the way water from a tank flows through pipes. The rate at which electric charge flows through a circuit is called current, and we measure it in units called amps. The size of the current depends on two main things: the strength of the driving force (called voltage or potential difference) that pushes electricity along, and how much resistance the electricity meets in the circuit.

Key facts

✓ Current is the rate of flow of electric charge. We measure it in units called amps (A).

✓ Current is measured by an ammeter, which is connected in series.

✓ Voltage (potential difference) is a measure of how strongly charge is pushed through a circuit. We measure it in volts (V).

✓ Voltage is measured by a voltmeter, which is connected in parallel.

✓ Resistance is anything that uses up electrical energy, reducing the flow of electric current. We measure resistance in ohms (Ω).

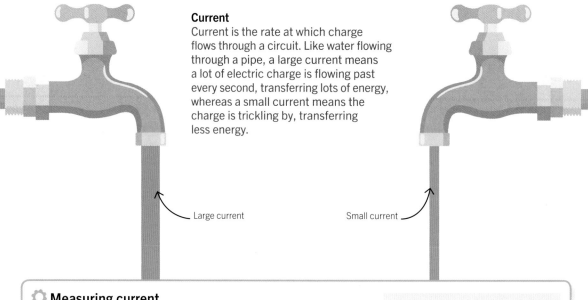

Current
Current is the rate at which charge flows through a circuit. Like water flowing through a pipe, a large current means a lot of electric charge is flowing past every second, transferring lots of energy, whereas a small current means the charge is trickling by, transferring less energy.

Large current

Small current

⚙ Measuring current

We measure current in units known as amps or amperes (A), using a device called an ammeter. An ammeter has to be connected in series wherever we want to measure the current. It doesn't matter where you put it in a series circuit as the current is the same in every part of the circuit. The symbol for an ammeter on a circuit diagram is the letter A in a circle.

Ammeter

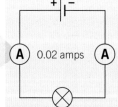

(A) 0.02 amps   (A) 0.02 amps

Voltage (potential difference)

A current can't flow unless something pushes it. The push comes from the difference in electric potential energy at the start and end of the circuit, which we call voltage or potential difference. It works a bit like water pressure. When a water storage tank is high up, the force of gravity creates a higher pressure, making the rate of flow of water through the tap bigger.

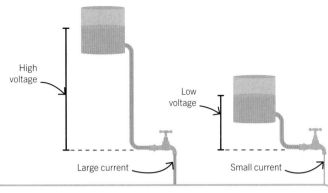

⚙ Measuring voltage

We measure voltage in units called volts (V), using a device called a voltmeter. The voltmeter must be connected in parallel with the component. The symbol for a voltmeter on a circuit diagram is the letter V in a circle.

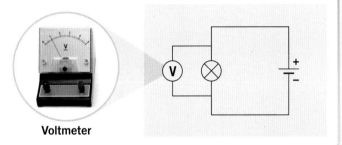

Voltmeter

Resistance

Anything in a circuit that uses up electrical energy reduces the flow of electric current. We call this resistance. Just as a narrow pipe reduces the flow of water, a thin wire creates resistance and reduces the current. Longer wires also increase resistance. We measure resistance in units called ohms (Ω).

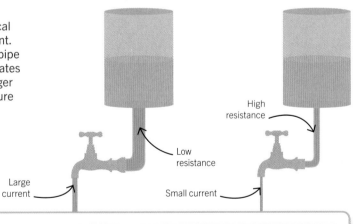

⚙ Resistors

In some circuits, a component called a resistor is added to ensure the current doesn't become high enough to damage other components. The symbol for a resistor in circuit diagrams is a rectangle.

Resistor

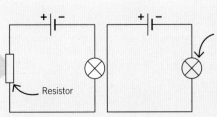

Resistor

The bulb is brighter in the circuit without a resistor because more current flows.

Series and parallel circuit rules

Here are the main rules that you need to know about currents and voltages in series and parallel circuits.

Rule 1: Current in equals current out
The sum of currents flowing towards any point in a circuit is always equal to the sum of currents flowing away from it. In the circuit below, a current of 250 mA (milliamps) flows towards A, where it splits into two. The two currents flowing away from A, 150 mA and 100 mA, add up to 250 mA.

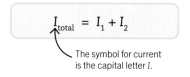

$$I_{total} = I_1 + I_2$$

The symbol for current is the capital letter I.

Circuit 1

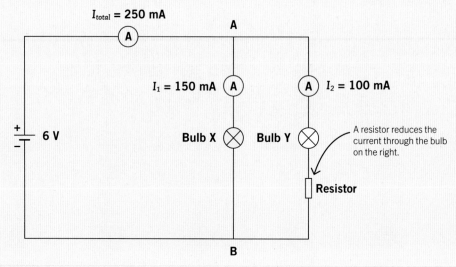

I_{total} = 250 mA

A

I_1 = 150 mA (A)

(A) I_2 = 100 mA

+ −
6 V

Bulb X ⊗   Bulb Y ⊗

A resistor reduces the current through the bulb on the right.

Resistor

B

 Calculating current

Question 1
In circuit 1, what's the size of the current flowing away from B?

Answer 1
Current in equals current out, so the answer is 250 mA.

Rule 2: Voltages in series add up

When components are connected in series, such as the two bulbs and the resistor shown here, the voltages across each component add up to the voltage of the power supply.

$$V_{total} = V_1 + V_2 + V_3$$

Circuit 2

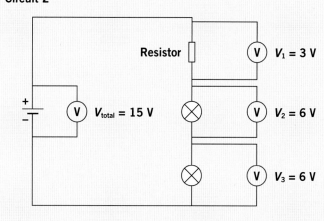

Rule 3: Voltages in parallel are the same

In a parallel circuit, each parallel branch has the same voltage across it. In the example shown here, the two bulbs have the same voltage across them.

Circuit 3

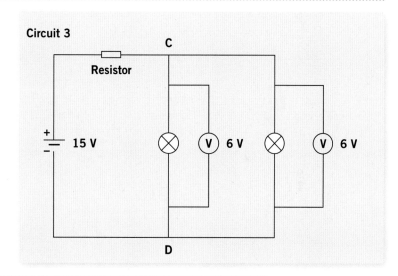

 Calculating voltage

Question 2
In circuit 3, what's the voltage across the resistor?

Answer 2
The circuit has a total voltage of 15 V, and the voltage between C and D is 6 V. The voltage across the resistor must therefore be 15 V – 6 V, which is 9 V.

Question 3
The voltage across the resistor in Circuit 1 is 4 V. What is the voltage across bulb Y?

Answer 3
The voltage across each branch of the circuit is 6 V. In the right branch, 6 V is divided between bulb Y and the resistor, so the voltage across bulb Y is 6 V – 4 V = 2 V.

Charge

Electrons all have negative charge. When a circuit is switched on, the moving electrons cause an electric charge to flow through it. We measure charge in units called coulombs. Electric current is the rate of flow of charge: a current of 1 amp means 1 coulomb of charge flows past every second. The equations on this page show how charge, current, voltage, and energy are related.

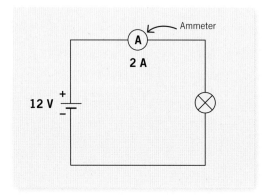

Charge and current

The size of an electric current tells you how much charge moves past any point in a circuit each second. In this circuit, the reading of 2 amps on the ammeter shows that 2 coulombs of charge pass through the cell and the bulb every second. This relationship between charge, current, and time is summed up in the equation below.

> charge (C) = current (A) × time (s)
>
> $Q = I \times t$

Charge and energy

Electrical devices do useful jobs by transferring energy. For instance, the circuit above transfers energy from the cell to light. If you know how much charge flows through a component and the size of the voltage (potential difference) pushing the charge, you can calculate how much energy the circuit transfers using the equation below.

> energy transferred (J) = charge (C) × voltage (V)
>
> $E = Q \times V$

Key facts

✓ The unit of electric charge is the coulomb (**C**).

✓ A current of 1 amp means 1 coulomb of charge passes through a circuit each second.

✓ When 1 coulomb of charge moves through a potential difference of 1 volt, it transfers 1 joule of energy.

▤ Calculating charge and energy

Questions

1. A torch bulb uses a 3 V battery and a current of 0.25 A flows through the bulb. The torch is turned on for 5 minutes. How much charge passes through the torch bulb?
2. How much energy is transferred from the battery to the bulb in that time?

Answers

1. First work out the time in seconds:
   5 minutes = 300 seconds.
   $Q = I \times t$
   $= 0.25 \text{ A} \times 300 \text{ s}$
   $= 75 \text{ C}$
2. Use the second equation to calculate energy transferred:
   $E = Q \times V$
   $= 75 \text{ C} \times 3 \text{ V}$
   $= 225 \text{ J}$

Changing resistance

Sometimes it's useful to change the resistance in a circuit to control how much current can flow. This makes it possible to change the brightness of a lamp, the speed of a motor, or the loudness of a radio.

Variable resistor

The component used to change resistance is called a variable resistor. It consists of a long, coiled wire that creates resistance and a sliding contact that can be moved to vary how much coil the current flows through.

Key facts

✓ A variable resistor consists of a resistance coil and a sliding contact.

✓ The current, voltage, and resistance of a circuit are linked by the equation voltage = current × resistance.

With the slider near the left end of the coil, the current does not have to pass through many turns of wire and the resistance is low.

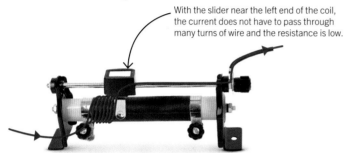

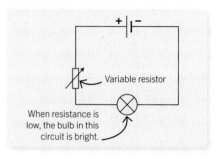

Variable resistor

When resistance is low, the bulb in this circuit is bright.

With the slider near the right end, the current has to pass through most of the coil and the resistance is high.

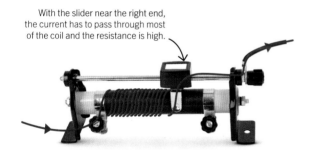

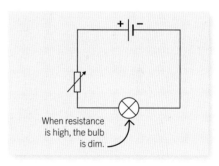

When resistance is high, the bulb is dim.

🖩 Calculating current, voltage, and resistance

The current, voltage, and resistance in a circuit or component are linked by the equation below, which is known as Ohm's law.

> **voltage (V) = current (A) × resistance (Ω)**
> $V = I \times R$

Question
A current of 0.5 A flows through a bulb when there is a voltage of 6 V across it. Calculate the resistance of the bulb.

Answer
Rearrange the equation to make resistance the subject:

$$R = \frac{V}{I}$$

$$R = \frac{6\ V}{0.5\ A}$$

$$R = 12\ \Omega$$

Investigating resistance in wires

The resistance of a component depends on many factors. This practical investigates how the resistance of a wire varies with the wire's length.

The circuit
The two crocodile clips in this circuit allow you to vary the length of a piece of wire through which the current flows. The voltmeter measures the voltage (potential difference) across this wire, and the ammeter measures the current flowing through the whole circuit.

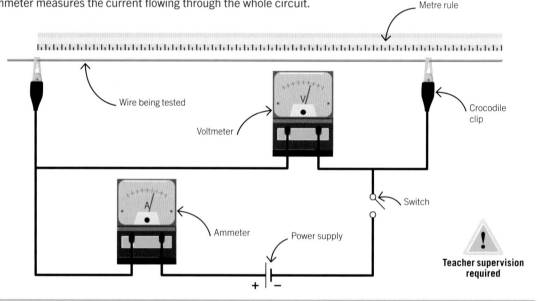

Metre rule

Wire being tested

Voltmeter

Crocodile clip

Ammeter

Power supply

Switch

⚠️ **Teacher supervision required**

📋 Method

1. With help from a teacher, set up a circuit as shown above.

2. Fasten one crocodile clip to the wire at the zero mark on the ruler. Fasten the other crocodile clip at 30 cm.

3. Set the power supply to a low voltage (3–4 V) or use a cell.

4. Switch on and note the readings on the ammeter and voltmeter. Switch off again as soon as you've done this to stop the wire becoming hot.

5. Write your results in a table with column headings for wire length, current, and voltage.

6. Move the crocodile clip to 40 cm and repeat steps 4 and 5.

7. Repeat every 10 cm up to 100 cm.

Warning
Your teacher will provide a special kind of wire (Constantan or Eureka wire with a diameter of about 0.5 mm) that is safe to be used as a resistor in this experiment. Do not use ordinary wire. The wire should either be raised or supported on a heat-resistant mat made of a material that does not conduct electricity. Take readings quickly and then disconnect the power to prevent the wire from heating up. Do not touch the naked wire when the circuit is switched on.

Results

1. Use Ohm's law (below) to calculate the resistance for each length of wire, and record the answers in a new table.

$$\text{resistance } (\Omega) = \frac{\text{voltage (V)}}{\text{current (A)}}$$

Wire length (cm)	30	40	50	60	70	80	90	100
Calculated resistance (Ω)	44	53	71	88	95	112	127	138

2. Draw a graph of resistance against length of wire, and join the points with a line of best fit. The points should be on a straight line that passes through the origin (0, 0). This shows that the resistance of the wire is proportional to its length. In other words, if its length doubles, its resistance doubles.

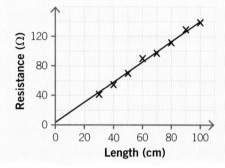

3. You may find that the straight line on your graph doesn't pass through the origin. This is caused by what's known as a systematic error – an error that affects all your readings. In this case, it could be that one crocodile clip was not exactly at the zero point on the ruler, so all your measurements of length are incorrect by the same amount. Another possible cause of systematic error is resistance from the other wires in the circuit, especially if they are long.

Resistance is useful
Resistance is caused by collisions between the free electrons in a wire and the lattice of fixed metal ions. The collisions transfer energy to the ions, increasing their store of thermal energy. Electric heaters and electric light bulbs exploit this process to generate heat and light. The filament in a light bulb gets so hot that it glows white hot, flooding its surroundings with light.

Resistance in wires

Why do some substances make it difficult for electricity to pass through them? Insulators have huge resistance because there are no free electrons to carry charge, but metals have lots of free electrons. However, electricity flows more easily through some wires than others.

Key facts

✓ Resistance in metals happens because free electrons collide with metal ions as they move through the wire.

✓ Short wires have less resistance than long wires.

✓ Thick wires have less resistance than thin wires.

✓ Some metals conduct better than others.

Wire length
Wires create resistance because the free electrons bump into the fixed metal ions as they move, transferring some of their energy to the ions. The longer the wire, the greater the resistance. Resistance is proportional to the length of the wire.

Short wire

Collisions between electrons and metal ions cause resistance.

Long wire

Longer wires cause greater resistance (like placing resistors in series; see page 165).

Wire thickness
In thicker wires there are more electrons to flow, allowing a greater current and therefore lower resistance. Resistance is inversely proportional to the cross-sectional area of a wire. If the cross-sectional area doubles, the resistance halves. If the diameter of the wire doubles, the resistance goes down by a factor of four.

Thin wire

Thick wire

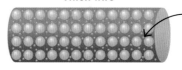

Thicker wires allow more electrons to flow (like placing resistors in parallel; see page 166).

⚙ Free electrons

Atoms in a metal are held together in a regular lattice. The atoms' outermost electrons can easily separate to become free electrons, leaving behind positively charged ions. These free electrons normally move randomly in all directions inside the metal, but when a voltage (potential difference) is applied, the electrons all flow in the same direction. Some metals (such as copper and silver) are better conductors than others because their atoms lose the outer electrons more easily.

Free electrons normally move randomly in all directions between the ions.

No current flowing

Current flowing

A potential difference makes electrons move in the same direction.

Investigating resistors in series and parallel

We use resistors to control the amount of current flowing through a circuit. This practical investigates how much resistance they create when multiple resistors are connected in series or parallel.

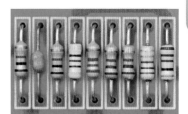

Resistors on a circuit board

Resistors in series
Use a circuit like the one below to find out what happens when you add resistors in series. This experiment shows that when resistors are added in series, the total resistance in the circuit increases.

Teacher supervision required

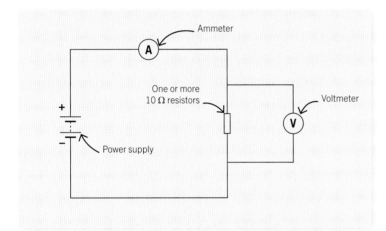

Method

1. Set up the circuit shown, with just one 10 Ω resistor held between two crocodile clips.

2. Switch on the power supply and record the voltage across the resistor and the current.

3. Switch off and add another 10 Ω resistor in series with the first. Switch on and record the current and voltage again.

4. Repeat step 3 until you've tested the circuit with four resistors in it.

5. Use the following equation to calculate the total resistance of the circuit for each test:

$$resistance = \frac{voltage}{current}$$

Results

Record your readings in a table like the one shown here. The results show that the resistance of the circuit increases by 10 Ω every time a 10 Ω resistor is added in series. The total resistance is the sum of the resistors in the chain. This is shown by the equation below.

$$R_{total} = R_1 + R_2 + ...$$

Number of 10 Ω resistors	Voltage (V)	Current (A)	Calculated resistance (Ω)
1	2.0	0.200	10
2	2.0	0.100	20
3	2.0	0.067	30
4	2.0	0.050	40

Resistors in parallel

We can investigate the effect of resistors in parallel using the circuits below. The bulbs serve as resistors here, but we would get similar results using actual resistors. This experiment shows that when resistors are added in parallel, the overall resistance of the circuit falls and the current in the main part of the circuit increases.

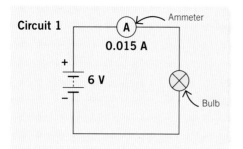

Circuit 1

Teacher supervision required

Method

1. Set up the circuit with a single bulb and note the current on the ammeter.

2. Turn off the power and add a second bulb in parallel. Switch on the power and note the new reading. The current will have doubled because the new path allows more electricity to flow through the circuit.

3. Add a third bulb in parallel and take another reading. The current will have tripled.

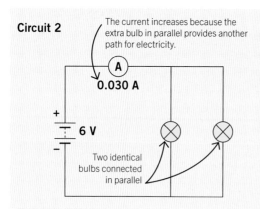

Circuit 2

The current increases because the extra bulb in parallel provides another path for electricity.

Two identical bulbs connected in parallel

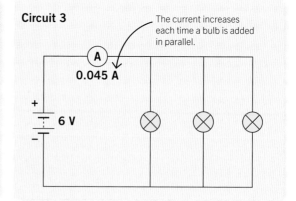

Circuit 3

The current increases each time a bulb is added in parallel.

Calculating resistance for components in parallel

The total resistance of components in parallel can be calculated using this equation:

$$\frac{1}{R_{total}} = \frac{1}{R_1} + \frac{1}{R_2} + \cdots$$

Question

Each bulb in the circuits above has a resistance of 400 Ω. What is the total resistance of the circuit with two bulbs?

Answer

$$\frac{1}{R_{total}} = \frac{1}{400\ \Omega} + \frac{1}{400\ \Omega}$$
$$= \frac{2}{400\ \Omega}$$
$$R_{total} = \frac{400\ \Omega}{2}$$
$$= 200\ \Omega$$

Note that this is half the resistance of one resistor by itself.

Check the answer using the equation $V = I \times R$ (voltage = current × resistance). For this circuit, $I = 0.030$ A and $V = 6$ V.

$$V = 0.030\ \text{A} \times 200\ \Omega$$
$$= 6\ \text{V}$$

Current and voltage calculations

Previous pages in this chapter have introduced lots of ideas about series and parallel circuits, and some equations. The calculations here show you some ways in which these ideas can be used. The first three questions feature series circuits. The rest are about parallel circuits.

Series circuits key facts

✓ Resistances of components in series add up to the total resistance: $R_{total} = R_1 + R_2$.

✓ Voltage = current × resistance: $V = I \times R$. This is known as Ohm's law.

✓ Ohm's law works everywhere in the circuit, whether we're looking at individual components, a part of the circuit, or the whole circuit.

Circuit 1

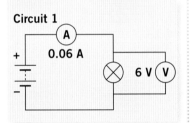

Circuit 2

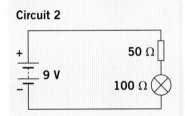

Circuit 3

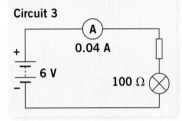

Question
What's the resistance of the bulb in circuit 1?

Question
What's the total resistance in this circuit? Use the answer to calculate the current that flows through the circuit.

Question
The bulb in this circuit has a resistance of 100 Ω. What's the resistance of the resistor?

Answer
You know the voltage across the bulb and the current flowing through it, so rearrange the equation $V = I \times R$ (Ohm's law) to calculate the resistance.

$$R = \frac{V}{I}$$

$$= \frac{6\ V}{0.06\ A}$$

$$= 100\ \Omega$$

Answer
The resistances of components connected in series add up.

$$R_{total} = R_1 + R_2$$
$$= 100\ \Omega + 50\ \Omega$$
$$= 150\ \Omega$$

You know the resistance and voltage, so rearrange $V = I \times R$ to calculate the current.

$$I = \frac{V}{R}$$

$$= \frac{9\ V}{150\ \Omega}$$

$$= 0.06\ A$$

Answer
Start by working out the total resistance of the circuit, using the voltage of the battery and the current.

$$R = \frac{V}{I}$$

$$= \frac{6\ V}{0.04\ A}$$

$$= 150\ \Omega$$

The resistances of the bulb and resistor add up to 150 Ω, so:

$$R_{resistor} = 150\ \Omega - 100\ \Omega$$
$$= 50\ \Omega$$

Circuit 4

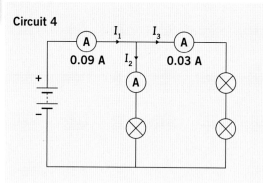

Parallel circuits key facts

✓ Current flowing into a junction equals current flowing out: $I_1 = I_2 + I_3$.

✓ The total resistance of components in parallel is smaller than the resistance of either of the components.

✓ Each branch of a parallel circuit has the same voltage across it.

Question

All the bulbs in this circuit are the same. What's the current I_2? Explain why I_2 is greater than I_3.

Answer

The current going into a junction equals the total current coming out of the junction.

$0.09 \text{ A} = I_2 + 0.03 \text{ A}$

$I_2 = 0.06 \text{ A}$

I_2 is flowing through one bulb, but I_3 flows through two. The two parallel branches have the same voltage, but two bulbs create twice as much resistance, so the current through I_3 is half the size.

Circuit 5

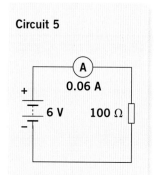

Circuit 6

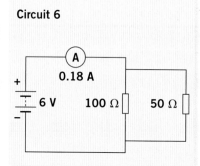

Circuit 7

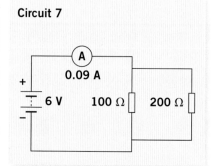

Questions

1. Which of the three circuits above has the smallest total resistance?
2. Which resistor has the highest voltage across it?
3. Explain why the current is highest in circuit 6.

Answers

1. Circuit 6. All the circuits have the same voltage supplied by the battery, and the current is biggest in circuit 6.
2. They all have 6 V across them. In the parallel circuits, each branch of the circuit has the same voltage across it.
3. The current through the 100 Ω resistor is the same in all three circuits. In circuits 6 and 7, more current can flow through the extra resistors. A higher current will flow through the 50 Ω resistor in circuit 6 than through the 200 Ω resistor in circuit 7, so the total current in circuit 6 is highest.

Current and voltage graphs

Resistors and wires are called ohmic conductors because they obey Ohm's law ($V = I \times R$). In other words, a resistor or a wire has constant resistance, and the current flowing through it is proportional to the voltage across it. Not all components obey this law, however. You can investigate the resistance of different components using the circuit below.

Teacher supervision required

Key facts

✓ The graph of current against voltage for an ohmic conductor is a straight line passing through the origin (0, 0).

✓ Filament bulbs and diodes are examples of non-ohmic conductors.

✓ The resistance of metals increases with temperature.

✓ Diodes only allow current to pass through in one direction.

 ## Method

1. Set up the circuit shown in the diagram.
2. Use the variable resistor to change the current to 10 different values. Make a note of the voltage for each different current. Write down your results in a table.
3. Swap the connections to the battery over, and repeat step 2. Your current and voltage readings will now have negative values.
4. Repeat steps 2 and 3 with a filament bulb instead of the resistor, and then with a diode.
5. Plot a graph of current against voltage for each component.

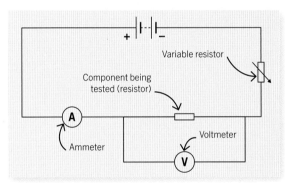

Results for a resistor

A graph of current and voltage for a resistor forms a straight line that passes through the origin (0, 0). As resistance can be calculated from voltage divided by current, this shows that the resistance is constant and doesn't change when the direction of the voltage and current changes. A resistor is an ohmic conductor.

Resistor

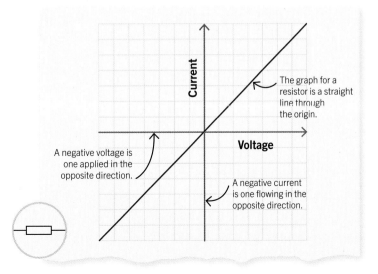

The graph for a resistor is a straight line through the origin.

A negative voltage is one applied in the opposite direction.

A negative current is one flowing in the opposite direction.

Results for a filament bulb

The graph for a filament bulb shows the line curving at higher voltages. This indicates that resistance is increasing, so a filament bulb is not an ohmic conductor. The filament in a light bulb gets white hot when current passes through, transferring electrical energy to light. Resistance increases because the metal atoms vibrate more as they get hotter, obstructing the flow of free electrons.

Filament

Bulb

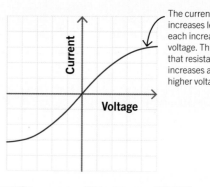

The current increases less for each increase in voltage. This shows that resistance increases at higher voltages.

Results for a diode

A diode is like a one-way street: current can flow freely in one direction but not the other. As the graph shows, a diode is not an ohmic conductor.

Resistance is very high when the voltage is applied in the reverse direction, so the current is zero.

The diode has an almost constant resistance above 0.7 V.

Diode

🖾 Rectification

Diodes are used in rectifier circuits, which convert alternating current (a.c.) from mains electricity supplies to direct current (d.c.) for electronic devices.

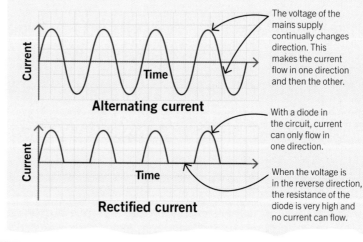

Alternating current

Rectified current

The voltage of the mains supply continually changes direction. This makes the current flow in one direction and then the other.

With a diode in the circuit, current can only flow in one direction.

When the voltage is in the reverse direction, the resistance of the diode is very high and no current can flow.

Power in circuits

Electrical devices transfer energy from a power supply such as a battery to components such as lamps, heaters, and motors. Electrical power is the amount of energy transferred each second. We measure it in watts (W).

Power equations
The energy transferred by an electrical device depends on the current and voltage. We can calculate power – the amount of energy transferred each second – using the equation below. The equation doesn't need to include a term for time as current is a measure of flow of the charge passing each second.

$$\text{power (W)} = \text{current (A)} \times \text{voltage (V)}$$
$$P = I \times V$$

If we combine the equation above with Ohm's law (voltage = current × resistance), we can derive two new equations for power. One, shown below, calculates power from current and resistance. The other calculates power from voltage and resistance:
power = (voltage)^2 ÷ resistance.

$$\text{voltage} = \text{current} \times \text{resistance} \qquad \text{power} = \text{current} \times \text{voltage}$$

$$\text{power (W)} = \text{current}^2 \text{ (A)}^2 \times \text{resistance } (\Omega)$$
$$P = I^2 \times R$$

 Calculating power

Question
A torch uses a 6 V battery, and the current through the lamp is 300 mA. What's the power of the torch? What's the resistance of the lamp?

Answer
Use the first equation to calculate power. Remember that 300 mA is 0.3 A.
$P = I \times V$
$\quad = 0.3 \text{ A} \times 6 \text{ V}$
$\quad = 1.8 \text{ W}$

To find resistance, rearrange either $V = I \times R$ or $P = I^2 \times R$ to make R the subject.
$$R = \frac{P}{I^2}$$
$$\quad = \frac{1.8 \text{ W}}{(0.3 \text{ A})^2}$$
$$\quad = 20 \ \Omega$$

Calculating energy

From torches and phones to electric cars and high-speed trains, all electrical devices transfer energy. The amount of energy transferred can be calculated using several related equations.

Key facts

✓ Energy transferred by a device equals power multiplied by the time the device is used for: $E = P \times t$.

✓ Energy transferred by a device equals the charge that has passed through it multiplied by the voltage across it: $E = Q \times V$.

✓ Energy transferred by a device equals current × voltage × time: $E = I \times V \times t$.

Equation 1

The power of a device is the energy used per second, so if you multiply the power by the number of seconds it is switched on, you can find the energy transferred.

$$\text{energy (J)} = \text{power (W)} \times \text{time (s)}$$
$$E = P \times t$$

Equation 2

The voltage of an electricity supply is the energy it transfers for each coulomb of charge, so you can work out the energy transferred by multiplying charge by voltage.

$$\text{energy (J)} = \text{charge (C)} \times \text{voltage (V)}$$
$$E = Q \times V$$

Equation 3

The power of an electrical device can be found by multiplying the current and the voltage. Combine this with energy = power × time and you get the following equation.

$$\text{energy (J)} = \text{current (A)} \times \text{voltage (V)} \times \text{time (s)}$$
$$E = I \times V \times t$$

Calculating energy, charge, and current

Question
This 3 kW oven took 30 minutes to cook an apple pie. The mains voltage is 230 V. Calculate the energy transferred, the total amount of charge that flowed during this time, and the current used.

Answer
There's a lot to work out here! Start by writing down what you know, but convert the information into the correct units:

   power = 3 kW = 3000 W
   time = 30 minutes = 1800 s
   voltage = 230 V

Use the first equation to calculate the energy transferred.

$E = P \times t$
   $= 3000 \text{ W} \times 1800 \text{ s}$
   $= 5\,400\,000 \text{ J (5.4 MJ)}$

Now you know the energy, you can use the second equation to calculate charge.

$E = Q \times V$

$Q = \dfrac{E}{V}$

   $= \dfrac{5\,400\,000 \text{ J}}{230 \text{ V}}$

   $= 23\,478 \text{ C} = 23\,000 \text{ C (2 s.f.)}$

Use the last equation (or just $P = I \times V$) to calculate the current:

$E = I \times V \times t$

$I = \dfrac{E}{V \times t}$

   $= \dfrac{5\,400\,000 \text{ J}}{230 \text{ V} \times 1800 \text{ s}}$

   $= 13 \text{ A}$

Electrified railway
High-speed trains, such as France's TGV (*Train à Grande Vitesse*), are powered by electricity supplied by overhead cables, giving the locomotive at the front of the train a power of 9.3 megawatts (9.3 million watts).

Light-dependent resistors

Light-dependent resistors (LDRs) are resistors that sense the brightness of light falling on them: as the light gets brighter, an LDR's resistance falls. LDRs have many applications. They are used in night lamps, streetlights, burglar alarms, and smartphone screen dimmers.

📌 **Key facts**

✓ The resistance of LDRs falls as the brightness of the light increases.

✓ LDRs are used in night lamps, streetlights, burglar alarms, and smartphone screen dimmers.

How LDRs work

Also known as photoresistors, LDRs are small circuit components made of a semiconductor material. When light shines on the semiconductor, electrons are released from atoms, allowing a larger current to flow and so reducing resistance. The higher the light intensity (brightness), the lower the resistance, as the graph here shows. In darkness, a typical LDR has a resistance of over 1 000 000 Ω, but this falls to a few hundred ohms in sunlight.

The circuit symbol for an LDR is a rectangle in a circle with arrows representing light.

LDR

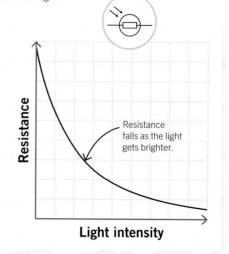

Resistance

Light intensity

Resistance falls as the light gets brighter.

⚙ **Investigating LDRs**

You can investigate how the resistance of an LDR changes using the apparatus shown here. Carry out the experiment in a darkened room so the only light falling on the LDR comes from the torch. Place the torch at different distances from the LDR, and use an ohmmeter connected to the LDR to measure resistance. Place a light meter next to the LDR to measure light intensity. Use your data to plot a graph of resistance against light intensity.

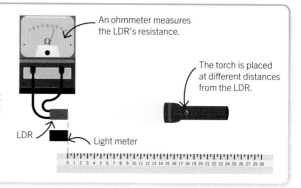

An ohmmeter measures the LDR's resistance.

The torch is placed at different distances from the LDR.

LDR

Light meter

Thermistors

Thermistors are resistors that react to a change in temperature. When the temperature rises, a thermistor's resistance may either rise or fall, depending on the type of thermistor. Thermistors are used as temperature sensors in many kinds of device, from digital thermometers to fridges, ovens, and thermostats.

📌 **Key facts**

✓ In thermistors, the resistance changes as temperature increases.

✓ Thermistors are used in devices that measure or control temperature.

How thermistors work
Thermistors are found in the tips of digital thermometers. These thermistors are made from a semiconductor material that releases more free electrons as it gets hotter, allowing more current to flow. The higher the temperature, the lower the resistance, as the graph shows.

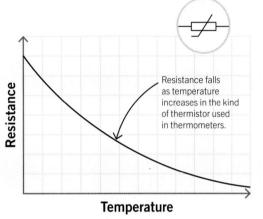

Resistance falls as temperature increases in the kind of thermistor used in thermometers.

Resistance (vertical axis)

Temperature (horizontal axis)

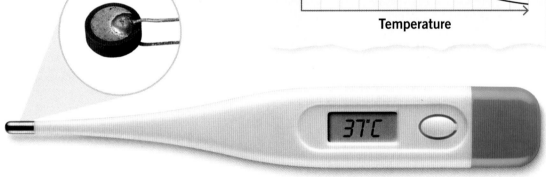

📑 Investigating thermistors

You can investigate how the resistance of a thermistor changes using this setup. Place a thermistor in a beaker of water and use a heat source to raise the water temperature. Record temperature and resistance at the same time at various temperatures. Use the data to plot a graph of resistance against temperature.

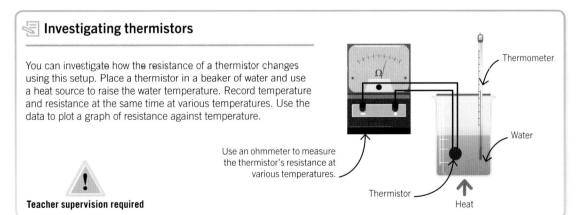

Thermometer

Water

Use an ohmmeter to measure the thermistor's resistance at various temperatures.

Thermistor

Heat

⚠️ **Teacher supervision required**

Sensor circuits

Sensor circuits are used to control electric devices automatically, such as streetlights that switch on when it gets dark and heating or cooling systems that keep the temperature in buildings comfortable all year round.

Potential dividers

Sensor circuits often use potential dividers. A potential divider is a circuit that uses resistors in series to control how much voltage is supplied to a parallel branch of the circuit. It works because voltage is divided between components in series but is equal across parallel branches. Changing the combination of resistors changes the voltage in the parallel branch.

Key facts

✓ LDRs and thermistors can be used as sensors to control lights, heaters, and other devices.

✓ The LDR or thermistor is connected in series with another resistor, forming a potential divider.

✓ A potential divider is a circuit that uses resistors in series to control the voltage supplied to a different part of the circuit.

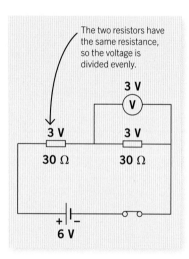

The two resistors have the same resistance, so the voltage is divided evenly.

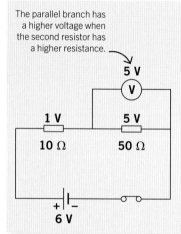

The parallel branch has a higher voltage when the second resistor has a higher resistance.

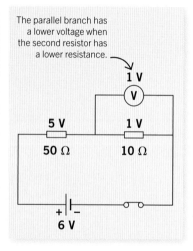

The parallel branch has a lower voltage when the second resistor has a lower resistance.

Control circuits

When a light-dependent resistor or thermistor is used as one of the resistors in a potential divider, the voltage in the parallel branch varies depending on the light level or temperature. This varying voltage can then be used to activate a control circuit that switches on when the voltage rises above (or falls below) a chosen level. The control circuit does not draw current from the sensing circuit – it has a different power supply and provides the much larger current needed to power a device such as a streetlight, heater, or fan.

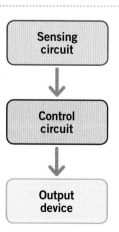

Sensing circuit

↓

Control circuit

↓

Output device

Controlling lights

The circuit below uses an LDR (light-dependent resistor) and a potential divider to send a signal to a control circuit that switches on a light at night as it gets darker.

Light-dependent resistor (LDR)

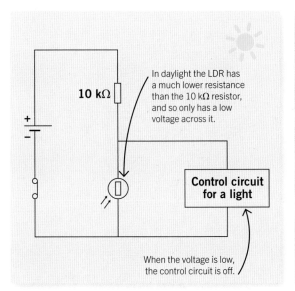

10 kΩ

In daylight the LDR has a much lower resistance than the 10 kΩ resistor, and so only has a low voltage across it.

Control circuit for a light

When the voltage is low, the control circuit is off.

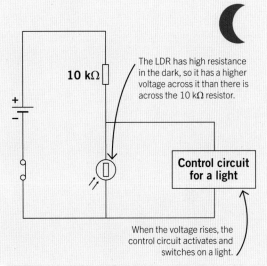

10 kΩ

The LDR has high resistance in the dark, so it has a higher voltage across it than there is across the 10 kΩ resistor.

Control circuit for a light

When the voltage rises, the control circuit activates and switches on a light.

Controlling temperature

The circuit below uses a thermistor and a potential divider to send a voltage signal to a control circuit that controls a fan. A similar circuit could be used to control an air-conditioning unit or a fridge.

Thermistor

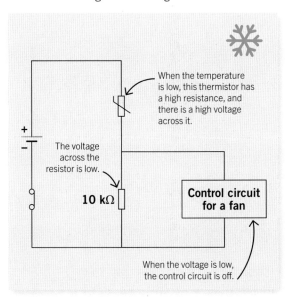

When the temperature is low, this thermistor has a high resistance, and there is a high voltage across it.

The voltage across the resistor is low.

10 kΩ

Control circuit for a fan

When the voltage is low, the control circuit is off.

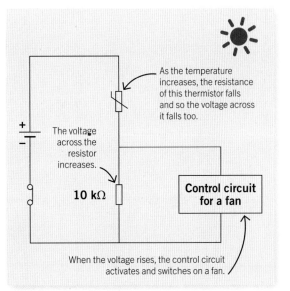

As the temperature increases, the resistance of this thermistor falls and so the voltage across it falls too.

The voltage across the resistor increases.

10 kΩ

Control circuit for a fan

When the voltage rises, the control circuit activates and switches on a fan.

Using electricity

Direct and alternating current

Depending on the way it's produced, electricity can take two different forms: direct current (d.c.) and alternating current (a.c.). Small portable devices typically use d.c., but the mains electricity supplied to our homes is a.c.

Key facts

✓ Direct current (d.c.) is electricity that flows in one direction only.

✓ Alternating current (a.c.) is electricity that reverses direction many times a second.

✓ The voltage of an a.c. current is continually changing.

Direct current

Batteries produce d.c. electricity. This is a continuous electric current that flows in one direction only. The d.c. electricity from a battery has a steady voltage, but devices that convert a.c. to d.c. produce a voltage that fluctuates but is always positive, ensuring the current always flows in the same direction.

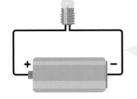

Alternating current

Power stations supply our homes with a.c. electricity. The voltage of a.c. electricity cycles from positive to negative and back 50 or 60 times a second (50 or 60 Hz), causing the current to reverse direction 100 or 120 times a second. Most electrical appliances in homes are powered by a.c. electricity, but electronic devices such as computers have power supply units that convert a.c. to d.c.

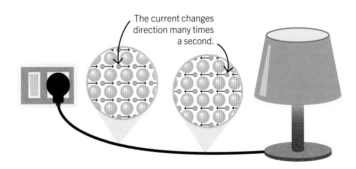

The current changes direction many times a second.

☼ Voltage graphs

The voltage of an a.c. electricity supply changes as shown in the graph. Depending on the country you live in, your mains electricity supply may have a stated voltage between 100 V and 240 V. This figure, shown by the dashed line, is a kind of average called a root mean square.

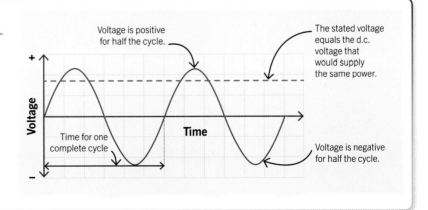

Voltage is positive for half the cycle.

The stated voltage equals the d.c. voltage that would supply the same power.

Time for one complete cycle

Voltage is negative for half the cycle.

Electrical wiring

Appliances are connected to the mains electricity supply via a cable and plug. Electricity cables have two or three different wires inside, each with a different function. These attach to two or three metal pins in a plug, which make contact with the mains when the plug is inserted in a socket.

Key facts

✓ The cables that join appliances to plugs have two or three separate wires inside them.

✓ The live wire carries the full mains voltage (between 100 V and 240 V, depending on the country).

✓ The neutral wire is usually at 0 V.

✓ The earth wire is for safety and is usually at 0 V.

Inside a plug
All plugs have at least two wires inside. The live wire and neutral wire create a circuit when an appliance is switched on, and the earth wire is for safety — it provides a path for electricity to flow away if an electrical fault occurs. Some devices don't need an earth wire and have two-pin plugs in many countries. For instance, "double-insulated" appliances have a layer of insulating plastic between the outer casing and the internal circuit, making them safe to touch even if a fault occurs.

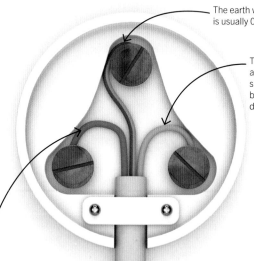

The earth wire's voltage is usually 0 V.

The live wire connects the appliance to the mains supply. This wire's voltage is between 100 V and 240 V, depending on the country.

The neutral wire completes the circuit when an appliance is switched on. Its voltage is normally 0 V.

Colour coding
It is important that each wire in a cable is connected to the correct pin in the plug and so to the correct part of the wiring in the electrical socket. For this reason, the wires in cables each have their own insulation colour. The colours vary in different parts of the world, but the functions of the three wires are the same. Colour-coding systems can change, so always consult your country's local guidelines or a qualified electrician before wiring a plug.

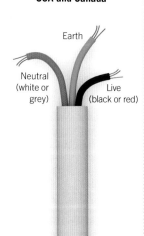

USA and Canada

Earth

Neutral (white or grey)

Live (black or red)

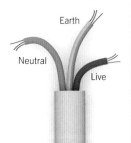

Europe, Australia, and New Zealand

Earth

Neutral

Live

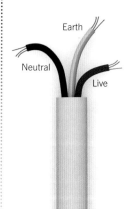

India and China

Earth

Neutral

Live

Fuses and circuit breakers

Fuses and circuit breakers are safety devices that automatically stop the flow of electricity if an electrical fault causes a dangerous surge in current.

Key facts

✓ Fuses and circuit breakers are used to protect electrical cables from overheating.

✓ Fuses must have the correct value for the appliances they are used for.

Fuses

If an electrical device develops a fault such as a broken wire, electricity can flow through the metal casing of the device, causing a dangerous surge in current that could start a fire or give someone an electric shock. Fuses contain thin wires that melt during a surge in current, breaking the circuit. It's important to choose a fuse with a rating in amps just above the current an electrical device normally uses. If the value is too low, the fuse will blow when the appliance is working normally. If the value is too high, too much current may flow, causing overheating.

This car fuse has blown – the wire inside it has melted.

This wire inside a fuse melts and breaks the circuit if the current gets too high.

⚙ Circuit breakers

A circuit breaker automatically disconnects the mains supply if the current flowing through the circuit is too high. Many circuit breakers use a coil of live wire to create an electromagnet. If the current surges, the electromagnet becomes powerful enough to separate two contacts, turning a "trip switch" to the off position and breaking the circuit.

The trip switch can be reset when the fault has been fixed.

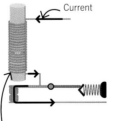

Current

In normal operation, the electromagnet is not strong enough to separate the contacts.

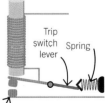

Trip switch lever   Spring

If a faulty appliance causes an increase in current, the electromagnet separates the contacts, breaking the circuit.

Preventing shocks

Sometimes a fault in an appliance can cause the outside of the appliance to become live – meaning that you can get a shock if you touch it. An electric shock hurts and can cause burns or even kill you. Earth wires and fuses (see page 181) can prevent this from happening.

Earth wires
If a fault happens in an appliance with metal casing, electricity can travel through the casing. When you touch the object, your body provides a route for electricity to reach the ground, creating a circuit and giving you a shock. Powerful devices such as washing machines have earth wires and three-pin plugs to prevent this from happening – the earth wire provides a low-resistance route to the ground. Appliances with plastic cases don't need earth wires as plastic is an insulating material.

Key facts

✓ The earth wire protects against electric shocks by providing a path for electricity to flow through if a fault happens.

✓ Appliances with plastic cases do not need to be earthed as plastic is an insulating material.

Faulty and not earthed

The person's body completes the circuit by providing a route for electricity to reach the ground.

Ground — Large current — A faulty wire allows electricity to flow through the washing machine case.

Faulty but earthed

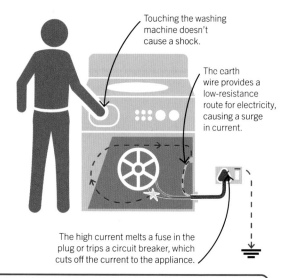

Touching the washing machine doesn't cause a shock.

The earth wire provides a low-resistance route for electricity, causing a surge in current.

The high current melts a fuse in the plug or trips a circuit breaker, which cuts off the current to the appliance.

🔍 Lightning rods

Tall buildings have lightning rods connected to the ground to provide a low-resistance route for electricity to flow during a lightning strike. Like the earth wire in an electrical appliance, this allows electrical energy to flow away safely, without harming the building or the people inside.

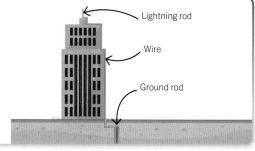

Lightning rod
Wire
Ground rod

Electrical appliances

Electrical appliances transfer the electrical energy supplied to them to sound, light, movement, or heat. The power rating on appliances tells you how much energy they use each second and therefore how expensive they are to run.

Power ratings

Electrical appliances usually have a power rating sticker on the base or on the back that tells you how much power they use in watts. The power needed depends on whether the device's main output is light, sound, movement, or heat. All appliances (except electric heaters) waste some energy as heat.

Digital radio
Appliances that transfer energy mainly to light or sound, such as radios, TVs, and light bulbs, use little energy and have a low power rating. This digital radio has a power rating of only 5 W.

ROY RADIOS 99
AC: 230–240 V~50 Hz
Power: 5 W
Made in UK

A power rating of 5 W means the radio transfers 5 J of energy every second.

Food mixer
Appliances that transfer energy mainly to movement, such as food mixers, drills, and fans, have a higher power rating.

CHOPRA CHOPPER Z50
AC: 220–240 V~50 Hz
Power: 500 W
Made in India

The blender uses 100 times as much energy per second as the radio.

Coffee maker
Appliances that transfer energy mainly by heating, such as coffee makers, ovens, and heaters, use the most energy and have high power ratings.

BARISTA BREWS 66
AC: 220–240 V~50 Hz
Power: 1200 W
Made in South Africa

The higher the power rating, the faster the coffee machine heats water.

Key facts

✓ The main power output from appliances may be light, sound, movement, or heat.

✓ All appliances (except electric heaters) waste some energy as heat.

✓ The power rating of an appliance in watts is how much energy is transferred each second.

Fuses

If an appliance is faulty, it may draw too much current from the mains supply and cause wires to overheat. To prevent this happening, high-power devices sometimes have fuses in their plugs. A fuse contains a delicate wire that melts in a power surge, breaking the circuit and switching off the appliance. You can work out the correct type of fuse to use from the device's power rating and the equation power = current × voltage ($P = I \times V$).

Question
A hairdryer runs off a 230 V mains supply and has a power rating of 1800 W. Which of the following fuses should be fitted in the plug: 5 A, 10 A, or 15 A?

Answer
Rearrange the equation to make current (I) the subject.

$$I = \frac{P}{V}$$
$$= \frac{1800 \text{ W}}{230 \text{ V}}$$
$$= 7.8 \text{ A}$$

The 5 A fuse is too small and the 15 A fuse is too large. The correct fuse rating is 10 A.

Energy use at home

The scientific unit for energy is the joule, but 1 joule is a small amount of energy – it takes at least 340 000 joules just to boil a litre of water. So instead of using joules, energy companies measure energy in kilowatt-hours (kWh).

Kilowatt-hours

Kilowatts are units of power, but kilowatt-hours are units of energy. 1 kWh is the energy transferred if you use a device with a power rating of 1 kW for an hour. Most household appliances have a power rating much lower than 1 kW. However, some devices, such as fridges and freezers, stay switched on all day, so they use a lot of energy. The amount of energy different households use varies a great deal and depends on the size of the house, the number of occupants, and the local climate, which affects heating and air-conditioner use.

Key facts

✓ The unit of energy used in energy bills is the kilowatt-hour (kWh).

✓ 1 kWh = 3 600 000 joules (3.6 MJ)

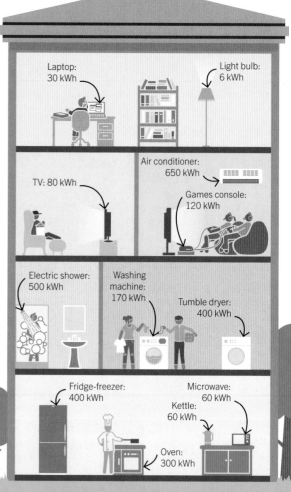

Laptop: 30 kWh

Light bulb: 6 kWh

Air conditioner: 650 kWh

TV: 80 kWh

Games console: 120 kWh

Electric shower: 500 kWh

Washing machine: 170 kWh

Tumble dryer: 400 kWh

Fridge-freezer: 400 kWh

Microwave: 60 kWh

Kettle: 60 kWh

Oven: 300 kWh

The amount of energy a house might use in one year

 Calculating energy usage

You can calculate how much energy an appliance uses by multiplying its power rating by the number of hours it's used:

> **energy transferred (kWh) = power (kW) × time (h)**

Question
An electric shower with a power rating of 7.2 kW is used for 15 minutes each day. How much energy does the shower transfer in a week?

Answer
Total number of hours used in a week = 0.25 h × 7 days
= 1.75 h
Energy transferred = 7.2 kW × 1.75 h
= 12.6 kWh

Wasted energy

All electrical devices waste some energy when we use them. Sometimes energy is wasted by sound or light, but most wasted energy is transferred to the surroundings as heat.

Heat and electricity

When electrons move through a wire or an electrical component, they collide with metal atoms and transfer some energy to them, causing the metal and its surroundings to heat up. Some devices transfer energy as heat deliberately, but in most devices the heat wastes energy. The amount of energy transferred by heating can be reduced by keeping wires short and by using good conductors, such as gold, silver, and copper.

Wasteful heating

Light bulbs transfer energy as heat and light, but only the light is a useful energy transfer.

Powerful computers use fans to dissipate unwanted heat from their central processing units.

Food mixers contain electric motors that waste some energy by generating heat and sound.

Useful heating

Kettles transfer most of the energy to the thermal energy store of the water inside, but some heat escapes to the surroundings.

Electric toasters use heat to toast bread, but a lot of energy escapes.

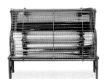

Electric heaters transfer nearly all the energy supplied to them as heat, making them very efficient.

🔍 Overheating

The heat produced by electrical devices or wires can be dangerous if it builds up – it can melt the plastic insulation around wires or start a fire. Never plug several powerful appliances into a single wall socket with an adapter as it can overload the socket and draw too much current, heating up the socket. Overheating can be prevented by using good conductors, short wires, and by plugging appliances into separate sockets. Extension cables should be unwound before use and fitted with appropriate fuses.

Overloading this extension lead caused the plastic to melt.

Power transmission

Power stations may be a long way from where electricity is used, so electricity has to be transmitted long distances by cables. All cables have resistance, which means they heat up and waste energy. The waste is reduced by using transformers to change the voltage and current of electricity in the cables.

Reducing the waste

The amount of power lost due to heating in cables can be calculated using the power equation from page 171: power loss = current² × resistance ($P = I^2 \times R$). Because power loss is proportional to current squared, the most effective way to reduce power loss is to reduce the current. This is what the transformers at electricity substations do. The same power can be transmitted with either high current and low voltage or low current and high voltage, so transformers raise the voltage for long-distance transmission and then lower it again for use in the home.

Key facts

✓ Energy is wasted when electricity is transmitted through cables.

✓ Energy loss is reduced by increasing the voltage of electricity and lowering the current.

✓ Step-up and step-down transformers in electricity substations change the voltage and current of electricity for long-distance transmission.

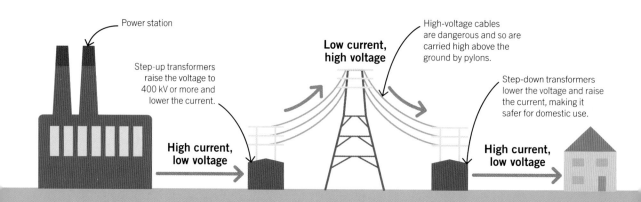

Power station

Step-up transformers raise the voltage to 400 kV or more and lower the current.

High current, low voltage

Low current, high voltage

High-voltage cables are dangerous and so are carried high above the ground by pylons.

Step-down transformers lower the voltage and raise the current, making it safer for domestic use.

High current, low voltage

 Calculating power loss

Question
If a transmission cable has a resistance of 20 Ω, how much power is wasted as heat when a current of 10 A flows? If the current is reduced by a transformer to 1 A, what will the wasted power be?

Answer
Use the equation $P = I^2 \times R$ to find both answers.

At 10 A:
$P = (10 \text{ A})^2 \times 20 \text{ Ω}$
$= 2000 \text{ W}$

At 1 A:
$P = (1 \text{ A})^2 \times 20 \text{ Ω}$
$= 20 \text{ W}$ ← The loss is 100 times smaller even though the cable has the same resistance.

Static electricity

Attracting and repelling

Have you ever noticed a jumper crackling when you pull it over your head or your hair standing on end after you brush it? These effects are caused by static electricity. Static charges can cause objects to attract or repel each other without touching.

Key facts

✓ Some objects can become charged with static electricity when rubbed.

✓ Objects can be given a positive or negative charge.

✓ Charged objects exert forces on each other: similar charges repel and opposite charges attract.

🔍 Static cling

Static electricity builds up most easily on insulating materials such as plastic and rubber. The effects are easiest to see on a dry day when there is little moisture in the air.

Plastic objects can become charged with static electricity when rubbed. For example, a comb can become charged when it moves through a person's hair.

Plastic wrap becomes charged when it unrolls. The static charge helps it cling to items of food or to itself.

Opposites attract
Static charges can be positive or negative. If two objects have opposite charges, they attract each other. Some objects become charged with static electricity when they are rubbed. For example, rubbing a glass rod gives it a charge that can attract water from a tap. The charge is caused by electrons (which are negatively charged) collecting on the glass from the material used to rub it.

The glass rod and the side of the water stream near it have opposite charges and attract each other.

The charged rod induces a charge in the water.

Similar charges repel

Objects with the same static charge repel each other. You can see this demonstrated with a Van de Graaff generator — a device that creates a positive charge on a metal dome. Anyone that touches the dome while insulated from the ground becomes positively charged too, which makes their hair stand on end.

Hairs stand on end because they all become positively charged, which makes them repel each other.

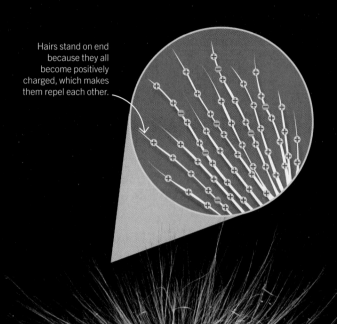

⚙ Van de Graaff generator

A Van de Graaff generator contains a moving belt made of an insulating material, such as rubber, that picks up a static charge as it moves around two nylon rollers. The charge is transferred via a small brush to an aluminium dome at the top.

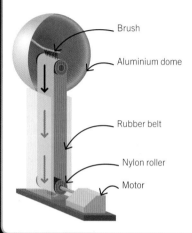

Brush

Aluminium dome

Rubber belt

Nylon roller

Motor

Attraction by induction

Rubbing a balloon on a woolly jumper causes a build-up of charge on the balloon. If you hold the balloon near a wall, it sticks to the wall. This happens because a charged object can induce an opposite charge in nearby objects.

Sticky balloon

Most objects contain equal amounts of positive and negative charge, resulting in no overall charge. However, when some objects are rubbed, electrons can break away from atoms and transfer from one object to another, giving both objects a charge. When a charged object is held close to something else, it can induce a charge in it, making them attract.

Key facts

✓ Electrons can be transferred between some objects through rubbing.

✓ Gaining electrons causes an object to become negatively charged, and losing electrons causes it to become positively charged.

✓ A charged object can induce a charge in another object, causing the two to attract.

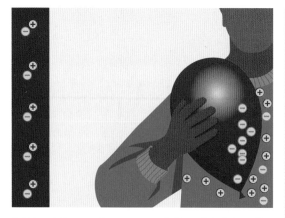

Rubbing a balloon on a jumper causes a build-up of electrons on the balloon, giving it a negative charge.

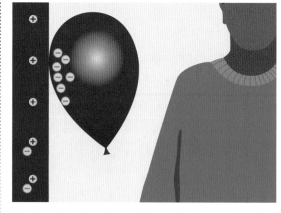

When the balloon is near the wall, the negative charge on the balloon repels electrons in the wall, making the wall's surface near the balloon positive. The two opposite charges attract and the balloon sticks to the wall.

⚙ Where static charge comes from

An atom normally contains equal numbers of protons (with a positive charge) in its nucleus and electrons (with a negative charge) surrounding the nucleus, making it electrically neutral. Rubbing some materials can transfer electrons from one object to another, causing a build-up of negative charge on one object and leaving the other object with an overall positive charge.

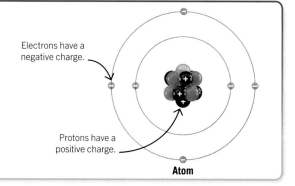

Electrons have a negative charge.

Protons have a positive charge.

Atom

Using static electricity

Static electricity is not as useful as current electricity, but some devices make use of it. For example, photocopiers, inkjet printers, and paint sprayers use static charges to guide a spray of chemicals.

Electrostatic paint sprayers
Car manufacturers use electrostatic sprayers to give cars an even coat of paint. The sprayer charges the mist of fine paint droplets, causing them to repel each other and spread widely and evenly. An opposite charge on the part being painted attracts the paint so that it coats the whole surface.

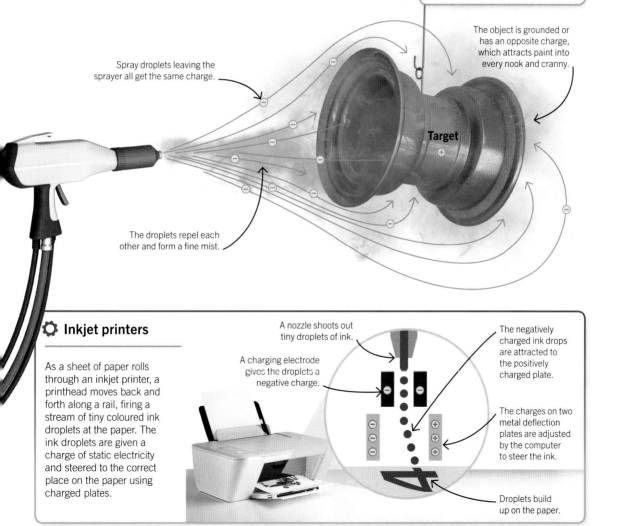

The object is grounded or has an opposite charge, which attracts paint into every nook and cranny.

Spray droplets leaving the sprayer all get the same charge.

Target

The droplets repel each other and form a fine mist.

⚙ Inkjet printers

As a sheet of paper rolls through an inkjet printer, a printhead moves back and forth along a rail, firing a stream of tiny coloured ink droplets at the paper. The ink droplets are given a charge of static electricity and steered to the correct place on the paper using charged plates.

A nozzle shoots out tiny droplets of ink.

A charging electrode gives the droplets a negative charge.

The negatively charged ink drops are attracted to the positively charged plate.

The charges on two metal deflection plates are adjusted by the computer to steer the ink.

Droplets build up on the paper.

Dangers of static electricity

Static electricity can sometimes be dangerous. If a large static charge builds up, it may cause sparks when it is released. These sparks can burn people or start fires.

Key facts

✓ Lightning and sparks are caused by the sudden discharge of static electricity.

✓ Sparks can burn people and start fires.

✓ A build-up of static charge when vehicles are being refuelled can be dangerous.

Lightning

Lightning is caused by a build-up of static electricity inside a thundercloud as water droplets and ice crystals rush past each other. It can be deadly if it strikes a person directly and can cause fires if it strikes buildings. Lightning can strike from cloud to cloud or from cloud to ground. The diagram below shows how a cloud-to-ground strike occurs.

Most lightning storms are caused by a type of cloud called cumulonimbus, which typically has a towering shape and a spreading top.

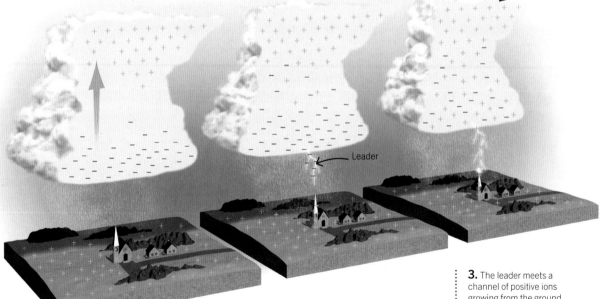

Leader

1. Strong winds inside a storm cloud cause ice crystals and droplets of water to tumble about, creating static charges. A negative charge builds up at the bottom of the cloud, inducing a positive charge in the ground.

2. Air normally acts as an insulator, but the growing electric field between the cloud and ground causes air molecules to ionize (split into charged particles). A channel of ionized air called a leader reaches down from the base of the cloud.

3. The leader meets a channel of positive ions growing from the ground and the two channels fuse, forming a charged path through which electricity can flow — a bolt of lightning.

Energy release

A bolt of lightning is a giant spark only a few centimetres wide but kilometres in length. The massive flow of electrical energy superheats the air to around 30 000°C, causing it to radiate brilliant light. The sudden release of heat makes the air expand explosively, producing the boom of thunder.

⚙ Earthing aircraft

A build-up of static electricity in fuel can be extremely dangerous – a spark could trigger an explosion. While a plane's fuel tanks are being refilled, wires are used to connect the plane to the filling truck. The wires prevent a charge building up between the two vehicles as a result of friction from the rapid movement of large volumes of fuel.

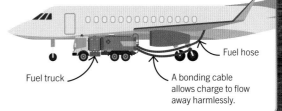

Fuel hose

Fuel truck

A bonding cable allows charge to flow away harmlessly.

Electric fields

All charged objects are surrounded by an electric field in which other charged objects experience a force. Attraction, repulsion, sparking, and other static effects are caused by electric fields.

Electric field diagrams

As electric fields are invisible, we use diagrams with lines and arrows to represent them. The arrows always show the effect the field would have on a positive charge placed within it. The three examples below show the fields around charges at a single point. The arrows show that a positive charge repels other positive charges, but a negative charge attracts positive charges. The density of the lines indicates how strong the field (and therefore the force) is.

 Key facts

- ✓ A charged object is surrounded by an electric field in which other charged objects experience a force.
- ✓ An object's electric field is strongest nearby and gets weaker with distance.
- ✓ Attraction, repulsion, and sparking are caused by electric fields.
- ✓ The strength and direction of electric fields can be shown in diagrams using arrows.

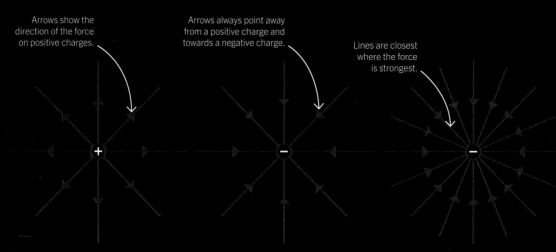

Arrows show the direction of the force on positive charges.

Arrows always point away from a positive charge and towards a negative charge.

Lines are closest where the force is strongest.

Field around a positive charge

Field around a negative charge

Field around a strong negative charge

🔍 **Parallel plates**

A pair of parallel plates with opposite charges produces a uniform electric field – the field strength is the same everywhere between the plates (except near both ends). In this photo, grains of semolina suspended in castor oil reveal the uniform electric field lines between two charged plates.

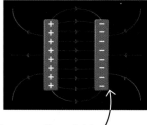

Charged plate   Grains of semolina   Charged plate

Magnetism and electromagnetism

Magnets

Magnets attract objects made from magnetic materials, such as iron, nickel, and cobalt. Magnets come in many shapes and sizes, but they all have two ends (or sides) called the north pole and the south pole.

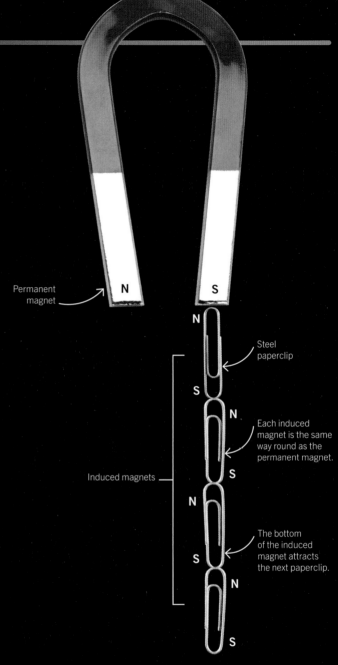

Permanent magnet

Steel paperclip

Each induced magnet is the same way round as the permanent magnet.

Induced magnets

The bottom of the induced magnet attracts the next paperclip.

Key facts

- ✓ A magnet has a north pole and a south pole.
- ✓ Opposite (unlike) poles attract each other. Similar (like) poles repel each other.
- ✓ When a piece of magnetic material is brought close to a magnet, it becomes an induced magnet.

⚙ Attracting and repelling

If you arrange two bar magnets so the north pole of one is close to the south pole of the other, they will attract each other. But bring two north poles close, or two south poles close, and the magnets will repel (push away) each other.

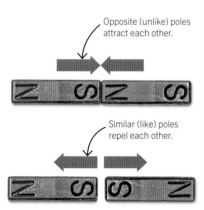

Opposite (unlike) poles attract each other.

Similar (like) poles repel each other.

Magnetism

Paperclips stick to a magnet because they are made of steel, which is a magnetic material. Magnetism is a force that works at a distance, so the paperclips are pulled even before they touch the magnet. Horseshoe magnets and bar magnets are permanent magnets – they are always magnetic. When a piece of magnetic material is brought close to a permanent magnet, it becomes a magnet itself. We call this induced magnetism. It stops being magnetic when it is taken away from the permanent magnet.

Magnetic fields

Magnetism is a force that can affect certain objects or materials from a distance, without physical contact. All magnets are surrounded by a magnetic field — a zone around the magnet in which it can exert forces on other magnets or on magnetic materials. The field around a bar magnet can be revealed by scattering iron filings over it.

Key facts

✓ **Magnets are surrounded by a magnetic field.**

✓ **The lines in a magnetic field always point from the north pole to the south pole of the magnet.**

✓ **A compass can be used to trace a magnetic field.**

Field around a bar magnet

A magnet produces a magnetic field — a zone in which magnetic materials are affected. The field curves out from the magnet's north pole and back to the south pole.

You can use a compass to trace the magnetic field around a magnet.

The compass needle points in the direction of the magnetic field.

Iron filings reveal the lines of the magnetic field around a magnet.

The closer together the lines are, the stronger the force on the iron filings at that point.

Iron filings can be harmful if they get in your eyes or are inhaled, so don't use them without teacher supervision.

The magnetic field is strongest near the poles.

⚙ Field lines

A magnetic field can be shown by drawing lines around magnets. Arrows show direction and always point from a magnetic north pole to a magnetic south pole.

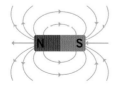

In a bar magnet, the field lines curve from the north pole to the south pole.

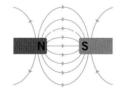

When opposite poles come close, the field lines run from the north pole of one magnet to the south pole of the other. The magnets attract each other.

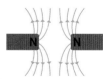

When similar poles of two magnets come close, the field lines point outwards. The magnets repel each other.

Earth's magnetic field

For many centuries, sailors navigated using compasses — tiny magnets that point north if allowed to swing freely. Compasses point north because Earth behaves like a giant magnet, with its own magnetic field.

The shape of Earth's magnetic field

At the centre of Earth is a hot, partially molten iron core that acts like a giant magnet, producing a huge magnetic field. This field extends thousands of kilometres into space and resembles the magnetic field around a bar magnet. Earth's magnetic field is dynamic — the poles are constantly moving, the strength changes over time, and every once in a while (on average, every few hundred thousand years) the north and south magnetic poles flip places.

> **Key facts**
>
> ✓ Earth's magnetic field is similar in shape to that of a bar magnet.
>
> ✓ Compasses can be used to determine the shape of the magnetic field.

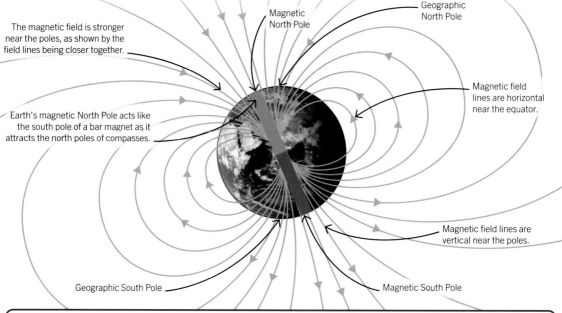

The magnetic field is stronger near the poles, as shown by the field lines being closer together.

Magnetic North Pole

Geographic North Pole

Magnetic field lines are horizontal near the equator.

Earth's magnetic North Pole acts like the south pole of a bar magnet as it attracts the north poles of compasses.

Magnetic field lines are vertical near the poles.

Geographic South Pole

Magnetic South Pole

> ⚙ **Magnetic dip**
>
> A compass contains a small magnetic needle mounted on a pivot that allows it to swing. The needle aligns with Earth's magnetic field, so as well as pointing north it tilts downwards in the northern hemisphere and upwards in the southern hemisphere. The angle of tilt, called magnetic dip or magnetic inclination, varies from 0° at the equator to 90° at the poles. Studying magnetic dip allowed scientists to work out the shape of Earth's magnetic field.
>
>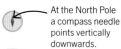
>
>
> At the North Pole a compass needle points vertically downwards.
>
> At the equator a compass needle stays horizontal relative to the ground.

Electromagnets

Electricity and magnetism are linked. An electric current creates a magnetic field around it, and we can use a coil of wire (called a solenoid) to strengthen this magnetic field. Adding an iron core to a solenoid makes the field even stronger, forming a powerful electromagnet. Electromagnets are useful because they are magnets that can be switched on and off.

Key facts

✓ A current flowing through a wire creates a circular magnetic field around the wire.

✓ When a current flows through a solenoid, the magnetic fields from the loops combine to strengthen the field inside the coil.

✓ An iron core inside the solenoid strengthens the field of an electromagnet.

Magnetic field around a wire
When an electric current flows through a wire, it forms a circular magnetic field around the wire. You can see the shape of the magnetic field by holding a compass near the wire. If you increase the current, the strength of the magnetic field increases. If you change the direction of the current, the direction of the magnetic field changes.

The magnetic field lines are closer together near the wire, where the field is strongest.

Direction of current

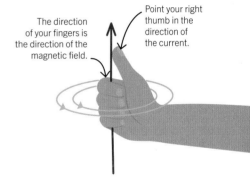

You can use your right hand, with your fingers curled, to help remember the direction of the magnetic field around a current.

The direction of your fingers is the direction of the magnetic field.

Point your right thumb in the direction of the current.

Magnetic field around a coil
The magnetic field around a single wire is weak, but if the wire is wound into a coil (called a solenoid), the fields around each loop reinforce each other. This creates a strong, uniform magnetic field inside the coil. The field outside the coil is similar to the field around a bar magnet, with north and south poles at the ends.

The magnetic field is weaker outside the coil.

The shape of the magnetic field is similar to that of a bar magnet.

The more loops of wire in the coil, the stronger the magnetic field.

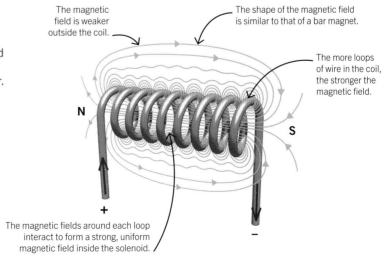

N

S

The magnetic fields around each loop interact to form a strong, uniform magnetic field inside the solenoid.

Iron core

One type of electromagnet is a solenoid with a core made of a magnetic material, which makes the magnetic field stronger. The core is usually iron, which is easy to magnetize but also loses its magnetism very easily. This is ideal for electromagnets, because it means they can be switched on and off.

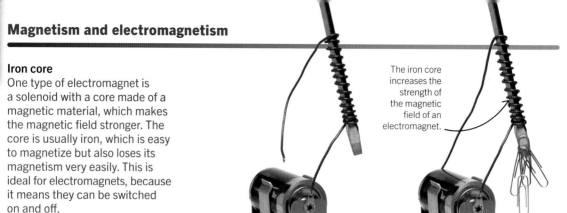

The iron core increases the strength of the magnetic field of an electromagnet.

No current   **Current flowing**

Scrapyard magnet

The grab magnets used in scrapyards are powerful electromagnets. They are used to separate magnetic metals such as iron and iron alloys from non-magnetic metals such as copper, aluminium, and lead. Separating materials this way allows them to be recycled.

Only scrap metals rich in iron are attracted to the grab magnet.

Using electromagnets

Electromagnets are very useful as they can be switched on and off and can create a variable magnetic force. They are used in many electrical devices, including loudspeakers, electric bells and buzzers, relays, and maglev trains.

Relays

A relay is an electrical switch in which a small electric current is used to turn on another circuit that has a larger current. For example, when a driver turns the key in a car, it switches on a low-current circuit with a relay switch. The relay then activates the high-current circuit that starts the motor.

Key facts

✓ Electromagnets can be switched on and off and can create a variable magnetic force.

✓ Relays allow a switch in one circuit to be used to turn a separate circuit on or off.

✓ Maglev trains use electromagnets to float above the track, allowing them to reach high speeds.

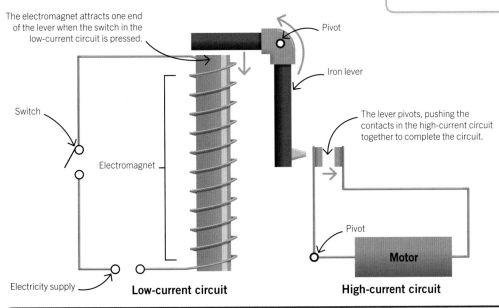

The electromagnet attracts one end of the lever when the switch in the low-current circuit is pressed.

Pivot

Iron lever

Switch

The lever pivots, pushing the contacts in the high-current circuit together to complete the circuit.

Electromagnet

Pivot

Motor

Electricity supply

Low-current circuit

High-current circuit

⚙ Maglev trains

Maglev (magnetic levitation) trains use electromagnets on the train and the track to make the train float above the track. Some of the electromagnets are also used to make the train move. Maglev trains can reach speeds of 400 km/h – far faster than conventional trains – as there is no physical contact between the train and track and therefore no friction.

Opposite poles on the train and track attract, pulling this part of the train upwards slightly to make the whole train hover.

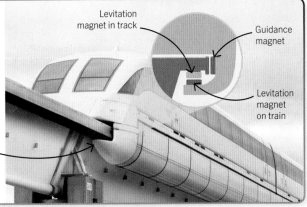

Levitation magnet in track

Guidance magnet

Levitation magnet on train

The motor effect

When a current flows through a wire, it creates a magnetic field around the wire. If the wire is also placed near a permanent magnet, the two magnetic fields interact and cause the wire to move. This is called the motor effect.

Jumping wire

In the jumping wire experiment shown below, a coil of wire is wrapped around a permanent magnet. When the circuit is switched on, the magnetic field around the wire is pushed by the permanent magnet and the wire jumps. This shows the motor effect in action.

Teacher supervision required

Key facts

✓ A wire carrying a current through an existing magnetic field experiences a force.

✓ The force caused by the interaction between a current-carrying wire and a magnet is the motor effect.

✓ You can work out the direction of the force using Fleming's left-hand rule.

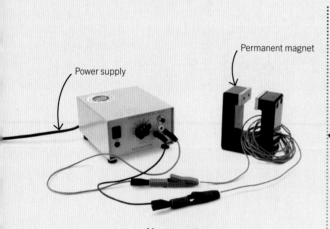

Power supply

Permanent magnet

No current

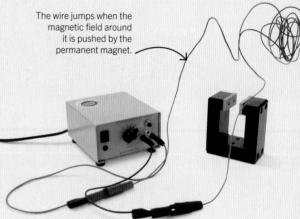

The wire jumps when the magnetic field around it is pushed by the permanent magnet.

Current flowing

⚙ Direction of the force

The force produced by the motor effect is greatest when the wire is at right angles to the permanent magnetic field. The direction of the force is at right angles to both the current and the magnetic field. Fleming's left-hand rule (see next page) helps you remember how the force, current, and magnetic field are oriented.

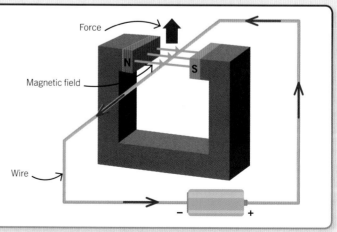

Force

Magnetic field

Wire

📑 Fleming's left-hand rule

You can work out the direction of the force produced by the motor effect by using Fleming's left-hand rule. Using your left hand, hold your thumb, index finger, and second finger at right angles. Your thumb shows the force, your index finger represents the magnetic field, and your second finger is the current.

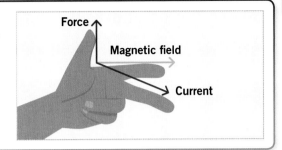

The force equation

The size of the force produced by the motor effect depends on the strength of the current, the strength of the existing magnetic field, and the length of the wire. The equation below shows how all these are related. The strength of the magnetic field is also called magnetic flux density and is measured in units called teslas (T).

The units for magnetic field strength are teslas (T), and the symbol is B.

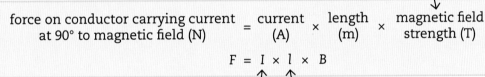

force on conductor carrying current at 90° to magnetic field (N) = current (A) × length (m) × magnetic field strength (T)

$$F = I \times l \times B$$

The symbol for current is I (upper case i).

This is a lower case L.

📑 Using the equation

Question 1
A magnet produces a magnetic flux density of 0.4 T. If a 2 m wire is at right angles to the magnetic field, with a current of 3 A flowing through it, what is the size of the force on the wire?

Answer 1
$F = I \times l \times B$
$= 3\,A \times 2\,m \times 0.4\,T$
$= 2.4\,N$

Question 2
There is a force of 1 N on a wire carrying a current of 0.2 A at right angles to a magnetic field. The length of wire in the field is 0.5 m. Calculate the magnetic flux density of the magnetic field.

Answer 2
Rearrange the equation:
$$B = \frac{F}{I \times l}$$
$$= \frac{1\,N}{0.2\,A \times 0.5\,m}$$
$$= 10\,T$$

Electric motors

Electric motors use the motor effect (see page 202) to turn a coil of wire in a magnetic field. There are many designs of motor, from the tiny ones used in watches to the large ones that power electric cars. All types depend on a wire carrying current in a magnetic field.

Key facts

✓ An electric motor uses the motor effect to make a coil of wire spin.

✓ The magnetic field is provided by permanent magnets or electromagnets.

✓ The direction of the current must be reversed every half-turn in order for the coil to keep rotating.

A simple electric motor

When a current flows through a coil of wire in a magnetic field, the force produced by the motor effect makes the coil rotate. The direction of the current needs to be switched every half-turn to prevent the coil coming to a halt. This is achieved by using a split-ring commutator.

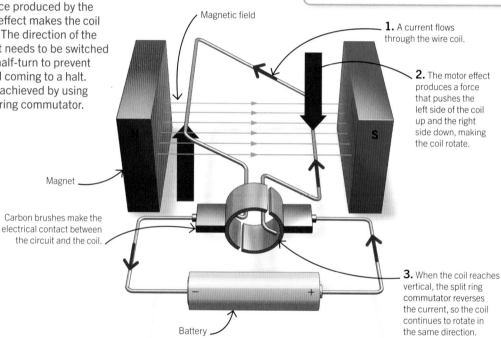

Magnetic field

Magnet

Carbon brushes make the electrical contact between the circuit and the coil.

Battery

1. A current flows through the wire coil.

2. The motor effect produces a force that pushes the left side of the coil up and the right side down, making the coil rotate.

3. When the coil reaches vertical, the split ring commutator reverses the current, so the coil continues to rotate in the same direction.

⚙ Powerful motors

Electric motors can be made more powerful by adding more turns to the coil, by increasing the current, or by increasing the power of the magnet. Electric drills also use multiple coils at different angles to maximize the force produced by the motor effect.

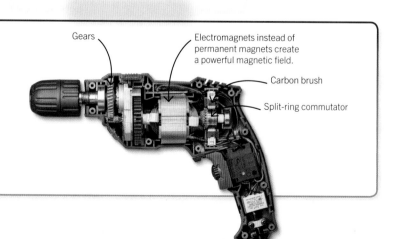

Gears

Electromagnets instead of permanent magnets create a powerful magnetic field.

Carbon brush

Split-ring commutator

Electromagnetic induction

Electricity can be generated by a process known as electromagnetic induction. When a wire that is part of a circuit is moved across a magnetic field (or when a magnetic field is moved across a wire), a voltage is "induced" in the wire, causing a current to flow.

Key facts

✓ When a wire that is part of a circuit moves through a magnetic field, a voltage is induced in the wire.

✓ The size of the induced voltage depends on the magnetic field strength and on how fast the wire is moving.

✓ The direction of the induced voltage changes if the direction of movement changes.

Moving wire experiment

In the experiment shown here, a wire connected to an ammeter is moved so it cuts through the magnetic field of a permanent magnet. Moving the wire down creates a small current, making the needle on the ammeter swing. Moving the wire up makes the needle swing the other way, and moving the wire parallel to the magnetic field induces no current. A larger current is induced by using a stronger magnet or moving the wire faster.

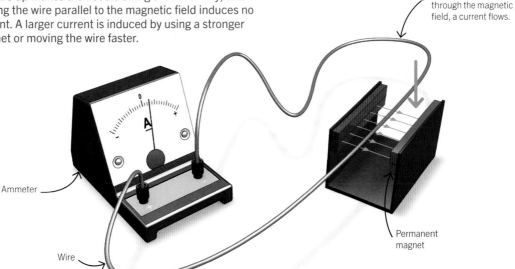

When the wire cuts through the magnetic field, a current flows.

Ammeter

Wire

Permanent magnet

⚙ Opposing forces

Moving a magnet into a coil of wire has just the same effect as moving a wire through a magnetic field – it induces a current in the wire. The induced magnetic field always opposes the movement of the original magnet, whichever way it is moving.

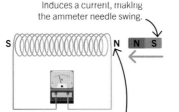

Moving a magnet into a coil induces a current, making the ammeter needle swing.

The induced magnetic field opposes the magnet's motion.

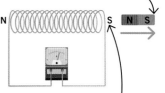

Pulling the magnet out reverses the current, making the needle swing the other way.

The induced magnetic field still opposes the magnet's motion.

Generators

Generators are devices that harness the kinetic energy of a moving object to generate electricity by electromagnetic induction (see page 205). Generators that produce alternating current (a.c.) are called alternators. Generators that produce direct current (d.c.) are called dynamos. Nearly all the electricity that powers our homes comes from generators.

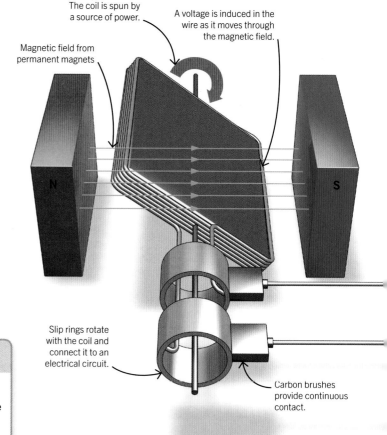

The coil is spun by a source of power.

A voltage is induced in the wire as it moves through the magnetic field.

Magnetic field from permanent magnets

N

S

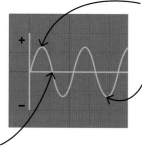

Slip rings rotate with the coil and connect it to an electrical circuit.

Carbon brushes provide continuous contact.

Key facts

✓ Generators are devices that use electromagnetic induction to generate electricity from kinetic energy.

✓ The voltage induced in a generator's coil varies as the coil spins round.

✓ An alternator produces alternating current.

✓ A dynamo produces direct current.

Alternators

An alternator has a large coil of wire that spins round within a magnetic field. As it turns, a current is induced in the wire. With each half turn, the coil's own magnetic field flips over and so the direction of the current reverses. A current that changes direction like this is called an alternating current (a.c.).

⚙ Producing alternating current

An oscilloscope (see page 115) shows that as the coil of wire in an alternator spins round, the voltage induced in it varies. The voltage peaks when the coil is orientated parallel to the magnetic field but drops to zero when the coil is perpendicular to the field. The current changes direction as the coil flips over, causing the voltage to change from positive to negative.

When the coil is orientated parallel to the magnetic field, the induced voltage is at its maximum.

No voltage is induced when the coil is perpendicular to the field.

The induced voltage reaches maximum again but with current flowing in the opposite direction.

Dynamos

Many electrical devices need direct current – current that always flows in the same direction. If a generator is connected to the external circuit by a split-ring commutator, the connections swap over each time the current in the coil reverses. As a result, the current in the external circuit always flows in the same direction instead of reversing every half-turn. A generator like this is called a dynamo.

The coil is spun by a source of power.

N

S

The split-ring commutator swaps the connections over every half turn so the current always flows in the same direction.

Carbon brushes make electrical contact between the ring and the circuit.

 Producing direct current

Unlike alternators, dynamos produce direct current (d.c.) electricity. An oscilloscope shows that the voltage rises and falls with each half-turn of the coil, but it remains positive as the direction of the electric current doesn't change.

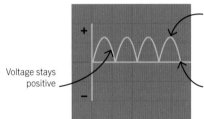

Voltage peaks when the coil is orientated parallel to the field.

Voltage stays positive

Voltage is lowest when the coil is perpendicular to the field.

Power station generators

The huge generators used in power stations use electromagnets rather than permanent magnets as they can produce a much stronger magnetic field. Instead of using the source of power to spin a coil inside a magnet, they spin electromagnets inside a huge coil of copper wire. The picture here shows a coil under construction.

When this generator is complete, electromagnets will be fitted in the centre.

Loudspeakers and microphones

Loudspeakers and headphones (which are really just small loudspeakers) use the motor effect to convert a changing electrical current into sound waves. Microphones do the opposite – they convert sound waves into a changing current using electromagnetic induction.

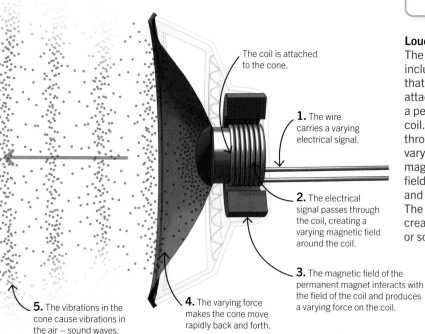

The coil is attached to the cone.

1. The wire carries a varying electrical signal.

2. The electrical signal passes through the coil, creating a varying magnetic field around the coil.

3. The magnetic field of the permanent magnet interacts with the field of the coil and produces a varying force on the coil.

4. The varying force makes the cone move rapidly back and forth.

5. The vibrations in the cone cause vibrations in the air – sound waves.

Loudspeakers
The key parts of a loudspeaker include a large cone (diaphragm) that can vibrate; a coil of wire attached to the cone's base; and a permanent magnet around the coil. A varying current passes through the coil, creating a varying magnetic field. This magnetic field interacts with the field of the permanent magnet and causes the cone to vibrate. The moving cone (diaphragm) creates variations in air pressure, or sound waves (see page 114).

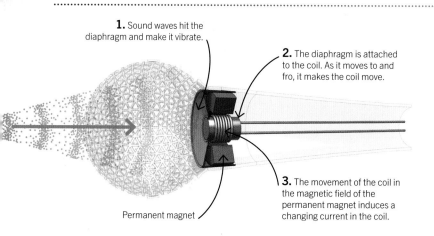

1. Sound waves hit the diaphragm and make it vibrate.

2. The diaphragm is attached to the coil. As it moves to and fro, it makes the coil move.

3. The movement of the coil in the magnetic field of the permanent magnet induces a changing current in the coil.

Permanent magnet

Microphones
A microphone contains similar components to a loudspeaker – a diaphragm, a coil attached to the diaphragm, and a permanent magnet – but they act in reverse. They convert variations in air pressure (sound waves) into a changing electrical signal by using electromagnetic induction (see page 205).

Transformers

A transformer is a device that changes the current and voltage (potential difference) of electricity by using electromagnetic induction. Huge transformers are used to reduce energy losses when electricity is transmitted over long distances, while smaller ones are used in electrical devices in the home. Transformers only work with alternating current (a.c.).

Key facts

✓ Transformers change the voltage of an a.c. supply.

✓ Step-up transformers increase the voltage; step-down transformers reduce it.

✓ The voltage output of a transformer depends on the ratio of the number of turns in its two coils.

✓ For a transformer with 100% efficiency, the power output is equal to the power input.

How transformers work

Transformers are made from two coils of wire (a primary coil and a secondary coil) on an iron core. The alternating current in the primary coil produces a magnetic field that changes direction many times each second. This induces an alternating current in the secondary coil. The two coils have a different number of loops, resulting in a change in voltage.

2. The iron core concentrates the magnetic field and carries it to the secondary coil. It does not conduct electricity between the coils.

1. When an alternating current is supplied to the primary coil, it produces an alternating magnetic field.

5 V input

10 V output

3. The changing magnetic field induces an alternating current in the secondary coil. This secondary coil has twice as many loops as the primary coil, which causes the voltage to double.

As well as housing a transformer, this camera's power supply converts alternating current (a.c.) to direct current (d.c.).

Magnetism and electromagnetism

Calculating voltage

The change in voltage made by a transformer depends on the number of turns (loops) of wire in the two coils. The ratio of the voltages in the primary and secondary coils is the same as the ratio of the number of turns on each coil.

$$\frac{\text{voltage across primary coil (V)}}{\text{voltage across secondary coil (V)}} = \frac{\text{number of turns in primary coil}}{\text{number of turns in secondary coil}}$$

$$\frac{V_p}{V_s} = \frac{N_p}{N_s}$$

Primary coil
Secondary coil

Transformer calculations

Question 1
A television uses the 230 V mains supply but only needs 46 V. Its transformer has 200 turns in the secondary coil. How many turns of wire does it have in the primary coil?

Answer 1

$$\frac{V_p}{V_s} = \frac{N_p}{N_s}$$

$$\frac{230\ V}{46\ V} = \frac{N_p}{200\ \text{turns}}$$

$$5 = \frac{N_p}{200\ \text{turns}}$$

$$N_p = 5 \times 200\ \text{turns}$$
$$= 1000\ \text{turns}$$

Question 2
A step-up transformer outside a power station has 3200 turns in its primary coil and 51 200 turns in its secondary coil. The voltage across the primary coil is 25 000 V. What's the voltage of the electricity supplied by the transformer?

Answer 2

$$\frac{V_p}{V_s} = \frac{N_p}{N_s}$$

$$\frac{25\,000\ V}{V_s} = \frac{3200\ \text{turns}}{51\,200\ \text{turns}}$$

$$\frac{25\,000\ V}{V_s} = 0.0625$$

$$V_s = \frac{25\,000\ V}{0.0625}$$
$$= 400\,000\ V$$
$$(400\ kV)$$

Power input and output

Energy cannot be created or destroyed, so if a transformer is 100 per cent efficient, its power output equals its power input. Since power = voltage × current, the relationship between the voltage and current entering and leaving a transformer can be written as shown in the equation below. (In reality, no transformer is perfectly efficient as some energy is lost to things like resistance.)

$$\begin{array}{c}\text{voltage across} \\ \text{primary coil (V)}\end{array} \times \begin{array}{c}\text{current in} \\ \text{primary coil (A)}\end{array} = \begin{array}{c}\text{voltage across} \\ \text{secondary coil (V)}\end{array} \times \begin{array}{c}\text{current in} \\ \text{secondary coil (A)}\end{array}$$

Primary coil — $V_p \times I_p = V_s \times I_s$ — Secondary coil

Using the power equation

Question
A transformer has a voltage across the secondary coil of 12 V and a current of 0.8 A. The current in the primary coil is 0.04 A. Calculate the voltage across the primary coil.

Answer
$$V_p \times I_p = V_s \times I_s$$
$$V_p \times 0.04\ A = 12\ V \times 0.8\ A$$
$$V_p = \frac{12\ V \times 0.8\ A}{0.04\ A}$$
$$= 240\ V$$

Matter

States of matter

All matter is made of billions of tiny particles. Solids, liquids, and gases have different properties because of the way their particles are arranged.

 Key facts

✓ **All matter is made of billions of tiny particles.**
✓ **The particles in solids are held close together in fixed arrangements.**
✓ **The particles in liquids are close together but can move around.**
✓ **The particles in gases are a long way apart, with relatively weak forces between them.**

Solids
The particles in a solid are held closely together in fixed arrangements by powerful forces. This is why solids keep their shape and are difficult to compress (squash).

Gold

Particles in a solid

Liquids
The particles in a liquid are close together but the forces between them are not as strong as in solids. As a result, liquids can be poured and take the shape of the container, but they are difficult to compress.

Water

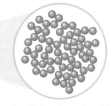

Particles in a liquid

Gases
The particles in a gas are a long way apart and there are only very weak forces between them. Gases spread out to fill their containers and are easy to compress.

Iodine vapour

Particles in a gas

🔍 Conservation of mass

When an ice cube melts, its particles end up in a different arrangement. But all the same particles are still present, so the mass of the water is the same as the mass of ice. We say that the mass is conserved. The same thing happens when the water evaporates to form a gas or the gas condenses back into a liquid.

Changes of state

Solids, liquids, and gases are three states of matter. Each state has its own characteristics, and a material can change from one state to another. A change of state is a physical change rather than a chemical change as no chemical reactions take place.

Changing state

Water can exist in three different states: as a solid (ice), a liquid, and a gas (steam or water vapour). The temperature at which water boils is called the boiling point. The temperature at which it freezes is called the freezing point.

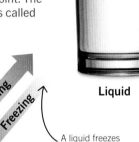

Liquid

A solid melts to form a liquid.

Melting

Freezing

A liquid boils or evaporates to form a gas.

Boiling

Condensing

The mist from a boiling kettle is condensed water. Water vapour is invisible.

A liquid freezes (solidifies) to form a solid.

A gas condenses to form a liquid.

Solid

Gas

Steam (water vapour)

Deposition is a gas changing straight to a solid without becoming liquid first.

Deposition

Sublimation

Sublimation is a solid changing straight to gas without becoming liquid first.

🔍 **Clouds and steam**

Steam is an invisible gas. The white cloud we often call steam actually consists of lots of tiny drops of liquid water floating in the air.

Steam emerging from a boiling kettle is invisible. As it cools, it condenses to form clouds of liquid drops.

The clouds we see in the sky are made up of water drops or tiny ice crystals.

When humans or other animals breathe out on a cold day, water vapour in breath condenses into liquid droplets, forming visible mist.

Particles in motion

The particles in fluids (liquids and gases) are continually moving. As a result, they gradually spread from areas of high concentration to areas of low concentration – a process called diffusion. Particle movement also causes Brownian motion – the random jiggling motion of small specks of matter (such as dust particles) floating in air or water.

Diffusion

Diffusion causes different liquids or gases to gradually mix together. Think of spraying perfume into the air. A breeze will spread the smell quickly, but the smell will spread even in still air. This happens because the particles in fluids are moving all the time. A substance will spread out from a place where it is concentrated into places where it is less concentrated.

 Key facts

✓ **Particles in fluids (liquids and gases) are moving around all the time.**

✓ **Particle movement causes different fluids to mix by diffusion.**

✓ **Substances diffuse from places with a high concentration to places with a low concentration.**

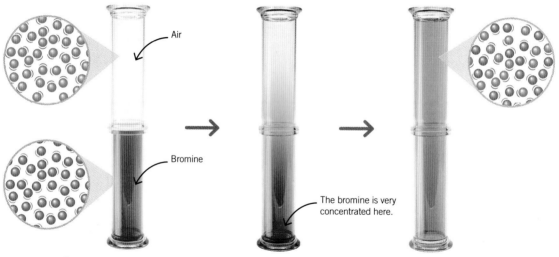

Air

Bromine

The bromine is very concentrated here.

1. A jar of bromine gas and a jar of air are placed together, with a glass barrier between them.

2. When the barrier is removed, bromine diffuses into the air, and air diffuses into the bromine.

3. Eventually, the gases are evenly mixed by diffusion.

⚙ Brownian motion

Have you ever noticed specks of dust dancing about in a beam of light? Most of the movement is due to air currents, but dust and smoke particles also jitter around in still air. This effect is called Brownian motion, after the Scottish scientist Robert Brown. He studied it in 1827, but it wasn't until 1905 that Albert Einstein explained what causes it: the specks of dust keep being hit by fast-moving air particles, making them move randomly.

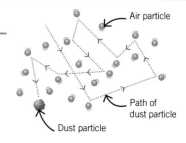

Air particle

Path of dust particle

Dust particle

Heat expansion

The way particles move depends on their temperature. When a substance is heated, its particles move faster, which makes the substance take up more space – it expands.

Expanding solids

Unlike gas and liquid particles, which move about separately, the particles in solids are fixed in place. However, they are not motionless – they continually vibrate (move back and forth). When solids are heated, the particles vibrate faster and further, making the solid expand.

 Key facts

✓ Particles in solids vibrate all the time, and particles in fluids move around.

✓ Particles vibrate or move around faster when a material is warmer.

✓ Materials expand when they are heated and contract when they cool.

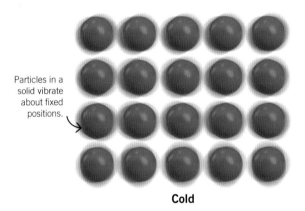

Particles in a solid vibrate about fixed positions.

Cold

The particles vibrate more after heating and take up more space.

Heat

The space between particles increases.

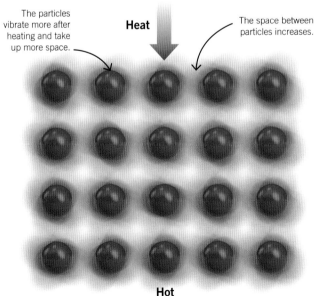

Hot

⚙ Thermal expansion

The expansion of materials as they get hotter is called thermal expansion. Thermal expansion can be useful, but it can also be a nuisance at times.

Hot-air balloons use a burner to heat up the air inside the balloon. The hot air expands, which makes it less dense than the air outside. This makes the balloon rise.

Thermometers use thermal expansion of liquids to measure temperature. As the liquid inside the bulb gets hotter, it expands up the thin glass tube inside the thermometer.

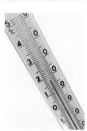

Expansion joints allow bridges to expand a little in hot weather and contract in cold weather. If these mobile joints were not used, the forces caused by expansion and contraction could bend or break the structure. Engineers design expansion joints to allow for these changes in size.

Density

We think of metal as being heavier than wood, but this is not always true. The weight of an object depends on its size as well as what it's made of, so a small piece of metal weighs less than a large piece of wood. Density is a way of comparing materials by saying how much mass there is in a certain volume.

Key facts

✓ Density is the mass of a substance in a certain volume.

✓ The density of a material depends on the mass of its particles and on how closely packed they are.

✓ Materials expand when heated, reducing their density.

Density and particles

A brick and a sponge have about the same volume, but the brick weighs much more because it is far more dense. The brick has more mass than the sponge because it has fewer air spaces within it and because it's made of elements with a greater atomic mass than those in the sponge.

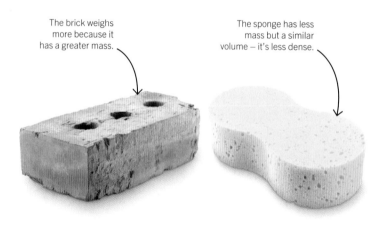

The brick weighs more because it has a greater mass.

The sponge has less mass but a similar volume – it's less dense.

🔎 Density and states of matter

When a substance is heated but its mass stays the same, it expands and its volume increases, making it less dense. Changes of state (such as melting or evaporating) also affect density. This is because the particles usually become less tightly packed when a substance melts to become a liquid or evaporates to become a gas.

The particles in solids are usually tightly packed, making solids more dense than liquids or gases.

The particles in liquids are usually less tightly packed than in solids, making liquids less dense than solids.

The particles in a gas spread out, giving gases very low density.

🔎 Water and ice

When most substances freeze, the particles get a little closer together. This means that the solid is more dense than the same substance as a liquid. However, water is unusual. When it freezes, the particles link together in a way that spreads them further apart, which makes ice less dense than cold water. This is why ice cubes float in a drink and icebergs float in the sea.

Finding the density

The density of a substance is its mass divided by its volume. This is easy to find for a liquid, but to calculate the density of a solid you first need to measure its volume. There are two different ways of doing this, depending on whether the object has an irregular or a regular shape.

The displacement method

To measure the density of an irregular object, use a special container called a displacement can or eureka can. Fill the displacement can with water to just below the spout. Then lower the irregular object into the water. The volume of the object is equal to the volume of water displaced. Place the object on a balance to find its mass, and then use the formula below to calculate density.

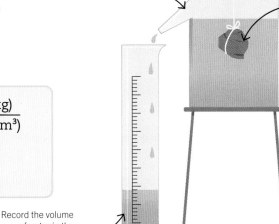

Displacement can

If the object floats, push it down until it is just under the surface.

$$\text{Density (kg/m}^3) = \frac{\text{mass (kg)}}{\text{volume (m}^3)}$$

$$\rho = \frac{m}{V}$$

The symbol for density is the Greek letter rho (pronounced "roe").

Record the volume of water in the measuring cylinder.

Density of a regular object

To calculate the density of a regularly shaped object, you first need to work out its volume. You can do this for a cube or a rectangular prism by measuring its dimensions and using the formula volume = length × width × height. Then use a balance to measure the object's mass, and finally use the density formula to work out the answer.

Question

Iron has a density of about 8000 kg/m³. What is the mass of a cube of iron with edges 5 m long?

Answer

1. First work out the cube's volume.
   Volume = 5 m × 5 m × 5 m
   = 125 m³
2. Rearrange the density equation to find the mass.
   Mass = density × volume
   = 8000 kg/m³ × 125 m³
   = 1 000 000 kg

Internal energy

The particles in objects are always in motion – either vibrating back and forth (in solids) or moving about separately (in liquids and gases). When you heat an object, the particles within it gain kinetic energy and move faster. The total kinetic and potential energy of all the particles in an object make up its store of internal energy (thermal energy).

Internal energy and temperature

The internal energy of an object is not the same as its temperature. Temperature is a measure of the average kinetic energy of the particles – the faster the particles are moving, the higher the temperature. But temperature is not a measure of an object's total internal energy. A large object can store more internal energy than a small object even if its temperature is lower.

Key facts

✓ Heating transfers energy to the kinetic energy stores of particles in an object, making them move faster.

✓ The internal energy (thermal energy) of an object is the total kinetic and potential energy of all its particles.

✓ Temperature and internal energy are not the same thing.

✓ The temperature of an object is a measure of the average kinetic energy of its particles.

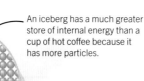

An iceberg has a much greater store of internal energy than a cup of hot coffee because it has more particles.

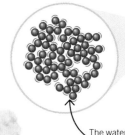

The water particles in a hot drink are moving faster than in ice, giving it a higher temperature. But a cup of coffee has less internal energy than an iceberg because it has fewer particles.

⚙ Cooling by evaporation

Why does a wet towel feel cold? The particles in water are always moving but not at the same speed – some move much faster than others. When water evaporates, it's the fastest particles that escape. The particles left behind therefore have a lower average speed. Since temperature depends on the particles' average speed, the temperature of the remaining water falls – the towel gets cold.

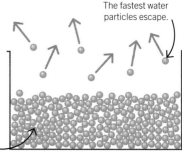

The fastest water particles escape.

The slowest particles are left behind.

Specific heat capacity

The amount of heat energy needed to make something hotter varies a lot from one substance to another. For instance, you need nearly 10 times as much energy to heat water by 1°C as you need to heat the same mass of iron by 1°C. We say that water has a higher specific heat capacity than iron.

Key facts

✓ Different substances require different amounts of heat energy to raise their temperature by the same amount.

✓ The specific heat capacity of a material is the amount of energy in joules needed to raise the temperature of 1 kg of the material by 1°C.

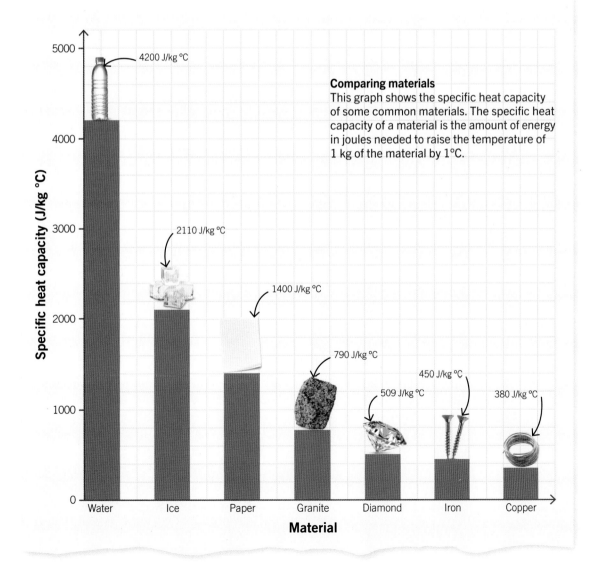

Comparing materials
This graph shows the specific heat capacity of some common materials. The specific heat capacity of a material is the amount of energy in joules needed to raise the temperature of 1 kg of the material by 1°C.

Formula for specific heat capacity

The formula below shows how we can use the specific heat capacity of a substance to work out how much energy is needed to raise its temperature.

$$\underset{\text{thermal energy (J)}}{\text{change in}} = \underset{\text{(kg)}}{\text{mass}} \times \underset{\text{capacity (J/kg °C)}}{\text{specific heat}} \times \underset{\text{temperature (°C)}}{\text{change in}}$$

$$\Delta E = m \times c \times \Delta T$$

The triangle symbol is the Greek letter delta and means a change in quantity.

This is the unit of specific heat capacity.

🖩 Calculating change in temperature

Question

This cup holds 300 g (0.3 kg) of tea. If the tap water used to brew the tea was 7°C, and the specific heat capacity of water is 4200 J/kg °C, how much energy was needed to bring the water to boiling point?

Answer

1. First work out the change in temperature (ΔT):
   $\Delta T = 100°C - 7°C = 93°C$.
2. Now work out the change in the water's store of internal energy (ΔE):
   $\Delta E = m \times c \times \Delta T$
   $= 0.3 \text{ kg} \times 4200 \text{ J/kg °C} \times 93°C$
   $= 117\,180 \text{ J} (117.2 \text{ kJ})$

⚙ Sea breezes

If you live near the coast, you've probably noticed that the wind often blows in from the sea on sunny days. This happens because the land has a lower specific heat capacity than the sea. When the Sun shines, it takes less energy to warm the land than the sea, so the land warms up faster and heats the air above it. The warmer air over the land rises in a convection current (see page 48), which draws in cooler air from the sea.

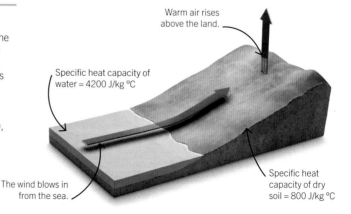

Warm air rises above the land.

Specific heat capacity of water = 4200 J/kg °C

The wind blows in from the sea.

Specific heat capacity of dry soil = 800 J/kg °C

Finding specific heat capacity

You can find the specific heat capacity of a substance by measuring the energy needed to heat up a known mass by a certain temperature. The accuracy of the result depends on how much energy escapes to the surroundings during the experiment.

Specific heat capacity of aluminium

This page shows how to measure the specific heat capacity of a 1 kg cylinder of aluminium, but you can use the same technique for a different mass or a different kind of metal. The metal is heated by an electric heater, and a joulemeter measures how much electrical energy is used. The method and results are shown on the next page.

Teacher supervision required

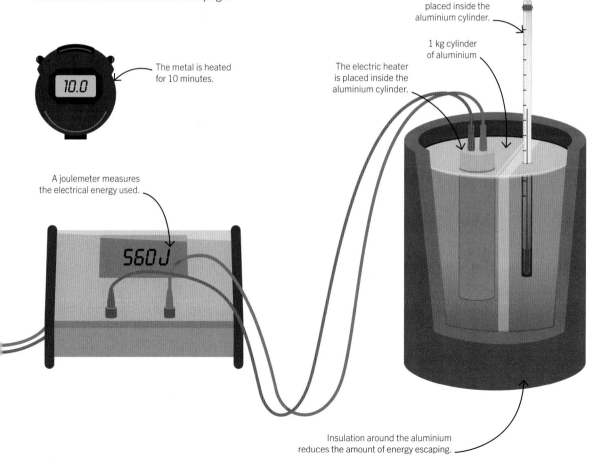

The thermometer is placed inside the aluminium cylinder.

1 kg cylinder of aluminium

The metal is heated for 10 minutes.

The electric heater is placed inside the aluminium cylinder.

A joulemeter measures the electrical energy used.

Insulation around the aluminium reduces the amount of energy escaping.

Method

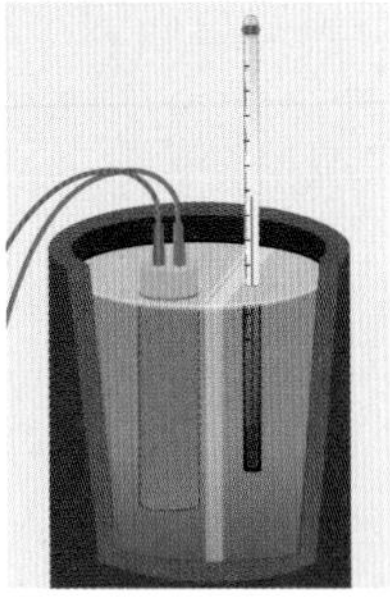

1. The aluminium cylinder has two holes drilled in it. Place the electric heater in the large hole and the thermometer in the small hole. Put a little oil in the thermometer hole to help conduct heat from the metal to the thermometer.

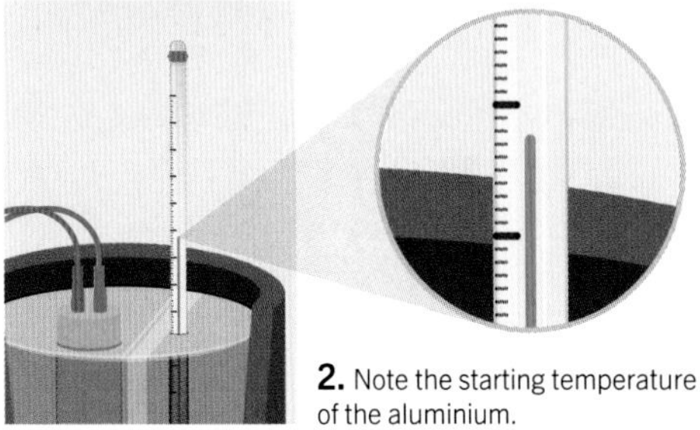

2. Note the starting temperature of the aluminium.

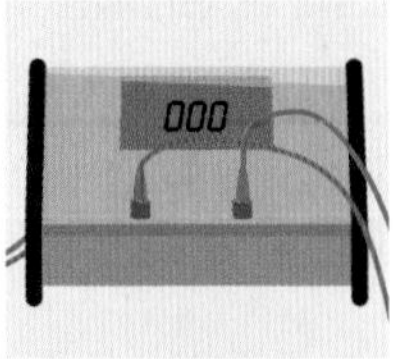

3. Zero the joulemeter and then switch on the heater.

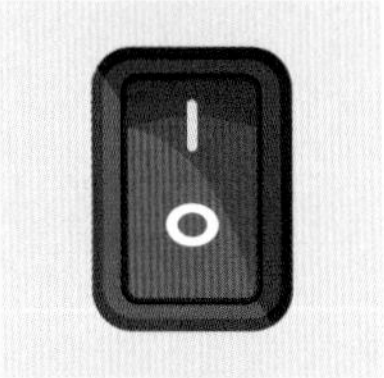

4. After 10 minutes, switch off the heater.

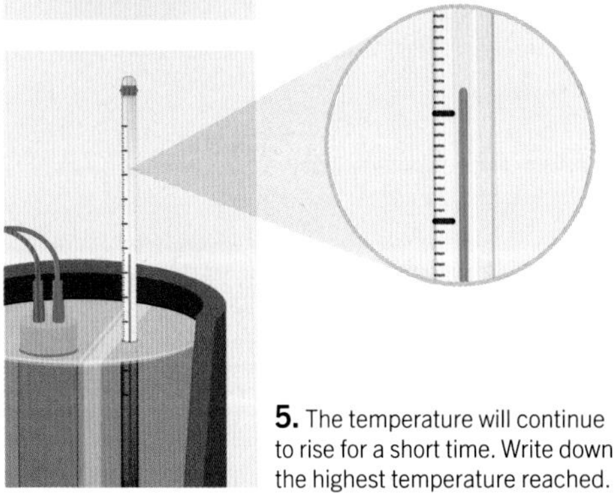

5. The temperature will continue to rise for a short time. Write down the highest temperature reached.

Results

1. Record your results in a table like this one.

Mass of aluminium	**1 kg**
Starting temperature	**18°C**
Highest temperature	**42°C**
Energy transferred	**22 313 J**

2. Calculate the temperature change:
$\Delta T = 42°C - 18°C = 24°C$

3. Now use the equation from page 220 to calculate the specific heat capacity. Rearrange it to calculate c:

$$\Delta E = m \times c \times \Delta T$$

$$c = \frac{\Delta E}{m \times \Delta T} = \frac{22\,313 \text{ J}}{1 \text{ kg} \times 24°C} = 930 \text{ J/kg °C}$$

Evaluation

You can work out how accurate your measurement was by comparing your result to the true specific heat capacity of aluminium, which is 897 J/kg °C. Some of the energy will have escaped to the surroundings during your investigation, so the energy value you used in your calculation is probably too high, giving an overestimate of aluminium's specific heat capacity. You could improve the accuracy of the experiment by putting insulation over the top of the metal block, leaving holes for the wires and the thermometer.

Heating curves

Transferring energy to a substance by heating normally makes its temperature rise. However, when solids melt or when liquids boil, they take in energy without a change of temperature. This practical investigates what happens when you heat ice to make it melt. The results form a graph called a heating curve.

Heating ice
A thermometer is placed in a tube of crushed ice, which is then placed in a beaker of hot water. The temperature is recorded regularly until after all the ice has melted.

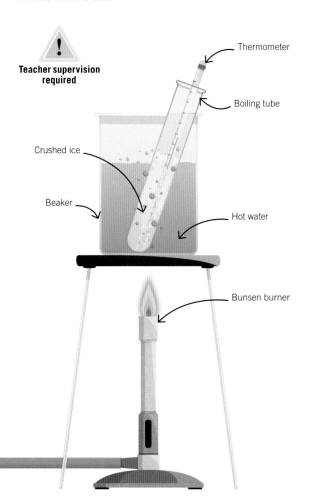

Teacher supervision required

- Thermometer
- Boiling tube
- Crushed ice
- Beaker
- Hot water
- Bunsen burner

🗐 Method

1. Half fill a boiling tube with ice and put a thermometer in it. Record the temperature of the ice.

2. Put the boiling tube into a beaker of hot water. Keep the water hot using a Bunsen burner.

3. Record the temperature of the ice every minute. Note the time when the temperature reaches 0°C and the ice starts to melt.

4. Note the time when the ice has completely melted. Keep taking the temperature for another three minutes.

🗐 Results

Use your results to plot a line graph of temperature (y-axis) against time (x-axis). When you put the tube of ice into the water bath, the temperature starts to rise, which is why the first part of the graph is an upward slope. When the temperature reaches 0°C, the ice starts to melt and the temperature remains constant even though energy is still being transferred from the hot water. This energy, called latent heat, melts the ice rather than raising the temperature, so the middle part of the graph is flat. After all the ice melts, the temperature rises again.

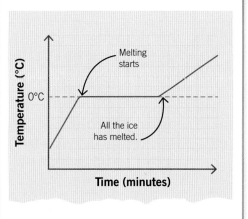

Temperature and changes of state

Energy is needed to melt a substance or make it boil. The energy needed to do this is called latent heat. When a gas condenses or a liquid solidifies, the latent heat is released again.

Heating and cooling curves

The graph below shows how temperature changes as a substance changes state. When a substance melts or boils, the energy supplied is used to overcome the forces between the particles, so the temperature remains the same, resulting in a flat section on the graph. When a gas condenses or when a liquid freezes, the formation of bonds releases energy and so keeps the temperature constant.

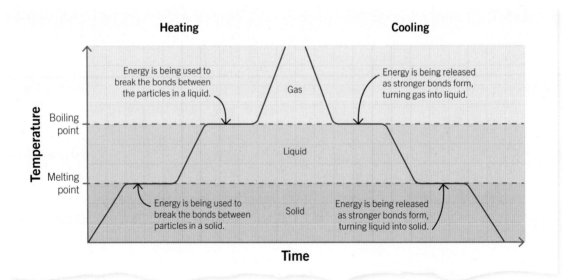

Heating   **Cooling**

Energy is being used to break the bonds between the particles in a liquid.

Energy is being released as stronger bonds form, turning gas into liquid.

Gas

Boiling point

Liquid

Melting point

Energy is being used to break the bonds between particles in a solid.

Solid

Energy is being released as stronger bonds form, turning liquid into solid.

Temperature

Time

⚙ Evaporation and boiling

Evaporation can happen from the surface of a liquid at any temperature. For example, puddles dry up even though the temperature of the water in them never reaches boiling point. Boiling happens when water turns to gas so quickly that lots of bubbles form deep within the liquid. These bubbles contain water vapour, not air.

Bubbles of water vapour

Latent heat calculations

Latent heat is the energy needed to change a solid to a liquid (called the latent heat of fusion) or a liquid to a gas (the latent heat of vaporization) without changing the temperature. When the reverse happens and a gas condenses or a liquid freezes, latent heat is released.

Key facts

✓ Latent heat is the energy needed to change a solid to a liquid or a liquid to a gas.

✓ The same amount of energy is released when the reverse state change happens.

✓ Specific latent heat is the energy needed to change the state of 1 kg of a substance at a constant temperature. Its unit is J/kg.

Latent heat of fusion
You can calculate how much energy is needed to melt a given mass of ice (without changing the temperature) by using the equation below. The equation uses a value called specific latent heat, which is the amount of energy needed to change the state of 1 kg of a substance. The example below uses the specific latent heat of fusion for water. Every substance has a different specific latent heat of fusion and vaporization.

energy for a change of state (J) = mass (kg) × specific latent heat (J/kg)

$$E = m \times L$$

For instance, to melt an ice igloo with a mass of 750 kg:
energy for a change of state (J) = 750 kg × 334 000 J/kg
= 250 500 000 J or 251 MJ

 Scalding steam

Be careful you don't scald yourself when your hand is near the spout of a boiling kettle. Steam can cause a nasty scald partly because it releases latent heat when it condenses. The latent heat of vaporization is much higher than the latent heat of fusion. This is because more energy is needed to separate particles completely to turn a liquid into a gas than is needed to turn a solid into a liquid.

Question
How much energy is transferred if 1 g of steam condenses? The specific latent heat of vaporization of water is 2 256 000 J/kg.

Answer
First convert the mass into kilograms: 1 g = 0.001 kg
energy released = $m \times L$
= 0.001 kg × 2 256 000 J/kg
= 2256 J

Pressure

Surface pressure

When you press on an object, the force might be spread across your hand or concentrated in the tip of one finger. Pressure is a measure of how much a force is concentrated by the surface area it acts through. What happens to an object when a force acts on it can depend on the pressure.

Raising the pressure
Pressing a balloon with a fingertip squashes it, but applying the same force with a pin bursts the balloon. The tip of the pin has an extremely small surface area, so the same force produces a much greater pressure. You can calculate pressure using the equation below. Pressure is the force per unit of surface area. We measure it in units called pascals: 1 Pa is 1 N of force applied over 1 m².

$$\text{pressure (Pa)} = \frac{\text{force (N)}}{\text{area (m}^2)}$$

$$p = \frac{F}{A}$$

Applying a force with a tiny surface area creates high pressure and bursts the balloon.

Key facts

✓ Pressure is the force per unit of surface area.

✓ The effect a force has on a surface depends on the pressure it exerts.

✓ The pascal (Pa) is a unit of pressure and represents 1 N of force per square metre.

 Calculating pressure

Question
A suitcase weighing 15 N is placed on a bed. Its base is 0.8 m long and 0.5 m wide. How much pressure does it exert on the bed?

Answer
First calculate the surface area in square metres:
$A = 0.8 \text{ m} \times 0.5 \text{ m}$
$\quad = 0.4 \text{ m}^2$
Now use the pressure equation to find the answer.
$p = \dfrac{F}{A}$
$\quad = \dfrac{15 \text{ N}}{0.4 \text{ m}^2}$
$\quad = 37.5 \text{ Pa}$

Atmospheric pressure

The atmosphere is the layer of air that surrounds Earth. Atmospheric pressure is the pressure on Earth's surface caused by the weight of this air. It is greatest at lowest altitudes and falls with increasing height above the ground.

Key facts

✓ Atmospheric pressure is the pressure on Earth's surface caused by the weight of air in the atmosphere.

✓ Atmospheric pressure falls with increasing altitude.

What is atmospheric pressure?

When a glass of water with a card on top is turned upside down, the card stays in place, held by atmospheric pressure. Air particles are continually flying around at hundreds to thousands of miles per hour and bouncing off things, creating pressure. Although we can't see or feel it, atmospheric pressure acts on us all the time from every direction.

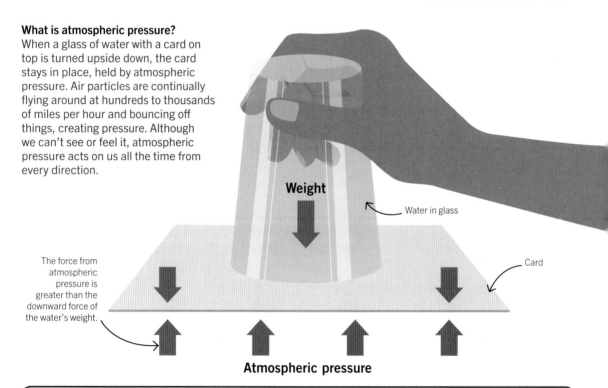

Weight

Water in glass

The force from atmospheric pressure is greater than the downward force of the water's weight.

Card

Atmospheric pressure

🔍 Pressure and altitude

When you climb a mountain, the pressure falls as you get higher. This is because pressure is caused by the weight of the atmosphere, and the higher you climb, the less air there is above you. As altitude increases, the air also becomes less dense, making it harder to breathe. This happens because gases, unlike liquids, are compressible. The higher pressure at sea level squeezes air into a smaller space than the lower pressure at high altitudes.

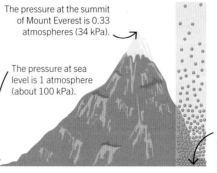

The pressure at the summit of Mount Everest is 0.33 atmospheres (34 kPa).

The pressure at sea level is 1 atmosphere (about 100 kPa).

Air particles are squeezed together, making air more dense.

Pressure in a liquid

The pressure on an object submerged in liquid is caused by the weight of the column of liquid above it. Pressure in liquids varies with depth and density: it's higher at greater depths and in denser liquids.

📌 Key facts

✓ Pressure in a liquid increases with depth and with density.

✓ Total pressure underwater equals pressure due to the water plus pressure due to the atmosphere.

Pressure at sea level = 100 000 Pa pressure

Depth and pressure
Divers experience more pressure the deeper they swim. This is because the height of the column of water above them increases. Unlike pressure in a gas, pressure in a liquid increases linearly: if a diver swims twice as deep, they experience twice the pressure. The total pressure on a diver equals pressure due to the water plus atmospheric pressure.

Depth = 5 m
Pressure = 150 000 Pa

Pressure acts on a diver from all directions.

Depth = 10 m
Pressure = 200 000 Pa

Pressure equation
You can calculate pressure on an object in a liquid with this equation. The height of the liquid above the object is h, the density of the liquid is ρ, and g is gravitational field strength (10 N/kg near the surface of Earth).

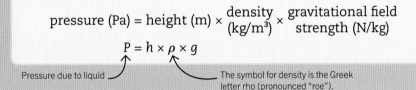

$$\text{pressure (Pa)} = \text{height (m)} \times \frac{\text{density}}{(\text{kg/m}^3)} \times \frac{\text{gravitational field}}{\text{strength (N/kg)}}$$

$$P = h \times \rho \times g$$

Pressure due to liquid

The symbol for density is the Greek letter rho (pronounced "roe").

🗐 Calculating pressure

Question
The density of water is 1000 kg/m³. Calculate the total pressure experienced by a penguin diving 30 m to catch fish if the pressure at sea level is 100 000 Pa.

Answer
First calculate the pressure due to the water at 30 m depth.
$P = 30$ m $\times 1000$ kg/m³ $\times 10$ N/kg
$= 300 000$ Pa
Then add the pressure at sea level to find the answer.
Total pressure $= 300 000$ Pa $+ 100 000$ Pa
$= 400 000$ Pa (400 kPa)

Floating and sinking

Apples float on the water surface, strawberries sink, but fish and dolphins do neither. Whether an object floats or sinks depends on the forces acting on it.

Upthrust

Because pressure increases as you go deeper underwater, a submerged object experiences greater pressure on its bottom surface than on top. This difference results in an overall upward force: upthrust. If the upthrust is greater than the object's weight, it will float. If the upthrust is less, it sinks.

The weight of the apple pushes down.

Upthrust on the apple is greater than its weight, so the apple floats.

The weight of the strawberry pushes down.

Upthrust on the strawberry is less than its weight, so the strawberry sinks.

Density and buoyancy

The upthrust on an object is equal to the weight of the water it displaces. If the object is less dense than water, the water it displaces weighs more than the object, so the upthrust exceeds its weight and it floats. Likewise, if the object is more dense than water, it sinks. Steel is denser than water, but a steel ship floats because it contains large air spaces, making it less dense overall than water. This is why ships weighing half a million tonnes don't sink.

Barometers and manometers

Barometers and manometers are instruments used to measure pressure in fluids. Barometers measure atmospheric pressure. Manometers measure the difference in pressure between two gases.

Barometers

There are several different types of barometer. A Goethe barometer (below) consists of a glass container that is half-filled with water and has a long, open-ended spout. When atmospheric pressure rises, the water level in the spout drops. Changes in atmospheric pressure can be used to predict the weather because high pressure usually brings fine weather, whereas low pressure brings changeable weather.

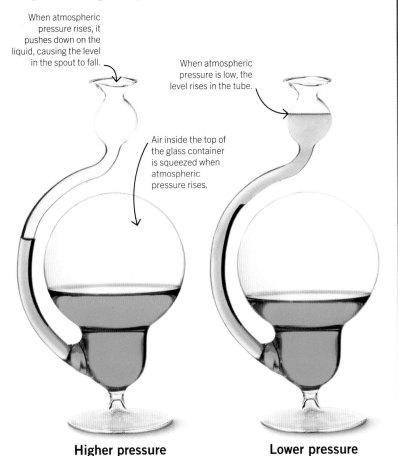

When atmospheric pressure rises, it pushes down on the liquid, causing the level in the spout to fall.

When atmospheric pressure is low, the level rises in the tube.

Air inside the top of the glass container is squeezed when atmospheric pressure rises.

Higher pressure

Lower pressure

Manometers

The simplest type of manometer is a U-shaped tube partially filled with liquid. When the manometer is not connected to anything, atmospheric pressure acts on both surfaces and the levels are equal. Applying gas pressure to one end pushes liquid around the tube.

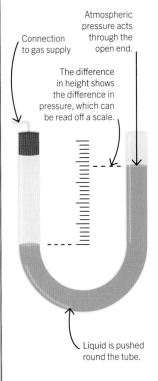

Connection to gas supply

Atmospheric pressure acts through the open end.

The difference in height shows the difference in pressure, which can be read off a scale.

Liquid is pushed round the tube.

Pressure in gases

A gas is made up of particles that are in random motion, colliding with each other and with other objects. This creates pressure.

Trapped gas

When a gas is trapped inside a container, the gas particles constantly collide with the walls of the container and exert tiny forces, creating pressure. The more gas particles there are in the container, the greater the number of collisions and the greater the pressure. This is why the pressure in a bicycle tyre rises when more air is pumped into it. If the temperature of a gas rises, the speed of the particles increases. This causes pressure to rise because the particles hit the walls of the container harder and more often.

Key facts

✓ A gas trapped in a container exerts pressure because the gas particles collide with the container walls.

✓ As the temperature of a gas rises, the speed of particles increases and so does the pressure.

✓ The theoretical temperature at which all the particles in a gas are still is called absolute zero.

✓ The Kelvin (K) scale for measuring temperature begins at absolute zero.

As a particle strikes the wall, it exerts a force.

Gas particles are in constant random motion.

As pressure inside rises, the tyre feels firmer.

⚙ Absolute zero

The temperature of a substance is a measure of the average kinetic energy of its particles. The faster the particles are moving, the more kinetic energy they have and the higher the temperature. The lowest temperature that is theoretically possible is the point at which every particle is completely still. This is known as absolute zero and is −273°C on the Celsius temperature scale. Absolute zero is also the starting point for the Kelvin temperature scale. An increment of one kelvin is the same as one degree Celsius.

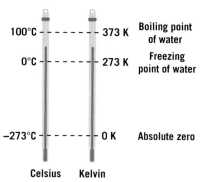

100°C	373 K	Boiling point of water
0°C	273 K	Freezing point of water
−273°C	0 K	Absolute zero

Celsius   Kelvin

Pressure and volume

The pressure exerted by a gas on its container depends on the container's volume. If the temperature doesn't change, squeezing a gas into a smaller volume increases the pressure. Allowing a gas to spread out in a larger volume reduces the pressure.

Key facts

✓ Increasing the volume of a gas at constant temperature reduces its pressure.

✓ Reducing the volume of a gas at constant temperature increases its pressure.

Changing volume

Gases exert pressure on their containers because the gas particles constantly collide with the container walls. The pressure is the total force from all the particles per square metre of container wall. Increasing the volume of a container gives the gas particles more room and so results in fewer collisions per square metre and therefore lower pressure. Reducing the volume has the opposite effect and pressure increases.

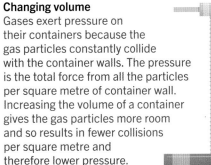
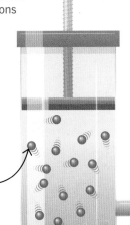

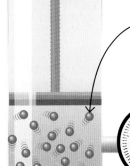

Collisions are spread over a larger area, resulting in lower pressure.

Collisions are concentrated in a smaller area, resulting in higher pressure.

📑 **Calculating change in pressure**

When either pressure or volume increases, the other quantity decreases. We say the two quantities are inversely proportional. This means that when you multiply them together, the product remains the same:

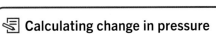

Pressure before   Pressure after

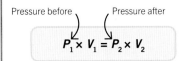

$$P_1 \times V_1 = P_2 \times V_2$$

Question

A container holds 0.25 m³ of air at a pressure of 100000 Pa. A piston is pressed down, reducing the volume of the trapped air to 0.1 m³. If the temperature remains the same, what is the new pressure?

Answer

Rearrange the equation to make the new pressure (P_2) the subject:

$$P_2 = \frac{P_1 \times V_1}{V_2}$$

$$= \frac{100000 \text{ Pa} \times 0.25 \text{ m}^3}{0.1 \text{ m}^3}$$

$$= 250000 \text{ Pa} = 250 \text{ kPa}$$

Pressure and temperature

Temperature is a measure of the average speed at which particles are moving. When the temperature of a gas rises, its particles move faster, causing the pressure to rise. The higher or lower the temperature, the higher or lower the pressure.

Key facts

✓ Changing the temperature of a gas at constant volume changes its pressure.

✓ Heating a gas increases its pressure and cooling it reduces its pressure.

Heating a gas

When a gas is heated, its particles gain kinetic energy and move faster. If the gas is trapped in a container and the volume does not change, the particles collide with each other and the container walls harder and more often. This results in increased force on the interior of the container and therefore greater pressure.

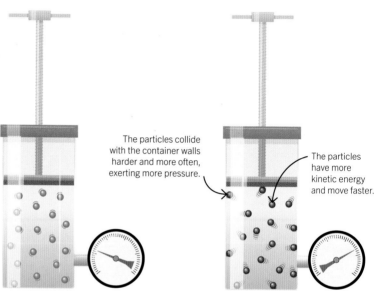

The particles collide with the container walls harder and more often, exerting more pressure.

The particles have more kinetic energy and move faster.

Low temperature   **High temperature**

Calculating change in pressure

The equation below shows how the temperature and pressure of a gas with a fixed volume are related. If temperature doubles, pressure doubles (pressure increases in direct proportion with temperature). This equation only works when using the Kelvin scale for temperature.

Pressure before → $$\frac{P_1}{T_1} = \frac{P_2}{T_2}$$ ← Pressure after

↳ Temperature in kelvin

Question

A sealed jar is filled with air. On a hot day, the temperature of the air increases from 20°C to 32°C. If the air starts at 100 000 Pa, what pressure does it reach?

Answer

First convert the temperatures to kelvin by adding 273:

20 + 273 = 293 K
32 + 273 = 305 K

Then rearrange the equation to make P_2 the subject:

$$P_2 = \frac{P_1 \times T_2}{T_1}$$

$$= \frac{100\,000 \text{ Pa} \times 305 \text{ K}}{293 \text{ K}}$$

$$= 104\,096 \text{ Pa} = 104 \text{ kPa (3 s.f.)}$$

Work and temperature

When energy is transferred by a force, we say the force is doing work. Pumping up a bicycle tyre does work on the trapped gas, increasing its store of energy and so making the temperature rise.

⚙ When a gas does work

While work can be done on a gas, a gas can also do work on other objects. In an internal combustion engine (the type of engine found in a petrol car), the expansion of hot gases in an enclosed chamber results in an increase in pressure. This pushes a piston, which transfers force to a rotating shaft (a crankshaft).

Hot gases are produced as fuel burns.

The gas does work on the piston, pushing it down.

The connecting rod and crank turn round a crankshaft.

Pump action

In physics, we use the word "work" to refer to the energy transferred when a force acts on an object (see page 55). The energy transferred is described as work done. When you inflate a bicycle tyre, the pump exerts a force on the air and transfers kinetic energy to the air particles. The air particles move faster, so the temperature of the air in the tyre rises.

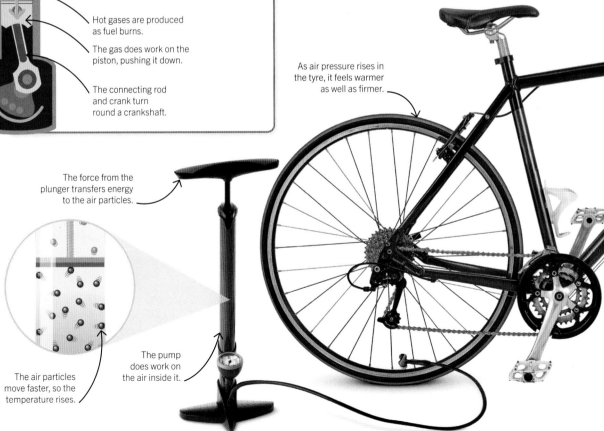

As air pressure rises in the tyre, it feels warmer as well as firmer.

The force from the plunger transfers energy to the air particles.

The air particles move faster, so the temperature rises.

The pump does work on the air inside it.

Atoms and radioactivity

Atomic structure

Scientists used to think that atoms were the smallest building blocks of matter. However, atoms can be divided further into three smaller particles: protons, neutrons, and electrons. Protons and neutrons form the nucleus at the centre of the atom. Outside this are even tinier particles called electrons.

Key facts

✓ Atoms are made up of three types of particle: protons, neutrons, and electrons.

✓ Protons and neutrons are bound together to form atomic nuclei.

✓ Electrons are outside atomic nuclei at distinct energy levels.

✓ Protons have a positive charge, electrons have a negative charge, and neutrons have no electrical charge.

Inside an atom

An atom has a nucleus in the middle containing a cluster of protons and neutrons. The nucleus is small compared to the atom – if an atom was the size of a sports stadium, the nucleus would be no bigger than a football – but it is dense and contains most of the atom's mass.

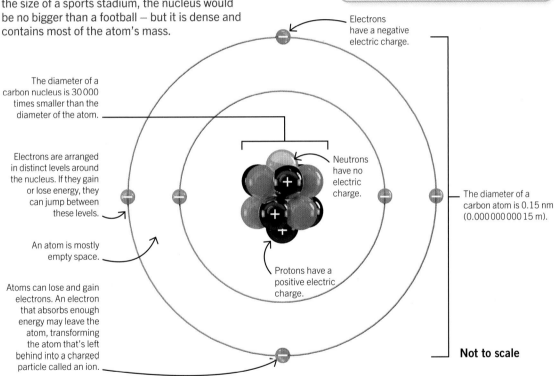

Electrons have a negative electric charge.

The diameter of a carbon nucleus is 30 000 times smaller than the diameter of the atom.

Electrons are arranged in distinct levels around the nucleus. If they gain or lose energy, they can jump between these levels.

An atom is mostly empty space.

Atoms can lose and gain electrons. An electron that absorbs enough energy may leave the atom, transforming the atom that's left behind into a charged particle called an ion.

Neutrons have no electric charge.

The diameter of a carbon atom is 0.15 nm (0.000 000 000 15 m).

Protons have a positive electric charge.

Not to scale

🔍 Particle properties

The protons and neutrons account for nearly all the mass of an atom and have the same mass as each other. Protons and electrons have opposite charges and so attract each other.

	Charge	Mass	Location
⊕ **Proton**	+1	1	Inside nucleus
Neutron	0	1	Inside nucleus
⊖ **Electron**	−1	0.0005	Outside nucleus

Elements and isotopes

Pure substances made of only one kind of atom, such as gold or oxygen, are called elements. The atoms of an element always have the same number of protons in the nucleus (the atomic number or proton number). However, the number of neutrons can vary. Atoms of the same element with different numbers of neutrons are called isotopes.

Key facts

✓ Pure substances made of only one kind of atom are called elements.

✓ The number of protons in an atom is its atomic number (proton number).

✓ The total number of protons and neutrons in an atom is its mass number (nucleon number).

✓ Isotopes are forms of an element with different mass numbers.

Carbon isotopes

Carbon is an element with six protons in its atomic nucleus but a varying number of neutrons. The total number of protons and neutrons is called the mass number (or nucleon number). There are three naturally occurring isotopes of carbon and these have mass numbers of 12, 13, and 14. All three have the same chemical properties, but they differ in other properties, such as mass and radioactivity.

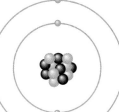

Isotope names are written using the name or symbol of the element followed by its mass number.

Carbon-13 makes up about one per cent of the world's carbon. It has 6 protons and 7 neutrons.

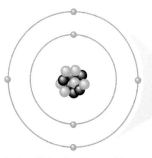

Carbon-12 has 6 protons and 6 neutrons. It is the most common carbon isotope, making up almost 99 per cent of naturally occurring carbon.

Diamond (a form of carbon)

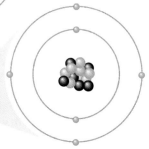

Carbon-14 is the rarest and heaviest carbon isotope. It has 6 protons and 8 neutrons and is radioactive.

⚙ Isotope symbols

Instead of writing out the name of an isotope in full, we can write it as a symbol. For example, carbon-14 is represented by the symbol $^{14}_{6}C$. This shows that it contains 6 protons and a total of 14 protons and neutrons. You can work out the number of neutrons by subtracting the atomic number from the mass number (14 − 6 = 8 neutrons).

Total number of protons and neutrons (mass number)

Element symbol

$$^{14}_{6}C$$

Number of protons (atomic number)

The atomic model

Over the last two centuries, the models we use to represent atoms have evolved as scientists have discovered more about how atoms work.

Key facts

✓ The scientific model of the atom has changed over time.

✓ The gold foil experiment showed that the mass of an atom is concentrated in the nucleus.

1. Dalton's "billiard ball"
The first model of the atom was devised by English chemist John Dalton. He suggested atoms were solid spheres that could not be divided.

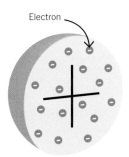

Electron

2. Thomson's "plum pudding"
British physicist J.J. Thomson discovered electrons in 1904. He proposed the plum pudding model, in which negatively charged electrons are embedded in a positively charged sphere.

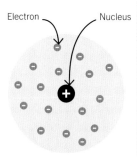

Electron   Nucleus

3. Rutherford model
British physicist Ernest Rutherford proposed an atomic model with a positive nucleus in the centre of a scattered cloud of electrons. He later discovered protons — the positively charged particles in the nucleus.

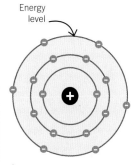

Energy level

4. Bohr model
Danish physicist Niels Bohr proposed the modern atomic model, with electrons arranged in energy levels at certain distances from the nucleus. This helped explain why atoms absorb or emit only certain wavelengths of light.

🔍 Discovery of the nucleus

In the early 1900s, physicists carried out an experiment to test the plum pudding model. They fired positively charged particles (alpha particles) at a thin piece of gold foil and discovered that while most of the particles flew straight through, a few were scattered in random directions, repelled by a positive charge. The results suggested that atoms have only a very small zone of positive charge and that most of the alpha particles had missed it. The scientists concluded that atoms are largely empty space, with most of their mass concentrated in small, positively charged nuclei.

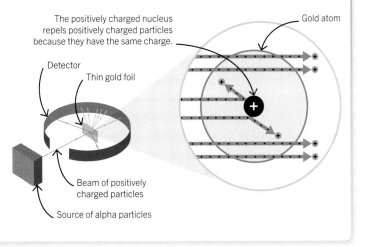

The positively charged nucleus repels positively charged particles because they have the same charge.

Gold atom

Detector

Thin gold foil

Beam of positively charged particles

Source of alpha particles

Radioactive decay

Some atoms are unstable, which means they can break down and release high-energy particles or waves known as radiation. We call such atoms radioactive. The release of radiation by radioactive atoms is known as radioactive decay and can make an unstable atomic nucleus more stable. Radioactive decay is a random process: it is impossible to predict when a particular atom will decay.

Key facts

✓ Unstable atomic nuclei decay and emit radiation.

✓ Radioactive decay is random.

✓ Radioactive decay can cause an atomic nucleus to change into a different element.

✓ Radiation can be detected by a device called a Geiger-Müller tube.

Detecting radiation
Radiation from a radioactive material can be detected using a device called a Geiger-Müller (GM) tube, which is pointed at the material. The rate at which nuclei in the source decay is known as activity and is measured in units called becquerels (Bq). One becquerel means that an average of one atom in the material decays each second.

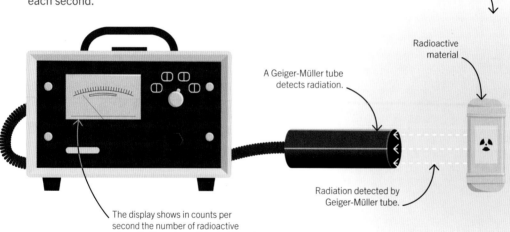

Radiation is emitted in all directions.

Radioactive material

A Geiger-Müller tube detects radiation.

Radiation detected by Geiger-Müller tube.

The display shows in counts per second the number of radioactive atoms that have been detected decaying.

⚙ Forming new elements

In some types of radioactive decay, the unstable atom changes from one element to another. For example, when uranium-238 decays, it emits something called an alpha particle, which consists of two protons and two neutrons. Because the remaining nucleus has two fewer protons, it is now the element thorium.

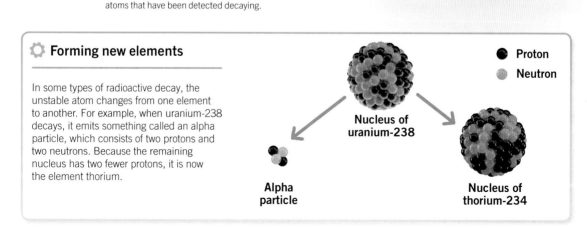

Nucleus of uranium-238

● Proton
● Neutron

Alpha particle

Nucleus of thorium-234

Different types of radiation

When radioactive atoms decay, they emit radiation. There are five kinds of radiation emitted by radioactive nuclei: alpha particles, beta particles, positrons, neutrons, and gamma radiation. All are known as ionizing radiation because they can knock electrons out of atoms, turning atoms into charged particles (ions).

Key facts

✓ There are five types of ionizing radiation emitted by radioactive nuclei: alpha particles, beta particles, positrons, neutrons, and gamma radiation.

✓ Most types of radiation emitted by radioactive nuclei are particles. However, gamma radiation is a form of electromagnetic radiation.

Alpha (α) radiation
Alpha radiation is made of particles – one alpha particle consists of two neutrons and two protons (a helium nucleus). It is highly ionizing but cannot penetrate far through materials. Even a sheet of paper, a few centimetres of air, or human skin can block it.

Beta (β) radiation
Beta radiation is made up of fast-moving electrons emitted from unstable atomic nuclei when neutrons change into protons. It is not as ionizing as alpha radiation but has greater penetrating power. It can travel a short distance through air and pass though paper but is blocked by a thin sheet of aluminium.

Gamma (γ) radiation
Like light or radio waves, gamma rays are a form of electromagnetic radiation. They are only weakly ionizing but penetrate materials much more powerfully than alpha or beta radiation. Several centimetres of lead or several metres of concrete or water are required to block gamma radiation.

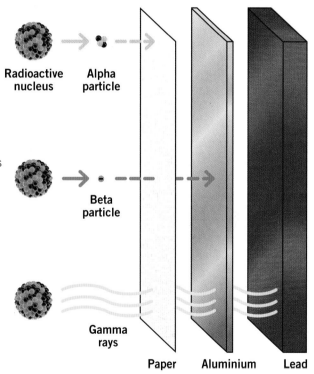

Radioactive nucleus   Alpha particle

Beta particle

Gamma rays

Paper   Aluminium   Lead

🔍 Ionizing radiation

All forms of ionizing radiation can knock electrons out of atoms. Because electrons have a negative charge, when an atom loses one, it is left with a net positive charge and so becomes an ion (a charged atom). Ionizing radiation can be dangerous as it can damage living tissue.

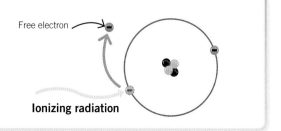

Free electron

Ionizing radiation

Nuclear equations

When radioactive decay takes place, the number of protons and neutrons in an atom may change, which causes the atom to transform into a new element. We can describe these changes by writing a nuclear equation.

Atomic number and mass number
The atomic number (proton number) of an atom is the number of protons in its nucleus. The total number of protons and neutrons is called the mass number or nucleon number. For example, carbon atoms have 6 protons and usually 6 neutrons, giving them an atomic number of 6 and a mass number of 12.

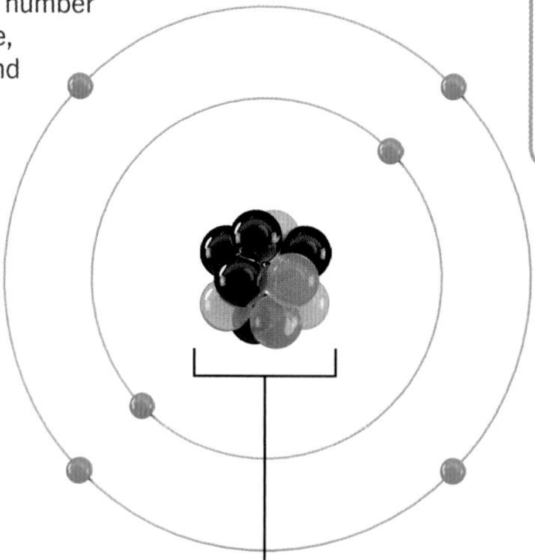

 + =

Atomic number (number of protons)	+	Number of neutrons	=	Mass number (protons + neutrons)
6		6		12

🔍 Symbols in nuclear equations

In nuclear equations, we write atomic number and mass number as small numbers next to the element's symbol.

Mass number → $^{12}_{6}C$

Atomic number →

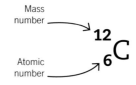

Alpha decay

An alpha particle consists of two protons and two neutrons. When an atom such as uranium emits an alpha particle, the atom's atomic number falls by 2 and its mass number falls by 4. The change in the number of protons causes the atom to become a different element (uranium, for instance, turns into thorium). The nuclear equation showing this change must be balanced – the mass numbers on both sides must add to the same value, and so must the atomic numbers.

The mass numbers on both sides of the equation must balance (238 = 234 + 4).

$$^{238}_{92}U \longrightarrow \,^{234}_{90}Th + \,^{4}_{2}He$$

The atomic numbers on both sides must balance (92 = 90 + 2).

The alpha particle is shown as a helium nucleus.

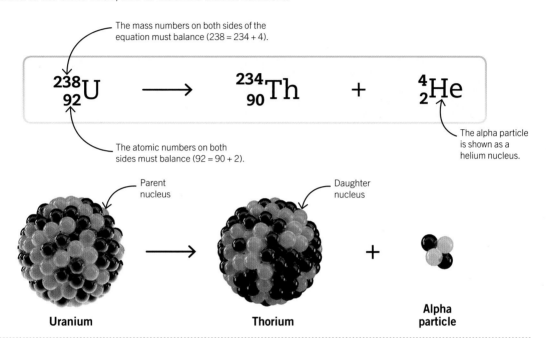

Parent nucleus

Daughter nucleus

Uranium → **Thorium** + **Alpha particle**

Beta decay

During beta decay, a neutron in the nucleus of an atom turns into a proton and emits a high-speed electron called a beta particle. The atomic number increases by 1, but the mass number remains the same (although the nucleus loses a neutron, it gains a proton). As with alpha decay, nuclear equations showing beta decay must balance.

A beta particle is written with −1 because it has a negative charge – the opposite of the positive charge carried by protons.

$$^{14}_{6}C \longrightarrow \,^{14}_{7}N + \,^{0}_{-1}e$$

Six protons

Seven protons

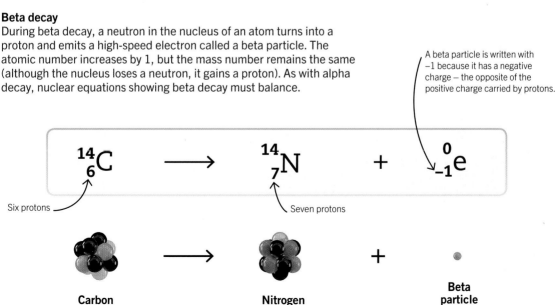

Carbon → **Nitrogen** + **Beta particle**

Half-life

Radioactive decay is random – it is impossible to predict when a particular atomic nucleus will decay. However, because there are so many atoms in a sample of a radioactive isotope, it is possible to predict what fraction of atoms will decay in a certain time. The time taken for half the atoms in a sample to decay is the half-life of that isotope.

Key facts

✓ Half-life is the time taken for half the unstable atoms in a sample of radioactive material to decay.

✓ Different isotopes have different half-lives.

Decay curve

After one half-life, the number of radioactive atoms is half the initial number. This falls to a quarter after two half-lives, an eighth after three half-lives, and so on, until there are barely any radioactive atoms left. The process can be shown on a graph called a decay curve. The half-lives of different isotopes vary from fractions of a nanosecond to trillions of times greater than the age of the Universe.

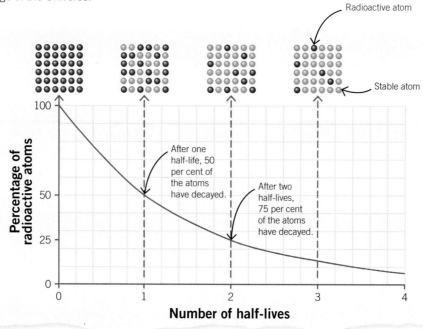

 Calculating radioactive decay

Question
The radioactive isotope iodine-131 has a half-life of 8 days. If you leave a 20 g sample for 24 days, how much iodine-131 remains?

Answer
Start: 20 g
After 8 days (1 half-life): 10 g
After 16 days (2 half-lives): 5 g
After 24 days (3 half-lives): 2.5 g

Background radiation

Anywhere you go you will find background radiation. This is the radiation emitted by natural sources such as the ground, rocks, and space, as well as by artificial sources such as medical treatment machines. Background radiation is usually harmless.

Sources of background radiation
The largest source of background radiation is the gas radon, which is found in the ground. Radon can be harmful if it seeps into buildings and becomes trapped. Earth is also constantly bombarded with cosmic radiation from the Sun and stars. About 20 per cent of background radiation comes from artificial sources such as medical treatment machines, nuclear weapons testing, coal-fired power stations, and nuclear accidents.

🔍 **Background radiation levels**

Background radiation levels vary from place to place. Because of this, people with certain jobs and lifestyles receive higher doses. For example, pilots and astronauts are exposed to higher levels of cosmic radiation from space because they are less shielded by Earth's atmosphere than people on the ground. To monitor background radiation in the environment, scientists use a Geiger-Müller tube. When measuring the activity of a radioactive material, the background reading is subtracted to find the true radioactivity of the material.

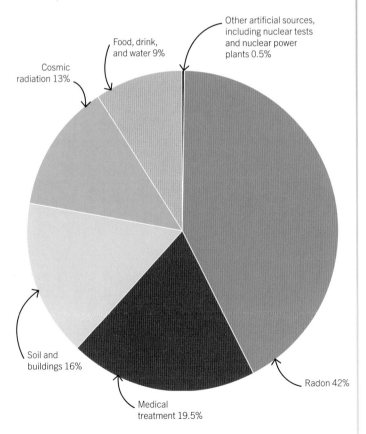

Other artificial sources, including nuclear tests and nuclear power plants 0.5%

Food, drink, and water 9%

Cosmic radiation 13%

Soil and buildings 16%

Medical treatment 19.5%

Radon 42%

Estimates of worldwide sources of background radiation

Using a Geiger-Müller tube

Radioactive hazards

Ionizing radiation can be harmful. Radioactive materials, such as those used in hospitals or nuclear power stations, must be handled, used, and stored carefully to prevent harm by irradiation or contamination.

Key facts

✓ Ionizing radiation can be harmful because it can kill cells and cause cancer.

✓ Contamination occurs when a radioactive material enters or gets onto a person's body.

✓ Irradiation is exposure to a radioactive material outside the body.

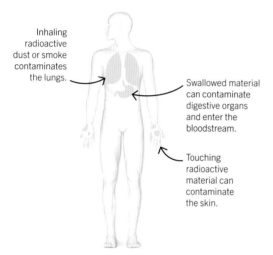

Inhaling radioactive dust or smoke contaminates the lungs.

Swallowed material can contaminate digestive organs and enter the bloodstream.

Touching radioactive material can contaminate the skin.

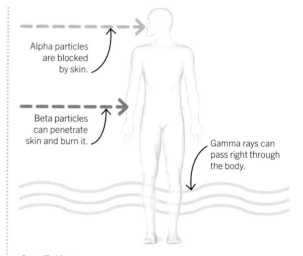

Alpha particles are blocked by skin.

Beta particles can penetrate skin and burn it.

Gamma rays can pass right through the body.

Contamination

Radioactive contamination occurs when radioactive material enters a person's body or gets on their skin or hair. Once inside the body, it is very difficult to remove and continues to release ionizing radiation, which can kill cells or cause mutations in DNA that lead to cancer.

Irradiation

Irradiation happens when a person is exposed to radioactive material outside the body. As with contamination, this can kill cells or cause cancer. It does not cause objects to become radioactive themselves, and it can be blocked with protective shielding. Irradiation stops as soon as the radioactive source is removed.

 Staying safe

There are three main ways to stay safe when working with a radioactive material. The precautions taken depend on the material's half-life and on the type of radiation it emits. Sources with a short half-life are the most dangerous as they can release huge amounts of radiation in a short time.

Limiting time spent near a radioactive material reduces the dose of radiation received.

Increasing distance from the radioactive source reduces the dose of radiation received.

Shielding to block radiation varies from gloves and face masks for alpha radiation to lead screens for gamma rays.

Using radioactive isotopes

Ionizing radiation is used for all sorts of purposes at home and in industry, including in food safety and manufacturing. The properties of different radioisotopes (such as their penetrating power) make them appropriate for different applications.

Key facts

✓ Ionizing radiation can be used for domestic and industrial purposes.

✓ Sources of alpha radiation are used in some smoke detectors.

✓ Beta radiation is used in paper mills to monitor the thickness of paper.

✓ Gamma radiation is used to irradiate food and medical equipment.

Smoke alarms

Smoke detectors contain americium-241, a radioactive isotope with a half-life of 460 years. It emits alpha radiation that ionizes air particles, making them electrically charged. This completes a circuit inside the alarm, allowing current to flow. If smoke enters the alarm, smoke particles attach to the ions and reduce the current, causing the alarm to sound.

Other uses

Measuring paper thickness
Beta radiation is used to measure the thickness of paper in paper mills. The thicker the paper, the less radiation passes through it to a detector, which then sends signals to a machine that adjusts the paper's thickness.

Irradiating food
Food can be preserved by exposing it to a source of gamma radiation. The high-energy gamma rays kill microorganisms in the food, preventing decay. Unlike heating, irradiating food does not affect its taste.

Sterilizing equipment
Gamma radiation is used in hospitals to sterilize surgical equipment, making it safe to use in operations.

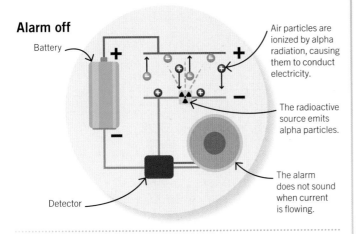

Alarm off

Battery

Air particles are ionized by alpha radiation, causing them to conduct electricity.

The radioactive source emits alpha particles.

The alarm does not sound when current is flowing.

Detector

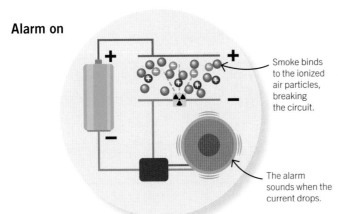

Alarm on

Smoke binds to the ionized air particles, breaking the circuit.

The alarm sounds when the current drops.

Nuclear medicine

Hospitals use radioactive substances both to diagnose and treat disease. In radionuclide scanning and PET (positron emission tomography) scanning, a radioactive material is put inside the body to help create images called scans. In radiotherapy, radioactive materials are used to kill cancer cells.

Diagnosing disease

Radioactive isotopes that emit gamma rays are used to help diagnose diseases. A radioactive substance, called a tracer, is injected into a patient's body. The tracer accumulates in certain areas and decays, releasing gamma rays, which are detected by a gamma camera. The image here, for instance, shows the isotope technetium-99m concentrating in bones affected by cancer.

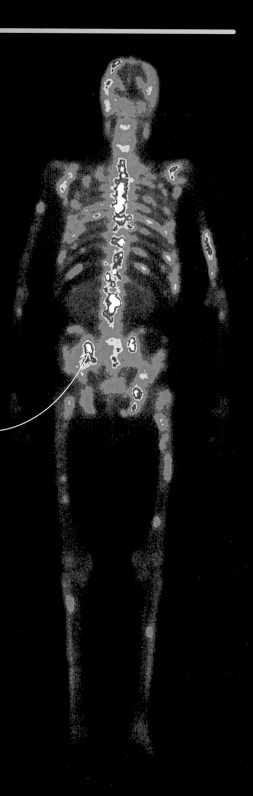

Bright areas show where the radioactive tracer has accumulated in tumours.

 Key facts

✓ Doctors use radiation to diagnose and treat disease.

✓ PET (positron emission tomography) is an imaging technology that uses radioactive isotopes attached to other molecules to reveal active tissues in the body.

✓ In radiotherapy, ionizing radiation is used to kill cancer cells.

✓ Radiation can be applied internally or externally.

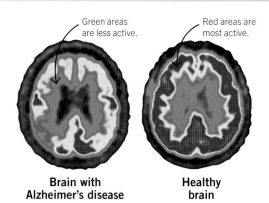

Green areas are less active.

Red areas are most active.

Brain with Alzheimer's disease

Healthy brain

PET scanning

In PET (positron emission tomography) scanning, doctors use radioactive isotopes attached to other molecules to highlight parts of the body that are active. For instance, the isotope fluorine-18 can be attached to sugar molecules to highlight tissues that are actively using blood sugar. This makes it possible to identify active tumours or organs that are less active than normal, such as a brain affected by Alzheimer's disease.

External beam radiotherapy

In external beam radiotherapy, narrow beams of radiation are directed through the body at cancer cells from many different angles. All the beams intersect at the site of the tumour, giving the cancer cells a large dose of radiation, but the surrounding areas of healthy tissue receive only a single beam each.

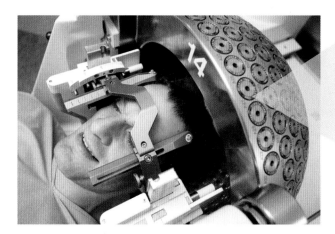

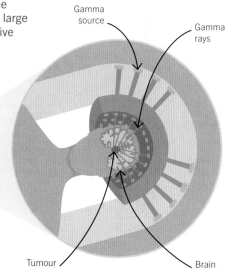

Gamma source

Gamma rays

Tumour

Brain

Internal radiotherapy

In internal radiotherapy, a radioactive source is implanted inside the body beside a tumour. This means that only the local area is affected, minimizing radiation exposure for the rest of the body. Radioisotopes that emit short-range radiation (alpha radiation) are ideal for this treatment.

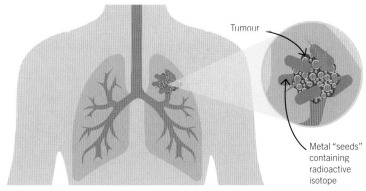

Tumour

Metal "seeds" containing radioactive isotope

Nuclear fission

Nuclear fission happens when an atomic nucleus splits into smaller nuclei and releases a large amount of energy. This energy can be used to generate electricity in nuclear power stations or to power spacecraft or submarines.

Key facts

✓ Nuclear fission is the splitting of an unstable atomic nucleus into two or more smaller nuclei.

✓ Fission normally occurs after a heavy, unstable nucleus absorbs a neutron.

✓ Nuclear fission releases a large amount of energy in the form of gamma radiation and heat.

✓ In a chain reaction, neutrons released during fission cause further fission reactions.

Fission of uranium

Nuclear fission is usually caused by a neutron colliding with an unstable atomic nucleus. Uranium-235, a naturally occurring isotope of the element uranium, is used in nuclear power stations. It splits to form the nuclei of new elements and releases energy along with two or three neutrons.

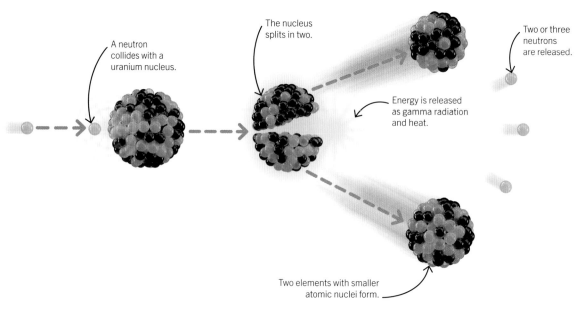

A neutron collides with a uranium nucleus.

The nucleus splits in two.

Energy is released as gamma radiation and heat.

Two or three neutrons are released.

Two elements with smaller atomic nuclei form.

🔍 Energy from fission

A vast amount of energy is released by the fission of uranium – millions of times more energy than is released burning the same mass of coal. This energy comes from a tiny amount of the mass of the original atomic nucleus that is converted into energy.

Uranium-235

Chain reactions

A nuclear chain reaction is a series of fission reactions, each caused by neutrons released in a previous fission reaction. Uncontrolled chain reactions, such as in a nuclear weapon, can cause the explosive release of a vast amount of energy.

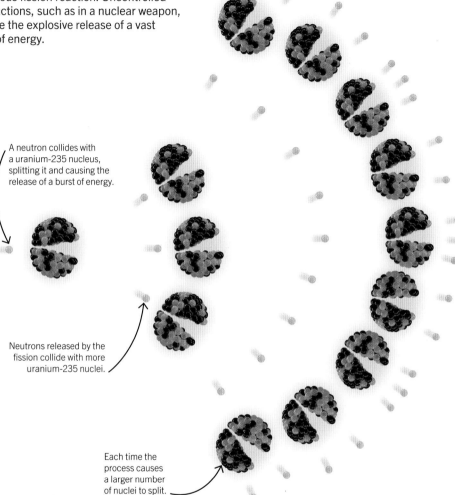

A neutron collides with a uranium-235 nucleus, splitting it and causing the release of a burst of energy.

Neutrons released by the fission collide with more uranium-235 nuclei.

Each time the process causes a larger number of nuclei to split.

⚙ Controlled chain reactions

Nuclear chain reactions can build, fade, or remain stable depending on how many fission reactions are caused by the products of a previous fission. If each fission reaction leads on average to only one more, this results in a stable (controlled) chain reaction. Nuclear power stations control chain reactions by inserting control rods into the reactor core. These absorb neutrons, slowing the reaction down.

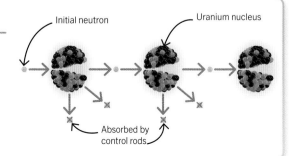

Initial neutron

Uranium nucleus

Absorbed by control rods

Nuclear power

Nuclear power is the generation of electricity using nuclear fission as a source of energy. Nuclear power plants generate about 10 per cent of the world's electrical power. Making use of nuclear energy means that we use less fossil fuel.

Nuclear reactor

A nuclear reactor contains radioactive uranium in fuel rods. Placing these close together triggers a chain reaction that releases large amounts of energy. The energy released boils water to make steam, which powers generators. The reaction is managed by moving control rods in and out of the reactor core. These absorb neutrons and slow the chain reaction down.

Key facts

✓ Nuclear power plants use the energy from nuclear fission to generate heat and electricity.

✓ Nuclear power does not generate carbon dioxide emissions.

✓ Nuclear power stations create hazardous radioactive waste that must be disposed of carefully.

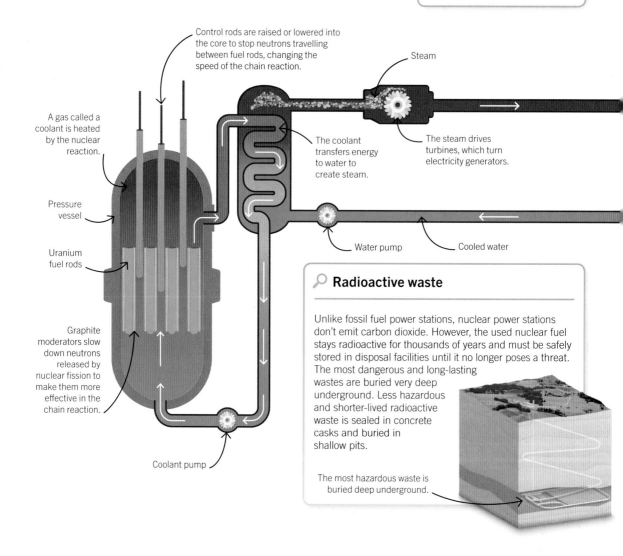

Control rods are raised or lowered into the core to stop neutrons travelling between fuel rods, changing the speed of the chain reaction.

Steam

A gas called a coolant is heated by the nuclear reaction.

The coolant transfers energy to water to create steam.

The steam drives turbines, which turn electricity generators.

Pressure vessel

Uranium fuel rods

Water pump

Cooled water

Graphite moderators slow down neutrons released by nuclear fission to make them more effective in the chain reaction.

Coolant pump

🔍 Radioactive waste

Unlike fossil fuel power stations, nuclear power stations don't emit carbon dioxide. However, the used nuclear fuel stays radioactive for thousands of years and must be safely stored in disposal facilities until it no longer poses a threat. The most dangerous and long-lasting wastes are buried very deep underground. Less hazardous and shorter-lived radioactive waste is sealed in concrete casks and buried in shallow pits.

The most hazardous waste is buried deep underground.

Fusion

Nuclear fusion – in which two or more atomic nuclei fuse to form a heavier nucleus – is the process that powers the Sun. Scientists and engineers are working on ways of harnessing this source of energy to generate electricity.

Key facts

✓ Nuclear fusion occurs when atomic nuclei are forced together to form a heavier nucleus.

✓ During nuclear fusion a small amount of mass is converted into energy.

✓ Extreme heat and pressure are required to initiate fusion.

Hydrogen fusion

During nuclear fusion, the nuclei of two atoms are forced together by very high temperatures and pressures. The reaction here shows the hydrogen isotopes deuterium (hydrogen-2) and tritium (hydrogen-3) fusing to create a helium nucleus. The new helium nucleus and the ejected neutron have slightly less mass than the two hydrogen nuclei. The lost mass is converted to energy.

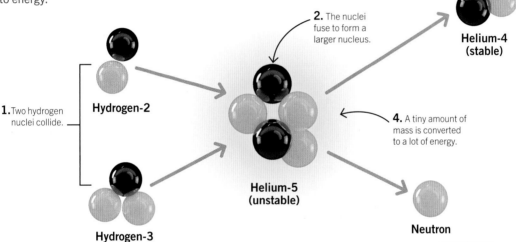

3. Helium is a product of the reaction.

2. The nuclei fuse to form a larger nucleus.

Helium-4 (stable)

1. Two hydrogen nuclei collide.

Hydrogen-2

4. A tiny amount of mass is converted to a lot of energy.

Helium-5 (unstable)

Hydrogen-3

Neutron

⚙ Harnessing fusion

The nuclei of atoms are positively charged and repel each other, so fusion can only take place if nuclei are pushed extremely close together, overcoming this repulsion. This is why fusion only occurs in extremely hot and high-pressure environments like the cores of stars. These requirements make it very difficult to build a fusion reactor on Earth to initiate and sustain fusion. Scientists working at experimental fusion reactors have briefly sustained fusion using powerful magnetic fields to confine the hot matter. However, it currently takes more energy to run the reactor than the reactor produces.

In the core of this fusion reactor, hot matter is confined by magnetic fields in a doughnut-shaped ring.

Space

Structure of Earth

Studies of seismic waves from earthquakes (see page 123) reveal that Earth's interior consists of distinct layers. Heavier elements, such as metals, are concentrated in the planet's centre, while lighter materials, such as rock, form the outer layers.

Inside Earth

Earth's interior consists of four distinct layers: the inner core, outer core, mantle, and crust. The crust and the uppermost part of the mantle are joined to form a rigid structure called the lithosphere, which is divided into sections called tectonic plates. These move very slowly over time, changing the shapes of continents and oceans.

Key facts

✓ Earth's interior has four distinct layers: the inner core, outer core, mantle, and crust.

✓ The crust and uppermost part of the mantle form a rigid structure that is divided into tectonic plates, which move slowly over time.

✓ The atmosphere is a layer of gases trapped by gravity.

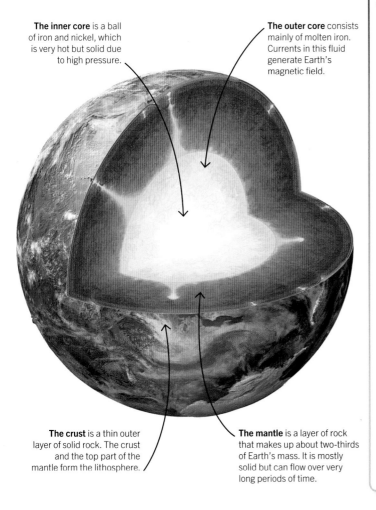

The inner core is a ball of iron and nickel, which is very hot but solid due to high pressure.

The outer core consists mainly of molten iron. Currents in this fluid generate Earth's magnetic field.

The crust is a thin outer layer of solid rock. The crust and the top part of the mantle form the lithosphere.

The mantle is a layer of rock that makes up about two-thirds of Earth's mass. It is mostly solid but can flow over very long periods of time.

The atmosphere

Earth's atmosphere is a mixture of gases that are held in place by gravity. The atmosphere is divided into layers with distinct properties. It has no clear upper edge and fades gradually into space.

Exosphere
This is the outermost layer and by far the tallest. Gas molecules can escape into space from here.

Thermosphere
The International Space Station orbits Earth in this layer.

Mesosphere
This is where meteors (shooting stars) burn up.

Stratosphere
Ozone gas in this layer absorbs harmful UV light from the Sun. Airliners fly in the lower stratosphere.

Troposphere
All weather occurs in this layer.

Seasons

It takes 365 days – which we call a year – for Earth to complete one orbit around the Sun. The cycle of seasons happens because Earth's axis of rotation is tilted. As a result, parts of the planet that tilt towards the Sun get more sunlight each day than parts tilted away from it.

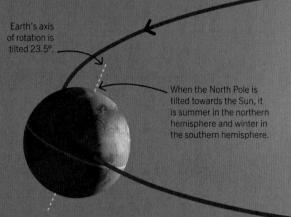

Spring in the northern hemisphere, autumn in the southern hemisphere

Earth's axis of rotation is tilted 23.5°.

When the North Pole is tilted towards the Sun, it is summer in the northern hemisphere and winter in the southern hemisphere.

Changing sunlight
Earth's axis of rotation remains at the same angle all year round. The hemisphere that is tilted towards the Sun experiences longer days and stronger heating from the Sun, while the one that is tilted away has shorter days and is heated less.

 The Sun's path

During summer, the Sun is visible for longer each day and reaches higher in the sky than in winter. This time-lapse photo from a northern-hemisphere location shows the Sun's path through the sky in midsummer (top) and midwinter (bottom). Between them is its path through the sky during the spring and autumn equinoxes – the two times of year when day and night are the same length.

East

West

Summer

Spring/Autumn

Winter

Key facts

- ✓ The cycle of seasons happens because Earth's axis is tilted.
- ✓ When the North Pole is tilted towards the Sun, it is summer in the northern hemisphere.
- ✓ When the South Pole is tilted towards the Sun, it is summer in the southern hemisphere.

Autumn in the northern hemisphere, spring in the southern hemisphere

When the South Pole is tilted towards the Sun, it is summer in the southern hemisphere and winter in the northern hemisphere.

The regular change from night to day is caused by Earth's rotation.

⚙ Solar heating

Because Earth is spherical, sunlight hits the planet's surface at an angle in the north and south, spreading the Sun's energy over a much larger area. As a result, the Sun feels much cooler at midday in winter than in summer, and tropical countries are usually much warmer than countries further from the equator.

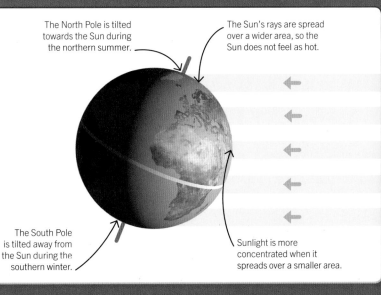

The North Pole is tilted towards the Sun during the northern summer.

The Sun's rays are spread over a wider area, so the Sun does not feel as hot.

The South Pole is tilted away from the Sun during the southern winter.

Sunlight is more concentrated when it spreads over a smaller area.

Solar system

The solar system is the region of space influenced by the Sun's gravity. It has eight major planets (including Earth), the moons that orbit them, and countless smaller objects such as dwarf planets, asteroids, and comets. All these objects are held in orbit around the Sun by its gravity.

Jupiter, Saturn, Uranus, and Neptune are giant gaseous planets that orbit the Sun beyond the asteroid belt.

Uranus

Mercury, Venus, Earth, and Mars are rocky planets and orbit near the Sun.

Jupiter

The Sun is our local star.

Earth

Mercury

Mars

Venus

Asteroids — small rocky bodies — are mostly confined to a broad circular belt between Mars and Jupiter.

Beyond Neptune's orbit is the Kuiper belt — a vast disc of small, icy bodies, including dwarf planets.

Neptune

Saturn

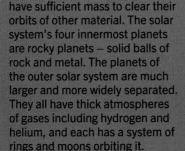

Key facts

✓ Objects in the solar system are held in orbit by the Sun's gravity.

✓ Planets are large, spherical objects that orbit a star and that clear their orbits of other material. There are eight in the solar system.

✓ Moons (natural satellites) are large bodies that orbit planets.

✓ Asteroids are small rocky bodies that are mostly found between Mars and Jupiter.

Smaller bodies

Pluto

Dwarf planets
Objects with enough mass to form a spherical shape, but not enough to clear their orbits of other material, are called dwarf planets. Pluto is the best-known dwarf planet.

Comet Lovejoy

Comets
Comets are made from a mix of rock and ice. They have long, elliptical orbits and often develop bright tails as they travel close to the Sun.

Asteroid Ida

Asteroids
Asteroids are usually irregular bodies made of rock and metal left over from the formation of the planets. Most asteroids orbit the Sun between the orbits of Mars and Jupiter.

Enceladus

Moons
Moons are large bodies that orbit planets and are sometimes called natural satellites. There are more than 200 moons in the solar system, most of which orbit the giant planets.

The planets
Planets are large, spherical objects that orbit a star and that have sufficient mass to clear their orbits of other material. The solar system's four innermost planets are rocky planets — solid balls of rock and metal. The planets of the outer solar system are much larger and more widely separated. They all have thick atmospheres of gases including hydrogen and helium, and each has a system of rings and moons orbiting it.

The Moon

The Moon is a natural satellite of Earth and orbits our planet once every 27.3 days. It doesn't produce its own light, but we can still see it because it reflects light from the Sun.

Lunar phases

Every 29.5 days, the Moon passes through a series of phases as we see different parts of its surface illuminated by the Sun. When the Moon is directly between Earth and the Sun, it cannot be seen from Earth and is called a new moon. When it's on the opposite side of Earth from the Sun, we see its whole face illuminated: a full moon. We always see the same face of the Moon because tidal forces exerted on the Moon by Earth slowed the Moon's period of rotation over millions of years until it matched the time it takes to orbit Earth once.

Key facts

✓ The Moon is a natural satellite of Earth.

✓ The Moon passes through a series of phases every 29.5 days.

✓ Tides are primarily caused by the pull of the Moon's gravity on Earth's oceans.

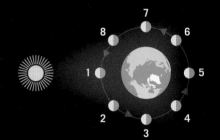

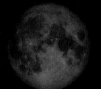

1. New moon

2. Waxing crescent

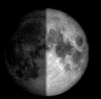

3. First quarter

4. Waxing gibbous

5. Full moon

6. Waning gibbous

7. Last quarter

8. Waning crescent

⚙ Tides

Ocean tides are caused mainly by the Moon's gravity. The Moon's gravity is strongest on the side of Earth facing the Moon as it is slightly closer. This force pulls the sea towards the Moon, causing a slight bulge. On the opposite side of Earth, where the Moon's gravity is weakest, inertia causes the water to bulge in the opposite direction as it tries to keep moving in a straight line. As a result, high tides occur twice a day.

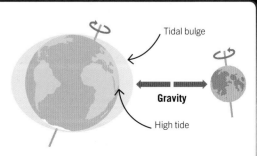

Tidal bulge

Gravity

High tide

Eclipses

Eclipses happen when Earth, the Sun, and the Moon line up in space. When the Moon passes directly between the Sun and Earth, it casts a shadow on Earth and creates a solar eclipse. A lunar eclipse happens when Earth casts its shadow on the Moon.

Key facts

✓ Eclipses occur when Earth, the Moon, and the Sun line up.

✓ Solar eclipses happen when the Moon casts a shadow on Earth.

✓ Lunar eclipses happen when Earth casts a shadow on the Moon.

Solar eclipse

Solar eclipses happen when the Moon comes directly between the Sun and Earth and so casts a shadow on part of Earth's surface. Although the Moon is much smaller than the Sun, it is much closer to Earth and can block the Sun completely, causing a total solar eclipse. When they occur, total solar eclipses are visible from only a small part of Earth.

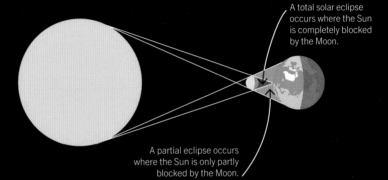

A total solar eclipse occurs where the Sun is completely blocked by the Moon.

A partial eclipse occurs where the Sun is only partly blocked by the Moon.

Lunar eclipse

Lunar eclipses occur during a full moon if the Moon passes through Earth's shadow. Sometimes only part of the Moon passes through Earth's shadow, but when the whole Moon falls in Earth's shadow, the Moon can turn a reddish colour. This is because light refracted (bent) through Earth's atmosphere can still reach the Moon's surface.

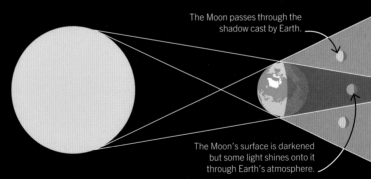

The Moon passes through the shadow cast by Earth.

The Moon's surface is darkened but some light shines onto it through Earth's atmosphere.

🔍 The Sun's atmosphere

When the Moon completely obscures the Sun during a total solar eclipse, astronomers can see the Sun's faint outer atmosphere – the corona. The corona extends millions of kilometres into space but is difficult to study because it is usually hidden by the Sun's glare.

Orbits

The planets of the solar system travel around the Sun because they are trapped by the force of gravity. The paths that planets follow around the Sun or that moons follow around planets are called orbits.

Shapes of orbits

The planets in the solar system have nearly circular orbits. The pull of gravity from the Sun provides the centripetal force (see page 96) that stops them flying away in a straight line. Smaller bodies, such as comets, have very elliptical orbits. Their speed increases as they get closer to the Sun.

Key facts

✓ An orbit is the path that an object takes as it moves around another object in space.

✓ The force of gravity causes objects in space to travel in orbits.

✓ Orbits can be circular or elliptical.

✓ In a circular orbit, an object's speed is constant but its velocity is always changing as its direction is changing.

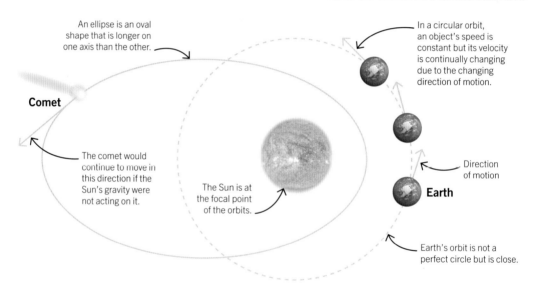

An ellipse is an oval shape that is longer on one axis than the other.

In a circular orbit, an object's speed is constant but its velocity is continually changing due to the changing direction of motion.

Comet

The comet would continue to move in this direction if the Sun's gravity were not acting on it.

The Sun is at the focal point of the orbits.

Direction of motion

Earth

Earth's orbit is not a perfect circle but is close.

🔍 Types of orbit

Artificial satellites are placed in different types of orbit depending on the job they do. Two common types of satellite orbit are geostationary and polar.

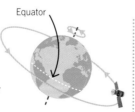

Equator

Geostationary orbits

Geostationary satellites stay above the equator and complete one orbit every 23 hours 56 minutes, matching Earth's period of rotation. This means they stay above the same point on the planet all the time. Geostationary orbits are used for weather and communications satellites.

Polar orbits

Satellites with polar orbits travel around the planet from pole to pole. Because Earth rotates beneath them while they orbit, they pass over different parts of the planet with each orbit. Polar orbits are used for Earth-monitoring satellites.

Galaxies

A galaxy is a spinning group of stars, held together by gravity. The Universe may have as many as 2 trillion galaxies, and each galaxy may hold billions or trillions of stars. Vast distances separate galaxies and the stars within galaxies.

Types of galaxy

Galaxies can be sorted into different kinds based on their shape. These include spiral, barred spiral, lenticular, elliptical, and irregular. The Sun is part of the Milky Way galaxy, which is a barred spiral galaxy — a spiral galaxy with a central bar shape made of stars. All the stars we see in the night sky belong to the Milky Way. The artist's impression below shows what it might look like from outside.

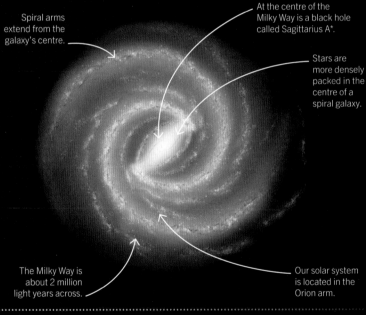

Spiral arms extend from the galaxy's centre.

At the centre of the Milky Way is a black hole called Sagittarius A*.

Stars are more densely packed in the centre of a spiral galaxy.

The Milky Way is about 2 million light years across.

Our solar system is located in the Orion arm.

Lenticular galaxies, like spiral galaxies, are disc-shaped with a central bulge. However, they lack spiral arms.

Elliptical galaxies are shaped like a squashed sphere. The stars in elliptical galaxies tend to be older than those in other galaxy types.

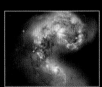

Irregular galaxies have no particular shape and lack spiral arms. About a quarter of all galaxies are irregular.

Key facts

✓ Galaxies are groups of stars held together by gravity.

✓ The different types of galaxy include spiral, barred spiral, lenticular, elliptical, and irregular.

✓ Our solar system is in the Milky Way galaxy.

🔍 Scale of the Universe

Distances in space are so great that we measure them in light years. One light year is the distance light travels in a year: about 9.5 trillion km.

The Sun is 8 light minutes from Earth.

Our nearest neighbouring star, Proxima Centauri, is 4.2 light years away.

Polaris, the North Star, is 320 light years away.

We are 26 000 light years away from the centre of the Milky Way galaxy.

Andromeda, the galaxy closest to us, is 2.5 million light years away.

Observing space

The main way we learn about the Universe is by capturing the visible light and other radiation that reaches Earth from far away. Telescopes are tools that collect this radiation and produce images that are brighter and more detailed than the naked eye can see.

Telescopes

Our understanding of space has been transformed over the past century thanks to powerful telescopes. Early astronomers had to draw what they saw, but today cameras record images and computers are used to analyse them. Astronomers use telescopes located both on Earth and in space to capture and study radiation from the whole electromagnetic spectrum.

Key facts

✓ Astronomers use different kinds of telescope to pick up different kinds of electromagnetic radiation from objects in space.

✓ Some telescopes are sent into space to give us clearer images.

Arecibo's primary dish is 305 m wide.

The curved shape of the dish focuses radio waves.

Telescopes on Earth
Earth-based telescopes, such as the Arecibo Observatory in Puerto Rico, can be much bigger than space telescopes because they don't need to be launched into space. Radio telescopes such as Arecibo need huge dishes because radio waves have a much longer wavelength than visible light.

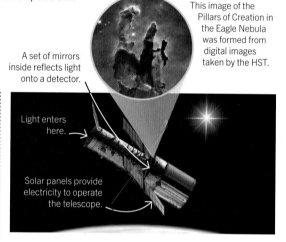

A set of mirrors inside reflects light onto a detector.

This image of the Pillars of Creation in the Eagle Nebula was formed from digital images taken by the HST.

Light enters here.

Solar panels provide electricity to operate the telescope.

Space telescopes
Like most modern telescopes, the Hubble Space Telescope (HST) uses mirrors rather than lenses to collect and focus light. Orbiting telescopes such as Hubble can observe space without clouds and dust in the atmosphere getting in the way and can detect types of radiation absorbed by Earth's atmosphere, such as infrared.

🔍 Invisible radiation

Stars and other space objects give off radiation across the whole electromagnetic spectrum. Astronomers can learn more about objects in space by studying images at different frequencies. These pictures show the Crab Nebula – the glowing remains of a star that exploded – in different electromagnetic frequencies.

Radio

Infrared

Visible light

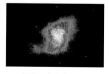

Ultraviolet rays

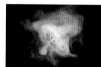

X-rays

Redshift

When astronomers analyse the light from distant galaxies, they find that its wavelength is slightly longer than that of light from closer objects. This difference, imperceptible to the naked eye, is caused by an effect called redshift, and it shows that the Universe is expanding.

Moving light

Light waves from objects that are receding (moving away) have a slightly elongated wavelength. The faster the object is receding, the greater the increase in wavelength. By studying redshift, astronomers discovered that the furthest galaxies are receding fastest. This shows that the whole Universe is expanding in a pattern that supports the big bang theory (see page 267).

Key facts

✓ Redshift is an increase in the wavelength of light from distant galaxies that are receding (moving away from us).

✓ Redshift studies show that the furthest galaxies are receding fastest.

✓ The observed redshift provides evidence that the Universe is expanding and supports the big bang theory.

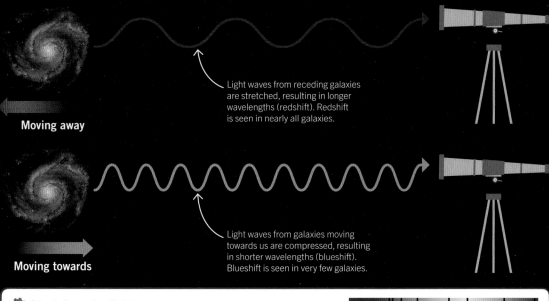

Light waves from receding galaxies are stretched, resulting in longer wavelengths (redshift). Redshift is seen in nearly all galaxies.

Moving away

Light waves from galaxies moving towards us are compressed, resulting in shorter wavelengths (blueshift). Blueshift is seen in very few galaxies.

Moving towards

⚙ Studying starlight

Astronomers study the light from stars and galaxies with a technique called spectroscopy. In one form of spectroscopy, the visible light from a star has distinctive black gaps because chemical elements in stars or in space absorb and block certain wavelengths. Redshift (or occasionally blueshift) causes these lines to shift, and the amount they move reveals how fast a star or galaxy is moving towards or away from us. Redshift affects all kinds of electromagnetic radiation, not just visible light.

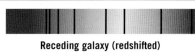

Receding galaxy (redshifted)

Laboratory spectrum (stationary)

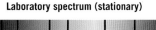

Approaching galaxy (blueshifted)

Expanding Universe

The light from stars and galaxies can be analysed to find out whether they are moving towards us or away from us. In 1929, astronomers including Edwin Hubble in the USA discovered that most galaxies are moving away from us at a speed that is proportional to their distance. We call this Hubble's law.

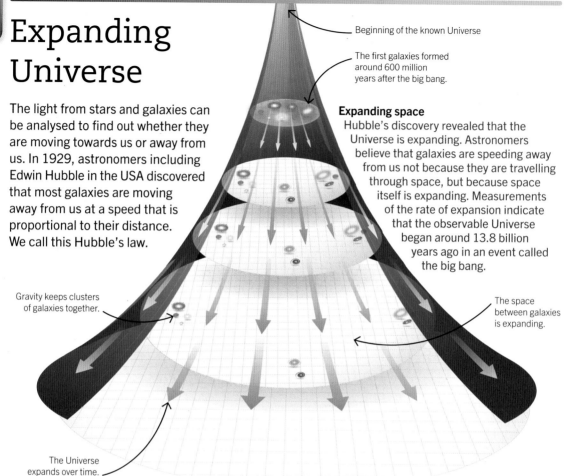

Beginning of the known Universe

The first galaxies formed around 600 million years after the big bang.

Expanding space
Hubble's discovery revealed that the Universe is expanding. Astronomers believe that galaxies are speeding away from us not because they are travelling through space, but because space itself is expanding. Measurements of the rate of expansion indicate that the observable Universe began around 13.8 billion years ago in an event called the big bang.

Gravity keeps clusters of galaxies together.

The space between galaxies is expanding.

The Universe expands over time.

Key facts

✓ **Most galaxies are moving away from us.**

✓ **The speed at which galaxies are moving away increases in proportion to their distance from us.**

✓ **Hubble's observations show the Universe is expanding and support the big bang theory.**

🔍 Dark matter and dark energy

Measurements of the light from supernovas in distant galaxies suggest that the expansion of the Universe is accelerating. Scientists think the acceleration is driven by an unknown source of energy, named dark energy. They also think there must be more mass in galaxies than we can see, as there isn't enough visible mass to properly explain the observed motion of stars and galaxies. The undetected mass is called dark matter.

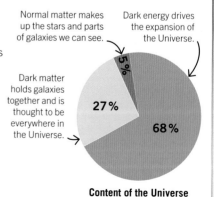

Normal matter makes up the stars and parts of galaxies we can see.

Dark energy drives the expansion of the Universe.

Dark matter holds galaxies together and is thought to be everywhere in the Universe.

5%

27%

68%

Content of the Universe

Big bang or steady state?

There are two different theories to explain the expansion of the Universe. The big bang theory says that the expansion can be traced back to a beginning at a single point. The steady-state model says that something is continuously creating matter and making the Universe expand.

The big bang theory

According to the big bang theory, space expanded suddenly from a single point of origin 13.8 billion years ago. All the matter and energy the Universe would ever have was present from the beginning. As the Universe expanded, matter and energy became ever more widely spread. Most evidence suggests the big bang theory is correct.

Matter formed as the Universe expanded and cooled.

The galaxies get further apart as space expands.

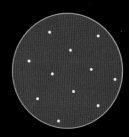

Steady-state model

According to this rival model, proposed in the early 20th century, the Universe has always existed and is continually expanding as new matter is created. However, scientific observations don't support the model, and it is now considered incorrect.

New matter is created as the Universe expands, so the density stays the same everywhere.

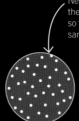

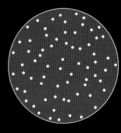

🔍 Cosmic microwave background radiation

In 1964, two radio astronomers discovered a weak radio signal coming from all over the sky. They realized they had picked up radiation from the big bang that is now spread thinly across the entire Universe. The existence of this energy had been predicted by the big bang theory but not the steady-state model, so its discovery supported the big bang.

Cosmic microwave background radiation

Star life cycles

Stars form inside gigantic clouds of gas and dust that contract due to the force of gravity until nuclear fusion reactions are triggered inside them. The life cycle a star passes through as it ages and uses up its fuel depends on the star's mass.

Different lives

The diagram here shows the typical life cycles of massive stars (along the top) and stars the size of our Sun (bottom). Massive stars shine brilliantly, use their fuel quickly, and die in a spectacular explosion. Smaller stars use their fuel slowly and shine for longer, before swelling as they age and then fading away.

Key facts

✓ **Stars form from clouds of gas and dust called nebulas.**

✓ **Planets form from the debris left behind after star formation.**

✓ **The stages in a star's life depend on its mass.**

When a massive star runs out of fuel, it swells to form a supergiant.

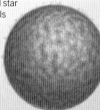

All stars form in nebulas -- giant clouds of gas and dust.

Massive star

A pocket of gas contracts to form a dense, spinning clump, eventually triggering nuclear fusion in the core.

As an average-sized star runs out of fuel, it swells to form a red giant.

Average-sized star

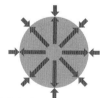

⚙ Stellar equilibrium

Stars shine stably as long as they can maintain a balance between the inward pull of their own gravity and the outward pressure of radiation from fusion reactions in the core. When the fuel inside the star begins to run out, the forces become unbalanced and the star changes, sometimes dramatically and violently.

Normal star
In a star like our Sun, the inward pull of gravity balances outward pressure from the core.

Red giant
In an ageing star the core heats up and the forces become unbalanced. The star swells in size until the forces balance again. It is now a giant star.

Black hole
When the most massive stars run out of fuel, the force of gravity far exceeds pressure from the core and the star collapses into a black hole.

⚙ Star formation

Stars form in vast, interstellar clouds of gas and dust called nebulas. If a nebula is disturbed, for instance by a shock from an exploding star, part of it may start to contract due to gravity to form a dense, rotating clump. As the clump becomes more dense, its gravitational pull grows stronger, drawing more material in, and its core heats up. Eventually the core is so dense and hot that nuclear fusion reactions are triggered, causing a star to shine. The remaining material orbits the star as a disc of dust and gas in which planets and other bodies form.

When a supergiant runs out of fuel, it collapses suddenly and then explodes. We call this explosion a supernova.

The remains of the core may contract to form an incredibly dense, fast-spinning star the size of a city. All matter is crushed to form neutrons, so such stars are called neutron stars.

When nuclear fuel in the core of an average star is used up, the star sheds its outer layers of gas into space and the core collapses into a hot, Earth-sized star called a white dwarf.

Cores of the most massive stars collapse to form a black hole – a region in which gravity is so strong that not even light can escape its pull.

Eventually, the star may cool to form a ball of carbon that emits no light or heat – a black dwarf. These take so long to form that none are thought to exist yet.

⚙ Making elements

Stars are made mostly of hydrogen, the simplest element in the Universe. They shine by nuclear fusion (see page 253): hydrogen nuclei are forced together to form larger atomic nuclei, such as helium, releasing energy in the process. Towards the end of a star's life, its core runs out of hydrogen and starts to fuse other elements instead. Sunlike stars fuse helium to make carbon, and more massive stars go on to make heavier elements such as nitrogen, oxygen, and iron. When massive stars explode as supernovas, elements even heavier than iron are produced, and the explosion scatters the elements through space to form new nebulas. Many of the chemical elements in our bodies formed this way.

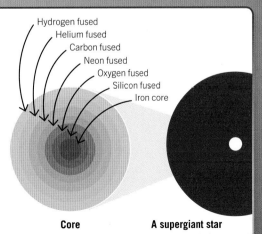

Hydrogen fused
Helium fused
Carbon fused
Neon fused
Oxygen fused
Silicon fused
Iron core

Core   **A supergiant star**

Classifying stars

Stars may look like pinpricks of light to the naked eye, but astronomers can use the light they emit to calculate their temperature, distance from Earth, diameter, and mass. These characteristics are used to classify stars and work out their age and how long they have left to live.

Key facts

✓ The light from a star can be used to calculate its temperature.

✓ Apparent magnitude is how bright a star appears from Earth.

✓ Absolute magnitude is how bright a star appears from a standard distance.

✓ A Hertzsprung–Russell diagram is a graph showing the temperatures of stars plotted against brightness.

Red supergiant

Blue hypergiant

Blue supergiant

Red giant

Orange giant

White dwarf

Red dwarf

The Sun

Star size

Stars vary enormously in size, from neutron stars no bigger than a city (but with more mass than our Sun) to supergiants and hypergiants millions or billions of times greater in volume than the Sun. The characteristics of a star depend mainly on its mass. The more massive a star is, the hotter, brighter, and bluer it will be for most of its life, but the shorter its lifespan. This is because massive stars burn through their nuclear fuel more quickly.

Colour and temperature

All objects emit radiation, whatever their temperature. As the temperature of an object rises, the amount of radiation it emits increases but the peak wavelength of the radiation decreases. That's why the light from a very hot object changes from red-hot to white-hot as its temperature rises. Astronomers use this principle to measure the surface temperature of stars. Although not always obvious to the naked eye, cooler stars emit red light more strongly and hotter stars emit blue light more strongly.

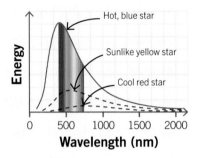

Hertzsprung–Russell diagrams

About 100 years ago, the Danish astronomer Ejnar Hertzsprung and the US astronomer Henry Russell independently discovered a pattern in the properties of stars. If stars are plotted on a graph of brightness against temperature, they form a distinctive pattern that reflects their stage of life. Most stars occupy a diagonal band called the main sequence. These are stars that are relatively small in volume and that fuse hydrogen in their cores. Other stars, such as ageing giant stars that are running out of fuel, form clusters away from the main sequence.

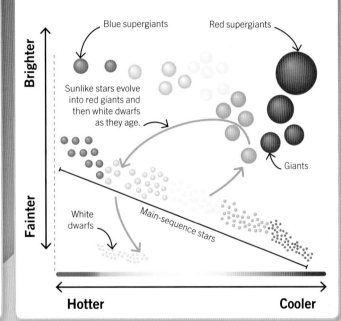

Magnitude

Astronomers use the word magnitude for the brightness of a star. There are two ways of measuring magnitude. Apparent magnitude is how bright a star looks from Earth, but this can be misleading as distant stars look fainter. Absolute magnitude is a standardized measure of how bright all stars would look from the same distance (32.6 light years).

These two stars look equally bright in the night sky, but in reality, star A is brighter but further away.

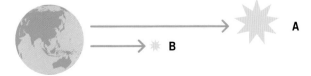

Earth

Glossary

Absolute magnitude The brightness of a star when observed from a standard distance. This is useful for comparing the brightness of stars regardless of their distance from Earth.

Absolute zero The lowest temperature possible, when all atoms stop moving. In the three main temperature scales (Kelvin, Celsius, and Fahrenheit), absolute zero is 0 K, −273°C, and −459°F.

Absorption spectrum A pattern of dark lines in the spectrum of light that has passed through a gas, such as in the outer layers of a star. These lines show the wavelengths of light absorbed by the gas, which represent elements present in the star.

Acceleration The rate of change of velocity. Acceleration can mean speeding up, slowing down, or changing direction. Acceleration is a vector quantity. Units are m/s².

Acceleration due to gravity The rate at which a falling object accelerates due to gravity in the absence of air resistance. On Earth this is about 9.8 m/s² and often rounded to 10 m/s².

Aerodynamic Relating to the way air moves over objects. It is often used to mean a smooth shape that reduces air resistance.

Air resistance The force that resists the movement of objects through the air. This force is mostly due to collisions with air particles.

Alpha decay A form of radioactive decay in which an atomic nucleus gives off an alpha particle.

Alpha particle A particle that consists of two neutrons and two protons (the same as a helium nucleus). Alpha particles are emitted from some atomic nuclei during radioactive decay.

Alternating current (a.c.) An electric current that reverses direction at regular intervals. *See also* direct current (d.c.).

Alternator An electric generator that makes alternating current from mechanical motion, usually by spinning a coil of wire in a magnetic field. *See also* generator.

Ammeter A device that measures electrical current.

Ampere (A) The unit of electrical current, often called an amp.

Amplitude The maximum displacement of a wave from its average position. It is the height of a wave's peak above the midline (half the vertical distance from the peak of a wave to a trough).

Angle of incidence The angle between the incident (incoming) light ray and the normal line.

Angle of reflection The angle between the reflected light ray and the normal line.

Apparent magnitude How bright a star appears to us on Earth. *See also* absolute magnitude.

Asteroid A rocky body that orbits the Sun. Most asteroids are in the asteroid belt between Mars and Jupiter.

Asteroid belt A region between the orbits of Mars and Jupiter where many asteroids exist. Jupiter's strong gravity prevents the asteroids from forming a new rocky planet.

Atmosphere The layer of air that surrounds a planet.

Atmospheric pressure The force of the atmosphere pressing on a square metre of Earth's surface, caused by the weight of air above. Units are Pascal (Pa), where 1 Pa = 1 N/m².

Atom The smallest part of an element that has the chemical properties of that element. An atom is made up of protons, neutrons, and electrons.

Atomic energy Sometimes referred to as nuclear energy, this is energy stored in the bonds between the neutrons and protons in an atomic nucleus. This energy may be released during nuclear fission or nuclear fusion.

Atomic number Sometimes called the proton number, this is the number of protons in an atom's nucleus. Each element has a different atomic number.

Average speed The average speed of a journey is the total distance travelled divided by the time taken. *See also* instantaneous speed.

Background radiation Low-intensity radiation that is around us all the time. Some of it is emitted by radioactive substances in rocks and other materials around us, and some comes from space (cosmic radiation).

Balanced forces The forces acting on an object are balanced if they add up to a net force of zero newtons. For example, the forces on a cyclist are balanced when the forward force from pedalling is equal to the forces of air resistance and friction.

Battery Two or more electrical cells connected in series make up a battery. *See also* cell.

Becquerel (Bq) A unit of radioactive decay. 1 Bq means that, on average, one atomic nucleus is decaying each second in the sample being measured.

Beta decay A form of radioactive decay in which an atomic nucleus gives off a beta particle.

Beta particle A high-speed electron. Beta particles are emitted from some atomic nuclei during radioactive decay.

Big bang The event in which the Universe is thought to have begun, around 13.8 billion years ago, rapidly expanding from a singularity (a single point).

Biofuel Any fuel made from recently living plant or animal matter, for example the conversion of sugar cane into ethanol fuel. If the sugar cane is regrown as quickly as it is harvested, then this biofuel can be considered renewable.

Bond A force between atoms or molecules that holds them together. Chemical reactions involve the making and breaking of bonds.

Braking distance The distance travelled by a vehicle from the moment the brake is pressed until the vehicle stops.

Cell A device that stores energy and produces an electric current when it is part of a complete circuit.

Celsius A temperature scale based on the freezing point (0°C) and boiling point (100°C) of water at sea level.

Centre of mass Sometimes called the centre of gravity, this is a point in an object where all its weight appears to be concentrated. You can balance a pencil halfway along its length because that's where its centre of mass is.

Centripetal force A pulling force that causes an object to move along a curved or circular path. For example, the tension force in a string tied to a heavy object that's being swung round in circles.

Chain reaction A chemical or nuclear reaction in which the products trigger similar reactions. Uncontrolled chain reactions can cause explosions.

Change of state A change between two states of matter (solid, liquid, gas).

Charge (or electric charge) A basic property of some particles, such as electrons or protons, that makes them feel a force in an electromagnetic field. Charge can be positive or negative. Similar charges repel, opposite charges attract.

Chemical Any element or compound, especially those produced or extracted in an industrial process. Water, iron, salt, and oxygen are all examples of chemicals.

Chemical change A chemical change occurs when atomic bonds are made and broken in a chemical reaction. This results in a new chemical substance being formed.

Chemical energy The energy stored in the bonds between atoms. It may be released during a chemical reaction, for example as heat and light. Food, fuels, and electrical cells store chemical energy.

Chemical reaction A process that changes substances into new substances by breaking and making chemical bonds.

Circuit The path through which an electric current can flow.

Climate The pattern of weather and seasons a place experiences in a typical year.

Climate change Long-term changes in Earth's weather patterns. *See also* global warming.

Closed system A system that matter does not leave or enter. However, energy may enter or leave the system. *See also* system.

Comet A mass of ice and rock that travels around the Sun in an elliptical orbit. Some of the dust may stream out to form a tail that points away from the Sun.

Compass A device containing a small magnetic needle allowed to rotate freely. The needle lines up with Earth's magnetic field.

Component of a force The part of a force that acts in a particular direction. For example, when pushing a wheelbarrow some of your push force moves the wheelbarrow forwards (horizontal) and some acts upwards, lifting the wheelbarrow (vertical).

Compound A substance consisting of two or more elements whose atoms have bonded.

Compression Pressing together or squeezing.

Concave lens A lens that curves inwards in the middle. Also called a diverging lens.

Concentration A measure of the amount of particles of a substance when mixed with another substance. For example, the concentration of carbon dioxide in air is about 412 particles for every million air particles.

Condensation The change of state when a gas turns into a liquid.

Conduction The movement of heat or electricity through a substance.

Conductor A substance through which heat or electric current flows easily.

Conservation of energy *See* Law of conservation of energy.

Conservation of momentum *See* Law of conservation of momentum.

Constant A quantity that does not vary, symbolized by a letter in an equation. Constants usually represent a physical property, such as how easily stretched a spring is (spring constant).

Contact force Any force delivered through direct contact. Examples include air resistance, friction, and tension.

Contamination Contamination occurs when unwanted, often toxic substances enter a system, such as radioactive material entering a human body. *See also* irradiation.

Continuous variable A variable that can take any value (between limits) and is not limited to whole numbers, such as a person's height. *See also* discrete variable.

Control variable A variable that needs to be kept constant in an experiment. This is done to see properly the effect of changing the independent variable on the dependent variable. For example, keeping room temperature constant during an experiment to measure the temperature of hot water as it cools.

Convection The transfer of heat through a fluid (liquid or gas), caused by particles rising from hotter, less dense areas and sinking from cooler, more dense areas.

Converging lens A lens that curves outwards in the middle. Also called a convex lens. Converging lenses make parallel beams of light come together.

Convex lens A lens that curves outwards in the middle. Also called a converging lens.

Correlation A correlation between two variables means that as one variable changes, the other also changes in a predictable way. Correlation does not necessarily mean that changing one variable causes the other to change.

Cosmic microwave background radiation (CMBR) Faint microwave radiation found throughout the Universe. It is thought to be energy left over from the big bang.

Cosmic rays Highly energetic particles, such as electrons and protons, that travel through space at close to the speed of light.

Coulomb (C) The unit of electrical charge. One coulomb is the quantity of charge moved in one second by a current of one amp.

Critical angle An angle of incidence greater than the critical angle causes total internal reflection (TIR) instead of refraction.

Crumple zone A safety feature in which parts of a vehicle are designed to deform (crumple) in a collision. This means that the vehicle decelerates over a longer period of time, reducing the chance of serious injuries.

Crust (Earth) The thin rigid outer surface of Earth, made of rock.

Current (electric) A flow of charged particles such as electrons or ions. The unit is the ampere (A).

Curve of best fit A smooth curve drawn through the points on a graph that comes as close to as many of them as possible. *See also* line of best fit.

Dark energy A poorly understood force that acts in the opposite direction to gravity, causing the Universe to expand. About two-thirds of the content of the Universe is dark energy.

Dark matter Invisible matter that can only be detected by its gravitational effect on visible matter. Dark matter helps to hold galaxies together.

Data Information gathered in an experiment.

Decay (radioactive) The process by which a radioactive atom's nucleus spontaneously emits ionizing radiation, often transforming into a different element.

Deceleration Slowing down. It may be called negative acceleration.

Density The mass (amount of matter) of a substance per unit volume. Units are kg/m³ or g/cm³.

Dependent variable The variable that you measure in an experiment.

Diffuse reflection This occurs when light is reflected in random directions from an uneven surface.

Diffusion The gradual mixing of two or more substances as a result of the random movement of their particles.

Diminished (of an image) An image that is smaller than the object.

Diode An electronic component that lets electricity flow in one direction only.

Direct current (d.c.) An electric current that flows in one direction only. *See also* alternating current (a.c.).

Discrete variable A variable that may only have certain values, such as months of the year.

Displacement 1. The straight line distance between two points in a particular direction (a vector quantity). Units are metres (m) or kilometres (km). 2. The moving aside of a medium by an object placed in that medium, such as bath water rising when a person gets in it.

Dissipate The process by which something spreads out, becoming less concentrated as it does so and effectively disappearing. For example, heat escaping from a poorly insulated house will dissipate into the atmosphere.

Distance–time graph A graph that represents a journey with distance on the vertical (y) axis and time on the horizontal (x) axis. The gradient of the line at any point is the speed at that moment.

Diverging lens A lens that curves inwards in the middle. Also called a concave lens. Diverging lenses make parallel beams of light spread out.

Drag Another name for air resistance or water resistance.

Dwarf planet A small, planet-like object that is massive enough to have become rounded by its own gravity but not massive enough for its gravity to have cleared the surrounding space of objects.

Dynamo A generator that produces direct current.

Earth wire A wire connected to the metal case of an appliance such as a kettle. If there is a fault and the case becomes "live", then a large current immediately flows from the case through the earth wire. This causes a fuse to melt or triggers a circuit breaker, making the appliance safe.

Earthed An electrical appliance is earthed if it is connected to an earth wire.

Efficiency A measure (usually a percentage) of how much of a system's input energy is converted into useful energy.

Effort A force applied against a load, such as the lifting force used to raise a wheelbarrow.

Elastic An object is elastic if it returns to its original size and shape after being stretched or compressed.

Elastic collision A collision between objects that spring back into their original shape after impact, with no loss of kinetic energy.

Elastic limit The maximum amount that a material can be stretched or compressed and still return to its original shape.

Elastic potential energy The energy stored in a stretched or compressed material, sometimes called strain energy. This stored energy comes from the work done in stretching or compressing the material.

Electric current A flow of charged particles such as electrons or ions. The unit is the ampere (A).

Electric field A region surrounding a charged particle (such as an electron or ion) in which other charged particles experience a force.

Electrical power The amount of electrical energy converted every second into other forms of energy. It is measured in watts (W).

Electricity The effects caused by the presence and/or movement of electric charge.

Electromagnet A coil of wire that becomes magnetic when electricity flows through it.

Electromagnetic induction The process by which a voltage is induced in a conductor when the conductor moves across a magnetic field. If the conductor is part of a complete circuit then a current will flow in that circuit.

Electromagnetic radiation A form of energy that travels at the speed of light, is a transverse wave, and can travel through a vacuum.

Electromagnetic spectrum The complete range of electromagnetic radiation from radio waves to gamma rays. *See also* spectrum and visible spectrum.

Electron One of the three main particles in an atom (with the proton and neutron). It has a negative charge.

Electron shell One of the layers in which electrons are arranged outside the nucleus of an atom.

Electrostatic force The force experienced by a charged particle when it is in an electric field.

Element A pure substance that cannot be broken down into other substances by chemical reactions. Examples include carbon, hydrogen, and oxygen.

Ellipse An oval shape like a flattened circle.

Energy The capacity to do work. Energy can be stored and transferred in different ways. For example, energy can be stored in the chemicals in a cell and transferred by electricity when the cell is put into a circuit.

Energy resource A store or source of energy that can be used.

Equilibrium A state of physical or chemical balance.

Evaporation A change of state in which a liquid turns into a gas (vapour).

Fair test A scientific experiment in which the only things that change are the independent and dependent variables.

Field The region in which a non-contact force such as gravity or magnetism has an effect.

Field lines Lines in a diagram of a force field that show the direction in which the force acts. The field is strongest where the lines are closest together.

Fluid A substance that can flow, such as a gas or liquid.

Focal length The distance between the focal point of a lens and the centre of the lens.

Focal point The point at which parallel rays of light are focused by a converging lens, or the point from which rays of light appear to have come from after passing through a diverging lens.

Force A push or a pull. Forces change the speed, direction, or shape of objects. Force is a vector quantity, and the units are newtons (N).

Force field The region in which a force can be detected.

Force meter Also called a newton meter, a force meter is any device that measures force.

Fossil fuel A fuel derived from the fossilized remains of living things. Coal, crude oil, and natural gas are fossil fuels.

Free body diagram A diagram showing all the forces acting on an object. The forces are represented by arrows showing the direction of the forces.

Freezing point The temperature at which a liquid turns into a solid. It is the same temperature as the melting point of the solid.

Frequency The number of waves that pass a point every second. The units are hertz (Hz).

Friction A force that resists or stops the movement of objects that are in contact with one another.

Fulcrum The point around which an object rotates. Also called pivot.

Fuse A safety device used in electrical circuits. It contains a thin wire that melts if too much current passes through, breaking the circuit.

g A measure of gravitational field strength. The value for Earth is 9.8 N/kg, which causes falling objects to accelerate at 9.8 m/s^2 in the absence of air resistance.

Galaxy A large collection of stars and clouds of gas and dust that are held together by gravity.

Gamma decay A form of radioactive decay in which an atomic nucleus emits gamma radiation – a dangerous, high-energy type of electromagnetic radiation.

Gamma rays Electromagnetic radiation with the highest energies, highest frequencies, and shortest wavelengths. It is emitted from the nuclei of decaying radioactive atoms.

Gas A state of matter in which the particles are far apart and move about randomly and quickly.

Gears Mechanical devices such as interlocking cogs that make the turning effect of a force bigger or smaller. Gears can make machines like cars move faster (but with less force) or slower (with more force).

Geiger-Müller (GM) tube An instrument used to detect and measure radiation. It consists of two plates with a high voltage across them. Ionizing radiation causes a spark to jump between the plates, which is detected by circuitry in the instrument. This circuitry and the GM tube are together called a Geiger counter.

Geocentric model A model of the Universe with Earth at its centre.

Geostationary orbit A satellite in geostationary orbit is positioned over the equator, moves in the same direction that Earth turns, and takes about 24 hours to orbit Earth once. To an observer on Earth, the satellite appears stationary in the sky.

Global warming A rise in the average temperature of Earth's atmosphere, caused by increasing levels of greenhouse gases. One of the main causes is the burning of fossil fuels, which releases the greenhouse gas carbon dioxide.

Gradient The steepness of a line. Gradient is measured by dividing the vertical distance between two points on the line by the horizontal distance between these same two points.

Gravitational constant (G) More commonly referred to as "big G", this is a tiny number used in gravity calculations. Its smallness tells us that gravity is a very weak force that needs very massive objects to produce a noticeable gravitational field.

Gravitational field The space surrounding an object with mass, in which another object with mass will experience an attractive, gravitational force.

Gravitational field strength The force with which a gravitational field pulls on a mass of 1 kg. Units are N/kg. *See also* acceleration due to gravity.

Gravitational potential energy (GPE) The energy that a body has as a result of its mass and position (usually height) in a gravitational field. Lifting an object increases its store of GPE.

Gravity A force of attraction between all objects that have mass. Earth's gravity keeps our feet on the ground and makes objects fall when we drop them.

Greenhouse effect The way in which gases such as carbon dioxide trap heat in Earth's atmosphere. The build-up of these gases leads to global warming.

Greenhouse gases Gases such as carbon dioxide and methane that absorb energy reflected by Earth's surface, stopping it from escaping into space.

Half-life The time taken for radioactivity in a sample to drop to half of its original value. In other words, the time taken for half the radioactive atoms in the sample to decay.

Heat Energy stored in the movement of atoms (vibrations for solids). Heat can be transferred by conduction, convection, and infrared radiation.

Heliocentric model A model of the solar system with the Sun at its centre.

Hertz (Hz) The SI unit of frequency. One hertz is one cycle (one complete wave) per second.

Hooke's law This law says that the deformation (stretching or squeezing) of a material is proportional to the force applied to it. This law applies up to the elastic limit, beyond which the material will not spring back into its original shape when the force is removed.

Hypothesis An educated guess or idea about how something works. Scientists test their hypotheses by carrying out experiments.

Incident ray The ray of light that enters a lens or shines upon ("is incident upon") a mirror.

Independent variable The variable in an experiment that is deliberately changed so its effect on the dependent variable can be measured.

Induced magnet A material that becomes temporarily magnetized when placed in a magnetic field. For example, the iron core of an electromagnet becomes an induced magnet when the electromagnet is switched on.

Industrialization The widespread development of industries in a country, often leading to the growth of cities and road or rail networks.

Inelastic collision A collision in which kinetic energy is lost and the colliding objects change shape permanently. *See also* elastic collision.

Inertia The tendency of an object to keep moving in a straight line or remain at rest until a force acts on it.

Inertial mass A measure of how difficult it is to change the velocity (speed and/or direction) of an object.

Infrared radiation Electromagnetic radiation with a lower frequency and longer wavelength than visible light. Infrared radiation transfers heat and is used by remote control devices for televisions.

Infrasound Sound with a frequency less than about 20 Hz. This sound cannot be heard as it is too low for the human ear to detect.

Instantaneous speed The speed at which an object is travelling at any particular moment. Speedometers on cars show instantaneous speed. *See also* average speed.

Insulator A material that reduces or stops the transfer of heat, electricity, or sound.

Interference The process whereby two or more waves combine, either reinforcing each other or cancelling each other out.

Internal energy The total kinetic and potential energies of all the particles in a system.

Inversely proportional If two variables (such as pressure and volume of a fixed amount of gas in a container) are inversely proportional, then as one increases the other decreases in such a way that their product (pressure × volume) remains constant. For example, if you double the pressure of a gas at constant temperature then the volume will halve.

Inverted image An image that is upside down in comparison with the object being viewed.

Ion An atom (or group of atoms) that has lost or gained one or more electrons and so become electrically charged.

Ionizing radiation Radiation (nuclear or electromagnetic) with enough energy to remove the electrons from the outer shells of atoms to form ions.

Irradiated An object or material that has been exposed to ionizing radiation.

Isolated system A system that matter and energy cannot leave or enter.

Isotopes Forms of an element that have different numbers of neutrons in the atomic nucleus but the same number of protons.

Joule (J) The unit of energy, equal to the work done by a force of 1 N moving 1 m in the direction of the force.

Kelvin (K) A scale of temperature that begins at absolute zero (−273°C). Its unit of measurement is the kelvin. A rise or fall of 1 K is the same as a rise or fall of 1°C.

Kilowatt (kW) A unit of power equal to 1000 watts.

Kilowatt-hour (kWh) A unit of energy used by utility companies in energy bills. 1 kWh is the energy transferred when a 1 kW appliance is used for 1 hour. 1 kWh is equal to 3 600 000 joules.

Kinetic energy The energy stored in an object because of its movement. Its value increases with the object's speed and mass.

Latent heat The energy transferred during a change of state at constant temperature. Latent energy is absorbed when ice melts and when water boils but is released when steam condenses and when water freezes.

Law of conservation of energy A law stating that you cannot create or destroy energy. Energy can only be stored or transferred.

Law of conservation of momentum A law stating that the total momentum of a system, before and after a collision, remains constant as long as no outside resultant forces are acting on the system.

Law of reflection This law says that when light is reflected from a plane (flat) mirror, the angle of incidence equals the angle of reflection.

LED Light-emitting diode. An electrical component that only allows currrent to flow in one direction and that emits light when current flows through it.

Lens A curved, transparent piece of plastic or glass that can bend light rays using refraction.

Lift The upward force produced on a wing when it moves through the air.

Light Electromagnetic radiation that our eyes can see. White light is a mixture of all the colours of the rainbow, which together make up the visible spectrum. Some scientists use the term "visible light" for radiation our eyes can see and "light" for all kinds of electromagnetic radiation.

Light gate A device that detects moving objects when they pass between a source of light and a light sensor, allowing precise measurements of time to be taken.

Light year A unit of distance used in astronomy. One light year is the distance travelled by light in one year, equal to 9.46 trillion km (9.46×10^{15} m).

Light-dependent resistor (LDR) A component whose resistance increases or decreases in a predictable way when the amount of light that it absorbs changes. LDRs are useful in control systems, for example in automatically switching street lights on when it gets dark.

Limit of proportionality If you stretch a material beyond this point then Hooke's law won't apply. The relationship between force and extension is no longer a straight-line graph (linear) but becomes curved (non-linear).

Line of best fit A line drawn through scattered data points on a graph so that it comes close to as many of them as possible. Drawing a line of best fit helps to identify the relationship between the independent and dependent variables.

Linear relationship Two variables have a linear relationship if the graph of this relationship is a straight line. For example, a material that obeys Hooke's law shows a linear relationship between the force applied to it and the extension.

Liquid A state of matter between a solid and a gas, in which the particles can slide around but remain close together and attract one another.

Live wire The wire in a mains electrical circuit that carries the electric current.

Load The total force pushing on an object or opposing the movement of an object, such as the weight of heavy material in a loaded wheelbarrow.

Longitudinal wave A wave in which particles vibrate back and forth along the direction of travel of the wave.

Long-sighted Unable to see nearby objects clearly. Long-sightedness can be corrected by wearing glasses with converging lenses.

Lubrication Using oil or other lubricants to reduce friction.

Luminous A luminous object emits its own light. For example, a candle, torch, or star.

Magnet Any object that produces a magnetic field.

Magnetic field The space around a magnet where it can affect magnetic materials. Magnetic fields decrease in strength as you move further from the magnet.

Magnetic poles 1. The two ends of a magnet, called the north and south poles. 2. The two points on Earth towards which a compass needle points.

Magnetism The property of some materials, especially iron, to attract or repel similar materials.

Main sequence star A star in the middle of its life. A main sequence star, like our Sun, emits energy by fusing hydrogen into heavier elements such as helium.

Mantle (Earth) The large part of Earth's interior between the outer core and the crust, made of rock.

Mass The amount of matter in an object, measured in grams, kilograms, or tonnes. Mass and weight are not the same. Weight is the gravitational force between Earth and the object with mass being considered.

Mass number Also called the nucleon number, the total number of protons and neutrons in the nucleus of an atom.

Matter Anything that has mass and occupies space.

Medium The matter through which a wave is travelling.

Megawatt (MW) A large unit of power equal to 1 million watts (10^6 W). This unit is commonly used in describing electricity generation.

Melting point The temperature at which a solid turns into a liquid. It is the same temperature as the freezing point of the liquid.

Microwaves Electromagnetic waves with a wavelength longer than that of infrared rays but shorter than that of radio waves. Microwaves are sometimes said to be a type of radio wave.

Molecule a particle of matter made of two or more atoms strongly bonded together.

Moment The turning effect of a force, such as a spanner turning a nut. The moment of a force is calculated by multiplying the force by its perpendicular distance from the pivot. The unit is the newton metre (Nm).

Momentum The tendency of an object to keep on moving, equal to its mass times its velocity. Units are kg m/s.

Motor A machine that uses electricity and magnetism to produce motion that is usually rotational.

Nebula A huge cloud of dust and gas in space in which new stars may form.

Net force When you add up the forces on an object and take into account their directions, the result is a single force that would have the same effect, called the net force or resultant force.

Neutral wire The wire that completes the circuit in mains electrical circuits. It is usually kept at zero volts.

Neutron One of the two main particles in the nucleus of an atom. It has no electric charge and a relative mass of 1.

Newton (N) The unit of force.

Newton metre (Nm) The unit of the moment of a force.

Non-contact force Any force that acts at a distance. Non-contact forces include gravity, magnetism, and electrostatic forces.

Non-linear A relationship between two variables that is not a straight line on a graph. For example, if you double the current flowing in an electrical device then the power of the device rises by four times.

Non-renewable resource A resource that will eventually run out, such as coal, oil, or gas.

Normal A line drawn at 90 degrees to the plane of a mirror or lens. Angles of light rays are measured from this line.

Normal force The part of a contact force that acts at 90 degrees to the surface being considered.

Nuclear energy 1. Energy stored in the bonds between the particles in an atomic nucleus. This may be released by nuclear fusion or nuclear fission. 2. Electricity generated by a nuclear power station.

Nuclear equation Similar to a chemical equation, a nuclear equation describes the changes that take place during nuclear reactions such as fission, fusion, and radioactive decay.

Nuclear fission A process in which the nucleus of an atom splits into two smaller nuclei, releasing energy.

Nuclear fuel The fuel for nuclear reactors. Most commonly this is enriched uranium (uranium-235), but some reactors use other fuels, such as plutonium or thorium.

Nuclear fusion A process in which atomic nuclei fuse (join) to form heavier nuclei, releasing energy. Stars such as the Sun are powered by the fusion of hydrogen nuclei to make helium.

Nuclear power station A power station in which energy released by nuclear fission reactions is used to generate electricity. This energy is used to heat water to make steam, which is used to drive generators to produce electricity.

Nucleon A proton or a neutron, i.e. any particle in an atom's nucleus.

Nucleon number The total number of protons and neutrons in the nucleus of an atom. Also called mass number.

Nucleus (plural nuclei) The centre of an atom, made up of protons and neutrons. It contains most of the atom's mass.

Ohm (Ω) The unit of electrical resistance.

Orbit The path of a body around another, more massive body, such as the path of Earth around the Sun.

Oscillation A regular movement back and forth.

Oscilloscope An instrument that shows electrical signals on a screen. It is often used to help us visualize waves, such as sound waves.

Outlier An item of data that does not fit the pattern of the other data points. Outliers are usually errors but may sometimes reveal something unexpected about a system. Ideally, an experimenter will return to the experiment and try to measure the outlier again.

Parallel (electrical circuits) Components connected in parallel are connected side by side in parallel branches rather than in a line (in series).

Particles Basic units from which all substances are made, such as atoms or molecules. Subatomic particles are those smaller than an atom, such as protons.

Pascal (Pa) The unit of pressure. 1 Pa is a force of 1 N spread over an area of 1 m^2.

PET scanner A machine used in medicine to form images of processes in the body to help diagnose diseases. PET stands for positron emission tomography.

Physics The scientific study of force, motion, matter, and energy.

Pivot The point around which an object rotates. Also called fulcrum.

Plane A flat surface.

Plate tectonics The theory that explains volcanoes, earthquakes, and other geological phenomena. It says that the surface of Earth is divided into large plates that are able to move against each other.

Potential difference Also called voltage, the difference in electric potential between two points. Potential difference can be thought of as providing the "push" that makes electric current flow. It is measured in volts (V).

Potential divider An electric circuit that uses resistors in series for controlling the voltage supplied to a parallel branch in the circuit. One of the resistors is usually a component such as an LDR or thermistor.

Potential energy Energy stored in the shape or position of something. Gravitational potential energy is the energy stored in an object because of its height. Elastic potential energy is stored in objects when they are stretched, squeezed, or twisted.

Power A measure of how quickly energy is transferred. For example, a bulb with a power rating of 100 W converts 100 J of electrical energy every second into heat and light energy. The unit of power is the watt (W).

Pressure The force per unit area. For example, the pressure exerted by you on the ground is equal to your weight divided by the total area of your soles and heels. The units are N/m^2 or pascals (Pa).

Prism A triangular wedge of glass or other transparent material that can split white light into a spectrum of colours.

Proportional Two variables are proportional to each other if their graph is a straight line through the origin. If one variable is multiplied by a number, the other variable is also multiplied by the same number (so if one doubles, the other doubles too).

Proton One of the two main particles found in the nucleus of an atom. It has a relative mass of 1 and a charge of +1.

Proton number Sometimes called the atomic number, the number of protons in an atom's nucleus. Each element has a different proton number.

Radiation An electromagnetic wave or a stream of particles from a source of radioactivity.

Radio waves The longest wavelength, lowest frequency, and lowest energy form of electromagnetic radiation. Uses include communication and radar.

Radioactive A material is radioactive if it contains unstable atomic nuclei that decay into smaller nuclei, releasing ionizing radiation as they do so.

Radiotherapy The use of radioactive materials to treat cancer by destroying cancerous body tissue. This radioactivity may be focused on a very small spot in the body so there is minimal damage to healthy surrounding areas.

Ray diagram A diagram that represents light rays and how they are affected by lenses or mirrors.

Real image An image formed when light rays are focused on a surface such as a screen. See also virtual image.

Red giant A late stage in a star's life when hydrogen in the star's core has been converted to helium, the core has collapsed, and outer parts of the star have cooled and greatly expanded, forming a large, red star.

Red supergiant An ageing star similar to a red giant but on a much larger scale. These are the largest stars in the Universe.

Redshift The apparent stretching of light waves from distant galaxies into longer wavelengths. This is strong evidence that these galaxies are moving away from us and from each other, which indicates that the Universe is expanding.

Refraction The bending of a wave as it speeds up or slows down on moving from one medium to another. Refraction of light makes a stick placed in water look bent at the point it enters the water.

Relative mass The mass of a particle or molecule in comparison to one-twelfth of the mass of a carbon-12 atom. It is a useful unit when working with very small masses. Carbon-12 is chosen as a standard for convenience and historical reasons. Protons and neutrons have a relative mass of 1.

Renewable energy A source of energy that will not run out, such as sunlight, wave power, or wind power.

Repeatable (experiment) An experiment is repeatable if making the same measurement with the same equipment gives the same result.

Reproducible (experiment) An experiment is reproducible if someone else follows your method with different equipment and gets the same result.

Resistance A measure of how much a material opposes the flow of electric current. The units are ohms (Ω).

Resultant force When you add up the forces on an object and take into account their directions, the result is a single force that would have the same effect, called the resultant force or net force.

Sankey diagram A diagram that uses arrows of different widths to represent the quantity of energy flowing into a system and the useful and wasted energy leaving it. It is useful in showing and calculating the efficiencies of devices.

Scalar A quantity that has a magnitude (size) but no direction. Mass and temperature are scalar quantities. *See also* vector.

Seismic wave A wave that travels through Earth from an earthquake, volcanic eruption, large explosion, or other source.

Semiconductor A material partway between an electrical conductor (such as a metal) and an insulator (such as glass). Semiconductors are used in most electronic circuits.

Series (electrical circuits) Components connected in succession in an electrical circuit are described as being in series. The same current flows through all of them. *See also* parallel.

Short-sighted Unable to see distant objects clearly. Short-sightedness can be corrected by wearing glasses with diverging lenses.

SI unit The standard, agreed international units for physical measurements. For example, the SI unit for mass is the kilogram. SI stands for Système International.

Significant figures The number of figures (digits) that an experimenter considers accurate in a measurement. For example, if timing a 100 m sprinter by hand with a stopwatch, including hundredths of a second would not be reasonable as a human cannot be that accurate. Three significant figures in this case would be sufficient (two for seconds and one for tenths of a second).

Solenoid A cylindrical coil of wire that becomes a magnet when an electric current is passed through it.

Solution A mixture in which the molecules or ions of a substance are spread out in a liquid. For example, salt water is a solution.

Sonar Sound navigation and ranging. A method of detecting objects underwater by sending out sound waves and interpreting their echoes.

Sound A kind of wave that travels through matter, alternately squeezing particles together and then pulling them apart. Sound waves in air are detected by the human ear.

Specific heat capacity The amount of energy it takes to heat 1 kg of a substance by 1°C. The same quantity of energy is released when 1 kg of the substance cools by 1°C. Units are J/kg °C.

Specific latent heat The amount of energy taken in or released when 1 kg of a substance changes state without a change of temperature. The units are J/kg. *See also* latent heat.

Spectrum (electromagnetic) The range of the wavelengths of electromagnetic radiation. The full spectrum ranges from gamma rays, with wavelengths shorter than an atom, to radio waves, whose wavelengths may be many kilometres long. The visible spectrum is the part we can see.

Specular reflection Regular reflection of light off a smooth surface, such as a mirror.

Speed The distance travelled in a particular time. Speed is a scalar quantity and does not have a direction. Units are m/s, km/h or mph. *See also* velocity.

Split-ring commutator A device in electric motors that reverses the electric current in the rotating coil at every half-turn of the coil. This means that the electromagnetic force acting on the coil is always pushing the coil in the same direction.

Spring constant A number describing the strength of a spring, usually represented by the letter k. The greater the spring constant, the more force is needed to stretch the spring. The units are N/m.

Standard form Also called scientific notation, a way of abbreviating very large or small numbers. The significant figures are written with a decimal point after the first figure, followed by the power of 10 this needs to be multiplied by. For example the speed of light, which is about 300 000 000 m/s, can be written as 3.0×10^8 m/s.

Standing wave A standing wave forms when a wave interferes with its own reflection, resulting in peaks and troughs that do not move. Waves formed in the bodies and strings of musical instruments are standing waves.

Star A massive ball of incandescent gas inside which nuclear fusion produces large amounts of electromagnetic radiation. The fusion processes in stars produce nearly all the chemical elements in the periodic table.

States of matter The different physical forms that matter can take, such as solid, liquid, and gas.

Static electricity An electric charge held on an object, caused by the gain or loss of electrons.

Stopping distance The total distance travelled between a driver seeing a hazard on the road and the car stopping. Stopping distance = thinking distance + braking distance.

Streamlined Shaped to reduce the force of air or water resistance. Streamlined objects are usually narrow, with smooth, tapering shapes.

Subatomic particle A particle that is smaller than an atom, such as a proton, neutron, or electron.

Sublimation A change of state from solid straight to gas without becoming a liquid.

Supernova An explosion caused by the collapse of a massive star. A supernova may be many billion times brighter than the Sun. The vast energies of supernovas are enough to produce elements heavier than iron by nuclear fusion.

System The environment in which physical phenomena being studied exist. For example, in studying gases we may choose a cylinder and piston as the system, but for studying climate change it may be the entire planet.

Systematic error An experimental error typically caused by faulty equipment, such as a balance that has not been zeroed correctly. This type of error is nonrandom and makes every measurement wrong by the same amount.

Temperature A scientific measure of how hot or cold something is. Temperature is a measure of the average kinetic energy of particles in a system, but not total internal energy. The units are °C (degrees Celsius) or K (kelvin).

Tension When forces pull an object in opposite directions, the object is in tension.

Terminal velocity The maximum velocity a falling object reaches when the force of air resistance balances the force of gravity pulling it downwards. For example, when the air resistance experienced by a parachutist becomes equal to their weight, they stop accelerating and fall at terminal velocity.

Tesla (T) The unit of magnetic flux density. It is closely related to the strength of a magnetic field.

Thermal image A picture produced using infrared radiation rather than visible light, with colours representing temperature. Hotter objects are usually depicted as redder and colder objects as bluer.

Thermistor A resistor whose resistance changes with temperature.

Thinking distance The distance travelled by a vehicle between a driver seeing a hazard on the road and pressing the brake. It depends on the reactions of the driver.

Total internal reflection Reflection of light within a medium such as glass or water when the angle of incidence is greater than a certain critical angle, resulting in an angle of refraction more than 90°. Total internal reflection is used to trap light in fibre-optic cables.

Transformer A device that uses electromagnetic induction to increase or decrease the voltage of an alternating electricity supply.

Transverse wave A wave in which the particles of the medium vibrate at right angles to the direction in which the wave travels. Waves on water are transverse.

Turbine A machine with blades like a fan that spins when air or liquid flows through it. Turbines are used to drive the generators in power stations.

Ultrasound Sound with frequencies above 20 000 Hz, which are too high for humans to hear.

Ultraviolet (UV) light Electromagnetic radiation with a shorter wavelength than visible light. Higher energy UV radiation is ionizing and can cause sunburn or even cancer. Uses of UV include security marking and disinfection.

Unbalanced forces Unbalanced forces produce a resultant (net) force on an object, causing acceleration or deformation (squashing or stretching).

Universe The whole of space and everything it contains.

Unstable isotope An isotope whose atomic nuclei are likely to break down and release radiation.

Upthrust The upward force exerted by a liquid or a gas on an object within it.

Uranium A radioactive element used as the fuel in nuclear power stations or as the active component in an atomic bomb.

Vacuum A space in which there is no matter.

Variables Things that might change in an experiment. Variables can be independent (the things you change), dependent (the thing you measure), or controlled (things you must keep the same).

Vector A quantity that has both magnitude (size) and direction, such as a force. *See also* scalar.

Velocity A measure of an object's speed and direction. Velocity is a vector quantity. The units are m/s or km/h.

Vibration Rapid to-and-fro movement. Musical instruments use vibration to generate sound waves.

Virtual image An image formed where light rays appear to be focused, such as a reflection in a mirror. Virtual images cannot be projected on a screen.

Visible spectrum The range of electromagnetic waves that we can see. The visible spectrum can be divided into seven colours: red, orange, yellow, green, blue, indigo, and violet.

Volt (V) The unit for potential difference (voltage).

Voltage A common term for electrical potential difference.

Voltmeter A device used to measure potential difference (voltage).

Volume The amount of space an object takes up. The units are m³ or cm³.

Water resistance A force that resists the movement of objects through water. Like air resistance, it always acts in the opposite direction to the object's motion.

Watt (W) The unit of power. 1 watt = 1 joule per second.

Wave Sound, light, and other energy transfers travel as waves – regular oscillations that spread out rapidly through matter or space.

Wavelength The distance between two successive peaks or two successive troughs in a wave.

Weight The force due to gravity felt by any object with mass. Weight is a force, so the units are newtons (N).

White dwarf The very hot, small, dense remains of a dead star.

Work The energy transferred when a force moves an object in a particular direction. The units are joules (J).

X-ray Electromagnetic radiation with high energy and frequency and very short wavelength. X-rays can penetrate most matter, which makes them useful for making images of bones and teeth.

Circuit symbols

Switch open (off)

Switch closed (on)

Cell

Battery

Bulb

Resistor

Variable resistor

Thermistor

LDR (light-dependent resistor)

Diode

LED

Fuse

Ammeter

Voltmeter

Motor

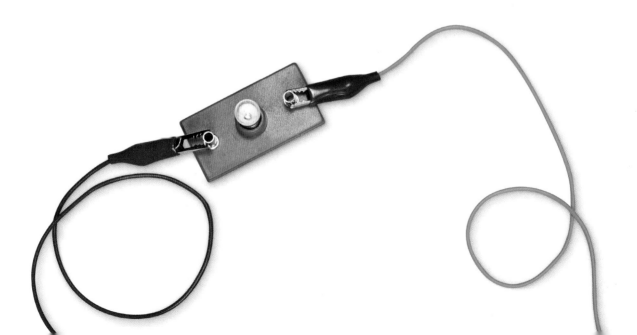

Index

Acknowledgments

The publisher would like to thank the following people for their help with making the book: Nayan Keshan and Sai Prasanna for editorial assistance; Mansi Agrawal, Tanisha Mandal, Baibhav Parida, and Lauren Quinn for design assistance; Peter Bull and Sanya Jain for illustrations; Neeraj Bhatia, Vijay Kandwal, Nityanand Kumar, Mohd Rizwan, Jagtar Singh, and Vikram Singh for CTS assistance; Harish Aggarwal, Suhita Dharamjit, Priyanka Sharma, and Saloni Singh for the jacket; Victoria Pyke for proofreading; and Helen Peters for the index.

The publisher would like to thank the following for their kind permission to reproduce their photographs:
(Key: a-above; b-below/bottom; c-centre; f-far; l-left; r-right; t-top)

1 Getty Images: Yamada Taro (c). 4 Getty Images / iStock: E+ / ThomasVogel (bl). 5 Science Photo Library: Dr Keith Wheeler (b). 6 Science Photo Library: (bc). 7 Dorling Kindersley: Stephen Oliver (b). 12 Alamy Stock Photo: Photo12 / Ann Ronan Picture Library (cla); Science History Images / Photo Researchers (br). Getty Images: Popperfoto (br). Science Photo Library: (cr); Royal Astronomical Society (ca). 13 Alamy Stock Photo: imageBROKER / Markus Keller (br); Stocktrek Images, Inc. / Roth Ritter (cra/Andromeda); Science History Images (bc). Dorling Kindersley: Science Museum, London (cl). NASA: JPL Caltech (cra); ROSAT, MPE (tr); JPL-Caltech / UCLA (ftr). Science Photo Library: Dr Eli Brinks (fcra). 14 Alamy Stock Photo: Hemis.fr / Francis Leroy (cra); mikecranephotography.com (cla). Dreamstime.com: Jim Parkin (crb). Science Photo Library: Cristina Pedrazzini (cra). 15 Dreamstime.com: Diadis (cl); Zhang Liwei (cr); Alf Ribeiro (clb); Flavio Massari (cra). 16 NOAA: (cra). 17 Alamy Stock Photo: sciencephotos (cra). Dorling Kindersley: Science Museum, London (bc). Dreamstime.com: Robert Davies (ca); Svetlana Zhukova (c); Yury Shirokov (tr). Getty Images / iStock: SchulteProductions (cr). 20 Dreamstime.com: Bizhan33 (br). 21 Alamy Stock Photo: Suchanon Sukjam (cl, clb). Dreamstime.com: Maxim Sergeenkov (clb/ruler, bl). Getty Images / iStock: didecs (br). 22 UNSCEAR: UNSCEAR 2008 Report Vol. I Sources And Effects Of Ionizing Radiation United Nations, Scientific Committee On The Effects Of Atomic Radiation (br). 29 123RF.com: Maria Tkach (cl, cla). Dorling Kindersley: Dave King / The Science Museum (crb). 32 123RF.com: olivierl (cr). Getty Images / iStock: E+ / ThomasVogel (cl). 34 Alamy Stock Photo: PhotosIndia.com LLC (cb); Science History Images / Photo Researchers (clb); Andrew Zarivny (br). Dreamstime.com: Konstantin Shaklein (ca). Getty Images: Corbis / VCG / Beau Lark (c); Moment / Sean Gladwell (cl). Getty Images / iStock: studiocasper (cla). 35 Getty Images: Photodisc / Creative Crop (bl). 36 Alamy Stock Photo: Cultura Creative (RF) / Mischa Keijser (bl). Dreamstime.com: Johan

Larson (clb). Getty Images / iStock: E+ / Mlenny (cla). 37 Alamy Stock Photo: Hemis.fr / Francis Leroy (cla). Dreamstime.com: Bborriss (clb). Shutterstock.com: Gary Saxe (tl). 38 Dreamstime.com: Hypermania37 (c); Peejay645 (cr). Getty Images / iStock: rancho_runner (cl). 40 Smil, V. 2017. Energy Transitions. Praeger.: bp Statistical Review of World Energy 2020. / © BP p.l.c. (c). 41 Dreamstime.com: Afxhome (c); Chukov (cb). 42 Alamy Stock Photo: Eye Ubiquitous / Paul Seheult (c). 43 Science Photo Library: Tony Mcconnell (cb). 46 Alamy Stock Photo: NASA Image Collection (br). 49 Alamy Stock Photo: David Wall (b). 50-51 Dreamstime.com: Julian Addington-barker (c). 51 Dreamstime.com: Destina156 (br). 54 Science Photo Library: Giphotostock (tr). 55 Dreamstime.com: Paul Prescott / Paulprescott (cl). 56 Getty Images / iStock: E+ / Abeleao (c, cr). 57 Getty Images / iStock: 3DSculptor (b). 58 Dreamstime.com: Wesley Abrams (b). 59 Dreamstime.com: Saletomic (b). 61 Alamy Stock Photo: DBURKE (bc). 69 Alamy Stock Photo: Malcolm Haines (b). 73 Dreamstime.com: Greg Epperson (b). 76 Alamy Stock Photo: parkerphotography (b). 78 Alamy Stock Photo: James Smith (c). 79 NASA: JPL-Caltech / MSSS (bc). Science Photo Library: Martyn F. Chillmaid (r). 81 123RF.com: Pumidol Leelerdsakulvong / lodimup (cra). Dreamstime.com: Jrtmedia (cra/Can). 84 Dreamstime.com: Lukawo (c). 85 Dreamstime.com: A-papantoniou (l). 86 Science Photo Library: (cl). 87 Alamy Stock Photo: imageBROKER / Norbert Eisele-Hein (b). 88 Alamy Stock Photo: LJSphotography (cl). 89 Dorling Kindersley: Ben Morgan (br). Dreamstime.com: Brad Calkins (cr); Andrei Kuzmik (ca); Nevinates (c); Joao Virissimo (cl). 90 Dorling Kindersley: Gerard Brown / Pedal Pedlar (br). Dreamstime.com: Tuja66 (c). 91 Dreamstime.com: Igor Yegorov (bl). 92 Dreamstime.com: Warrengoldswain (c). 93 NASA: NASA Earth Observatory (cr). 94 NASA: GSFC / Arizona State University (cr); NASA Earth Observatory (cl). 96 Getty Images: Moment / Photo by cuellar (br); Ezra Shaw (c). 97 123RF.com: Aleksei Sysoev (bl, cb). 99 Ariel Motor Company: (b). 101 Dreamstime.com: Chumphon Whangchom (r). 102 Science Photo Library: Gustoimages (c). 103 123RF.com: Sebastian Kaulitzki (c). 105 © The State of Queensland 2019: (b). 106 Alamy Stock Photo: WENN Rights Ltd (b). 109 Alamy Stock Photo: Bob Weymouth (b). 110-111 Alamy Stock Photo: Cultura Creative (RF) / Oliver Furrer. 113 Dreamstime.com: Le Thuy Do (cr). 114 Dreamstime.com: Gualtiero Boffi (cl). 117 Getty Images: Moment / Image Provided by Duane Walker. 121 Alamy Stock Photo: agefotostock / Plus Pix (br). Science Photo Library: Gustoimages (clb). 122 123RF.com: alexzaitsev (ca). Dreamstime.com: Kanok Sulaiman (cra). 123 Alamy Stock Photo: Mopic (cl, cr). 124 Science Photo Library: ER Degginger (c). 125 Science Photo Library: Dr Keith Wheeler. 127 Dreamstime.com: Mimagephotography (cr); Photographerlondon (cl). Getty

Images / iStock: invizbk (crb). 131 Science Photo Library: (c). 134 Alamy Stock Photo: Zoonar GmbH / Sebastian Kaulitzki (c). 135 Alamy Stock Photo: Nature Picture Library / Alex Mustard (b). Fotolia: Andrey Eremin / mbongo (c). 137 Alamy Stock Photo: sciencephotos (c). 138 Dreamstime.com: Robert Davies (clb/Goggles). Fotolia: apttone (clb). 146 Alamy Stock Photo: Westend61 GmbH / Ulrich Hagemann. 147 Dreamstime.com: Chumphon Whangchom (c). Getty Images: Moment / Photo by Benjawan Sittidech (bc). 149 Fotolia: Natallia Yaumenenka / eAlisa (cb). Shutterstock.com: biletskiyevgeniy.com (c). 151 Dreamstime.com: Itsmejust (br). 153 123RF.com: citadelle (fbr); iarada (cl, cr); scanrail (crb); lanych (br). Dorling Kindersley: Ben Morgan (bl). 156 Science Photo Library: GIPHOTOSTOCK (bc). 157 Science Photo Library: Giphotostock (ca). 161 Dreamstime.com: Arsty (cl, clb). 163 Dreamstime.com: James Warren (b). 164 123RF.com: iarada (cb, cb/same image). 165 Dreamstime.com: Thomas Lenne (tr). 167 Dreamstime.com: Kooslin (bl). 170 Dreamstime.com: Kooslin (bl); Vlabos (clb). 171 Getty Images / iStock: didecs (cr). 173 Getty Images: The Image Bank / Michael Dunning (b). 174 Science Photo Library: (cl). 175 Getty Images / iStock: E+ / malerapaso (cb). Science Photo Library: Andrew Lambert Photography (cl). 177 Science Photo Library: (tr); Andrew Lambert Photography (cr). 181 Dreamstime.com: Atman (c); Kirill Volkov (cl). Getty Images / iStock: E+ / Malca (bc). 183 Dreamstime.com: Fotoatelie (bl); Mphoto2 (cl); Msphotographic (clb). 185 Dorling Kindersley: Ben Morgan (c). Dreamstime.com: Georgii Dolgykh (cr); Gawriloff (c/Monitor); Luca Lorenzelli (br). 188 Dreamstime.com: Oleksiy Boyko (crb). Science Photo Library: Martyn F. Chillmaid; Giphotostock (cr). 189 Science Photo Library: Ted Kinsman (b). 191 Dreamstime.com: Loraks (bc). Science Photo Library: (cb). 192 Alamy Stock Photo: Universal Images Group North America LLC / QAI Publishing (c). 193 Dreamstime.com: Jim Reed Photography. 194 Science Photo Library: Andrew Lambert Photography (cr). 196 Dreamstime.com: Ilonashorokhova (clb, clb/opposite magnet); Timawe (cr). 197 Getty Images: Photographer's Choice RF / Gary S Chapman (tc). 197 Dorling Kindersley: Stephen Oliver (c). 198 NASA: NASA Earth Observatory (c). 200 Dreamstime.com: Dan Van Den Broeke / Dvande (b). Science Photo Library: Turtle Rock Scientific / Science Source (tc, tr). 201 Science Photo Library: Martin Bond (br). 202 Science Photo Library: Trevor Clifford Photography (cl, cr). 204 Science Photo Library: MARTYN F. CHILLMAID (bc). 207 Alamy Stock Photo: ITAR-TASS News Agency (cr). 209 Science Photo Library: Trevor Clifford Photography (b). 212 Dreamstime.com: Bblood (cb); Kyoungil Jeon (ca); Okea (c); Mykola Davydenko (br). 213 Dreamstime.com: Andreykuzmin (ca); Valentyn75 (cr); Romikmk (crb); Hasan Can Balcioglu (bc/kettle); Rudy Umans (bc);

Russelljwatkins (br). 215 Alamy Stock Photo: Brilt (crb); Andrew Wilson (cr); David R. Frazier Photolibrary, Inc. (cr). 216 Dreamstime.com: Norgal (cb); Petro Perutskyy (clb); Santiaga (bc). 218 123RF.com: Mariusz Blach (cr). Getty Images / iStock: E+ / Mlenny (b). 219 Alamy Stock Photo: Flas100 (clb); Somchai Somsanitangkul / Tank_isara (cla); Jaroslaw Grudzinski / jarek78 (crb/Iron). Fotolia: apttone (crb). 220 Getty Images / iStock: didecs (tr); E+ / julichka (c). 224 Science Photo Library: Turtle Rock Scientific (br). 225 Dreamstime.com: Geerati (c). 227 Dreamstime.com: Chernetskaya (b). 230 Dreamstime.com: Mr.siwabud Veerapaisarn (crb). Getty Images: Tomasz Melnicki (clb); Yamada Taro (c). 231 Science Photo Library: (bl, bc). 232 Dorling Kindersley: Gerard Brown / Pedal Pedlar (bl). 235 Alamy Stock Photo: Science Photo Library (cb). Dorling Kindersley: Gary Ombler / Stuart's Bikes (cr). 238 Fotolia: apttone (cb). 245 Science Photo Library: Public Health England (br). UNSCEAR: UNSCEAR 2008 Report Vol. I Sources And Effects Of Ionizing Radiation United Nations, Scientific Committee On The Effects Of Atomic Radiation (bl). 246 Dorling Kindersley: Arran Lewis / Zygote (cl, cr). U.S. Environmental Protection Agency: (cr). 247 Depositphotos Inc: microgen (crb). Dreamstime.com: Serg_velusceac (cr). Science Photo Library: Andrew Wheeler (cra). 248 Science Photo Library: ISM (cra). 249 Science Photo Library: Astier - Chru Lille (cl); Centre Jean Perrin, ISM (tl). 250 Science Photo Library: US Dept Of Energy (br). 252 Swiss Federal Nuclear Safety Inspectorate ENSI.: (br). 253 Science Photo Library: Claus Lunau (br). 255 Dorling Kindersley: Arran Lewis / NASA (cl). 256 Photo of Peter Wienerroither: https://homepage.univie.ac.at/~pw (b). 259 Dreamstime.com: Reinhold Wittich (cr). Getty Images: Stocktrek RF (crb/Enceladus). NASA: Johns Hopkins University Applied Physics Laboratory / Southwest Research Institute (cra); JPL / USGS (cb). 260 NASA: GSFC / Arizona State University (c/Used 8 times). 261 Science Photo Library: European Space Agency / Cesar / Observatorio Astrofisico Di Torino (br). 262 Dreamstime.com: Intrepix (cr, cra, crb). NASA: Soho - Eit Consortium / ESA (c). 263 NASA: ESA and The Hubble Heritage Team (STScI / AURA) (clb); JPL-Caltech (c); ESA / Hubble (crb); ESA, and The Hubble Heritage Team (STScI / AURA) (cb). 264 Alamy Stock Photo: Dennis Hallinan (cl). Dreamstime.com: Ivan Kokoulin (cl). NASA: ESA / ASU / J. Hester (bc); ESA / Hubble and the Hubble Heritage Team (cra); JPL-Caltech / R. Gehrz (bl); (br); CXC / SAO / F. Seward et al (fbr). NRAO: AUI (fbl). 265 NASA: ESA, S. Beckwith (STScI) and the Hubble Heritage Team (STScI / AURA) (cl, clb). 266 NASA: STScI / Ann Feild (br). 267 NASA: WMAP Science Team (br). 269 NASA: (tr). 271 from HyperPhysics by Rod Nave, Georgia State University: (cl)

All other images © Dorling Kindersley
For further information see:
www.dkimages.com